CRUCIAL IMAGES IN THE PRESENTATION OF A KURDISH NATIONAL IDENTITY

SOCIAL, ECONOMIC AND POLITICAL STUDIES OF THE MIDDLE EAST AND ASIA

(S.E.P.S.M.E.A.)

(Founding editor: C.A.O. van Nieuwenhuijze)

VOLUME 86

CRUCIAL IMAGES IN THE PRESENTATION OF A KURDISH NATIONAL IDENTITY

Heroes and Patriots, Traitors and Foes

BY

MARTIN STROHMEIER

BRILL
LEIDEN · BOSTON
2003

[redacted]

This book is printed on acid-free paper.

Library of Congress Cataloging-in-Publication Data

The Library of Congress Cataloging-in-Publication Data is also available.

Strohmeier, Martin.
Crucial images in the presentation of a Kurdish national identity : heroes and patriots, traitors and foes / by Martin Strohmeier.
p. cm.–(Social, economic, and political studies of the Middle East and Asia, ISSN 1385-3376 ; v. 86)
Includes bibliographical references (p.) and index.
ISBN 9004125841 (hard cover)
1. National characteristics, Kurdish. 2. Kurds–Middle East. 3. Nationalism–Middle East. I. Title. II. Series.

DS59.K86 S79 2003
320.54'089'91597 dc2l

2002032270

ISSN 1385-3376
ISBN 90 04 12584 1

PRINTED IN THE NETHERLANDS

[redacted]

For Angela

CONTENTS

PART THREE

A "NOVEL" APPROACH TO PRESENTING THE KURDISH NATION

PREFACE

A decade ago, while I was working at the Orient-Institut of the Deutsche Morgenländische Gesellschaft in Istanbul, I came across a small brochure in Ottoman with the title *Kürdler Türklerden ne istiyorlar?* ("What do the Kurds want from the Turks"?). It was the time following the Gulf War, when the plight of the Kurds in Iraq and their flight into Turkey had aroused world-wide attention, and the Kurdish question was being more openly discussed. I was intrigued by the booklet, actually an open letter, because it seemed to promise a historical reading of the Kurdish question. But I had no clue about the author, Dr. Meḥmed Şükrü. It took me some time to establish that the full name of the author was Dr. Meḥmed Şükrü Sekban and to gather details about his life. A staunch supporter of the Kurdish movement from its inception at the turn of the 19th to the 20th century, Sekban withdrew from the movement in the 1930's. He came to be considered a traitor by his former comrades. His bad reputation is probably the reason that his writings have been neglected. In this book I argue that he deserves scholarly attention.

Sekban's writings led me to a study of the wider context of the discourse on Kurdishness. An important source was the nascent Kurdish press. Among the other ethnic groups in the Ottoman Empire, the press was a crucial instrument in generating and maintaining a discourse on the respective nationalisms and the so-called awakenings. The study of the Kurdish press drew my attention to the family which was involved in most Kurdish newspapers between 1898 and 1919: the Bedir Khāns. In particular, three of its scions, Celādet, Kāmurān and Ṯüreyyā, became the most active advocates of the Kurdish movement after the establishment of the Turkish Republic. Driven by a cultural as well as a political mission, motivated by claims to leadership and legitimized by their noble descent, as they saw it, they created a Latin alphabet for Kurmanjī, established journals, wrote open letters to statesmen and supranational organizations, published propaganda brochures, and engaged in academia. Specifically, Kāmurān's literary activities aroused my interest. His novel *Der Adler von Kurdistan* ("The Eagle of Kurdistan"), ignored by students of the Kurdish national movement, constitutes my third major source. All three groups of sources, Sekban's writings, the press, and Kāmurān's novel have been used to analyze the evolving discourse of the Kurdish movement.

This study has grown out of lectures given at the Universities of Halle (1994), Bamberg (1994) and Freiburg (1995) as well as two papers delivered at the Congrès d'Association Française pour l'Etude des Mondes Arabe et Musulmans (AFEMAM) and the International Conference "Querelles privées et contestations publiques. Le rôle de la presse dans la formation de l'opinion publique au Proche-Orient", both held at Aix-en-Provence in 1996. The writing of the book took place at the University of Bamberg, for many years my home institution, where I had the privilege of a stimulating academic exchange with Bert Fragner, Roxane Haag-Higuchi, Klaus Kreiser, Maurus Reinkowski, Semih Tezcan and many others. Most of the manuscript was finished in spring 1998. Due to my move to Cyprus later that year I was only able in 2001 to get back to the manuscript. After updating and revising, the editor of the series Social, Economic and Political Studies of the Middle East and Asia (SEPSMEA), Reinhard Schulze, accepted it for publication.

I have profited immensely from the encouragement, support and constructive criticism of my wife Angela. The late Ulrich Haarmann read the manuscript at an early stage. Elizabeth Boleman-Herring (New York) and Nancy Kobrin (Minneapolis) made a number of valuable suggestions. The anonymous reader not only prevented me from making some unfounded speculations, but also provided helpful comments and bibliographical information. Malmîsanij (Stockholm) contributed some data on members of the Kurdish national movement. Winfried Riesterer (München) is my lifeline to libraries. Ludwig Paul (Göttingen) advised me on Kurdish transliteration, while Trudy Kamperveen of Brill Publishers (Leiden) kindly persevered with the project despite missed deadlines. My sincere thanks go to all of them, but, as usually, all responsibility lies with the author.

Nicosia, May 15, 2002
Martin Strohmeier

NOTE ON TRANSLITERATION

The transliteration of Oriental languages has always been a tiresome problem. German orientalists transcribe differently than their English speaking colleagues; Arabists use other systems than Ottomanists. Nor is the transcription of the authoritative *Encyclopaedia of Islam* followed by all scholars of Oriental Studies. This situation is further complicated in this study because terms and names from Kurdish, Arabic, Persian and Turkish resp. Ottoman are used. Moreover, since there is no unified Kurdish language, different ways of transliteration for Kurmanjī and Sorani are employed, e.g. the word for "hope" is in both Kurmanjī and Sorani, the same, but it is differently pronounced and transcribed, *hēvī* in Kurmanjī and *hīva* in Sorani. Under these circumstances any attempt to create a consistent transliteration runs into serious difficulties. Therefore, a certain degree of anarchy is inevitable. I have tried to cope with the situation in the following way: Since most of my sources are Ottoman, I have followed the transcription system of *İslam Ansiklopedisi* (generally used by Ottomanists) with the following exceptions, mainly on account of the English language context:

instead of "ḫ" "kh" is used
instead of "s̱" "ṯ" is used

Inconsistencies were unavoidable: In Ottoman texts "ş" was used, whereas in other contexts a "sh" like in sheykh was used. Again, in an Ottoman text "c" or "ç" were used, whereas I preferred to employ "j" as in *Hijaz*. In an Ottoman context the letter "g" of the Arabic alphabet was transcribed as "ġ" (like in *ġazete*), but throughout the book the transliteration *agha* (instead of *āġā*, the Kurdish *axa* or modern Turkish *ağa*) has been used.

In the transcription of Kurdish instead of ^ showing the length over certain vowels (such as in *hêvî*), macrons have been used as in *hēvī*. Many names and place names, esp. Kurdish ones, have been kept as they appear in the texts.

Words and geographical terms familiar to English readers are given in the English version and not in transliteration.

A special problem is the transcription of the names of some of the Kurdish newspapers analyzed in this book. The first Kurdish newspaper which I have transcribed *Kürdistān*, that is as an Ottoman word, could by the same token be transcribed as *Kurdistan* which would be the Kurdish spelling. There would be some justification for the Kurdish transliteration, since the first numbers of this newspaper were only in Kurmanjī, but later numbers were bilingual or carried mainly Ottoman articles. On the other hand, the newspaper by the same name, appearing in 1919, had only few Kurdish articles and the undertitle was in Ottoman too, so I thought it acceptable to transcribe both newspapers as *Kürdistān*.
Kreyenbroek in his introduction to Kreyenbroek and Allison (1996, pp. 5–6) has aptly described the problems in transcribing Kurdish, esp. in Arabic, Persian and Turkish contexts.

PREVIEW[1]

I

Once upon a time, the Auroritarian Empire was great and powerful, feared by all for its military prowess. However, the nations of Occidentaly had overtaken the once formidable state in almost every aspect of development. Disparagingly referred to as the "patient of Occidentaly", the empire had become incapable of preventing interventions in its internal affairs. Occidentaly seemed to be encouraging the dissolution of the vast empire of Auroritaria, particularly in supporting the claims of ethno-religious minorities aspiring to independence. Because the minorities and their champions in Occidentaly doubted the ability of Auroritaria to reform and modernize, they considered its demise inevitable.

Despite the force of disintegrating tendencies, a group of Auroritarians—let us call them patriots—became committed to saving the empire and to assuming important positions once the backward and destructive rule of the tyrant was overthrown. Painfully aware that the Occidentalians considered Auroritarian culture, religion, political and economic institutions to be inferior, these patriots sought to understand the source of Occidentalian strength in order to reproduce it in their own society and thus acquire the credentials for acceptance in the modern world.

Evidently, the states of Occidentaly derived their stamina from their particular nationhoods. But what exactly accounted for the discrepancy between their own and the Occidentalian states? Constitutions, civic rights, and above all a completely different sense of identity were the key concepts. The citizens of the respective Occidentalian nations felt themselves to be united by an ineffable something which

[1] Gellner (1991, pp. 58–62) delineates the course of a typical national movement in a fictive land in his chapter "The course of true nationalism never did run smooth". I have adopted the idea and the framework though little of the almost Swiftian satirical tone to provide a preview of the aspects of Kurdish nationalism discussed in this study.

dictated an allegiance and devotion at once transcendental yet material, sacred yet secular. Their nationality engendered pride and collective self-love. Auroritarian reformers divined the force of patriotism underpinning national identity as powering the motor of the superior Occidentalian model. If the Auroritarian patriots could instill in their fellow Auroritarians a commensurate sense of loyalty based on pride and reverence for the nation rather than on their traditional local and religious affiliations, then the Auroritarian Empire might yet recover and retain its vast holdings. Since you cannot love what you do not know, the patriots saw education as the first step in acquiring a national identity. The patriots' task was to first acquire and then disseminate the knowledge of their own neglected history and contributions to civilization in order to kindle a sense of pride. The examples of valiant heroes would foster love for and dedication to their nation. They would not have acknowledged it as such, but they had begun to invent the nation.

II

Among the ranks of the patriots were two ethnically distinct groups: the numerically dominant Turarians and the Kurarians, whose homeland was far to the east of the capital. Initially, the two groups did not focus on their differences. Both were united in their desire to modernize the empire, achieve some sort of synthesis of their own and Occidentalian culture, as well as in their need to carve out nîches for themselves in the future order. Their mutual opposition to the tyrant was a further cohesive force. The Kurarian patriots saw themselves as loyal Auroritarians. Their sense of being Kurarian, while never questioned, had not constituted an allegiance overriding their loyalty to the empire. But the imported agenda of patriotic concerns, with its emphasis on matters of language, literature and history, led to a growth of self-awareness in both groups. The exclusivity of Turarian self-concerns brought Kurarians to the realization that the very culture they had taken for granted, and even disparaged, stood little chance of surviving unless efforts were made to revitalize it. Very few among the Kurarian intelligentsia could read and write in their mother tongue as they had been educated in the Turarian language. Kurarians were pained that in Occidentaly they were considered to be primitive, wild and thus unfit for the modern world.

Inspired by imported concepts which had stood as models for other Auroritarian minorities, a very small group of Kurarian patriots began to envision the difference a self-aware Kurarian society could make. Their language was as distinctive as that of other Auroritarian minorities. Why should it not be the basis of a community striving for improvement through education? The Kurarians were a proud and valiant people, easily motivated to self-sacrifice in defence of their honour and their religion. What was needed was to transform the basis of their feelings of honour; to transfer their loyalty and love to the nation. From what the patriots had gleaned of the Occidentalian model, the first step in creating the Kurarian nation was to experience an "Awakening".

The educated Kurarian elite set about establishing newspapers and organizations to propagate a message of doom and redemption. The Kurarians were doomed if they persisted in their antiquated world view and social organization. Above all, their devotion to their religious leaders and to the tyrant had perpetuated their backwardness. Not fit for modern society, they would fall victim to it if they did not awaken to their true interests. Theirs was a distinctive and glorious history. There had been a golden time when they had been free. Guided by patriotic leaders they had developed their culture. They would do so again if they could recognize that the tyrant was their enemy and the patriots their rightful leaders.

There were, however, limits to imagining Kurarian nationality in public. Few other Kurarians were affected by the message. It was not that fear and insecurity regarding the future did not weigh heavily on them; it was simply inconceivable that they regard their religious leader as an adversary. He represented the dignity and ancientry of their religious identity. He was their hero against the Occidentalians and their protégés in the empire. The latter were the true enemy, having challenged the existing order and humiliated the Kurarians.

Widespread disapproval of Occidentalian civilization and values was not the only impediment to constructing and promoting a viable Kurarian national identity. Turarian patriots felt that all their co-religionists should be content with their Auroritarian heritage. Any efforts to delineate ethnic boundaries were perceived as a threat to Auroritarian solidarity. Kurarian patriots, not wishing to be seen as traitors to the Auroritarian cause, found themselves enmeshed in contradictions. Arguments for education in the mother tongue and the study of Kurarian history, hinged on the premise that Kurarians were distinct from Turarians. At the same time, they had to postulate the historical bonds between the two peoples and the primacy of Auroritarian identity.

III

The Great War fulfilled the worst nightmares of Auroritarian patriots. The empire would be partitioned and their patriotic mission extinguished. Radical Kurarians felt that it was time to emerge as a nation. All that seemed necessary was the good will of the Occidentalian leaders and their own resolve. But most Kurarians shared the shame and humiliation of the Turarians, and were easily motivated to remain within the Auroritarian fold when a great Turarian hero appeared to lead the battle against the Occidentalian invaders. A living hero was more persuasive than remote historical forebears, and the majority of Kurarian patriots threw in their lot with the Turarians, thus forfeiting whatever advantages might have been in store for them as autonomous Kurarians. The few patriots who continued to agitate for separate rights were denounced as traitors by the victorious Turarian patriots and forced to flee the empire, soon to be reinvented as the Turarian Republic.

Although the historic moment had come and gone, these Kurarian patriots persevered in their efforts to secure recognition and rights for their people, and to keep alive the image of a nation wronged. From their various places of exile they authored letters and pamphlets, organized new groups, supported rebellions. Curiously, although it was clear that the Turarian patriots had become their outspoken enemies, for some time it remained difficult to articulate the opposition. Even in exile, their definition of Kurarian identity was blurred at the edges. Yes, Kurarians were distinct, but they were also inseparable from Turarians.

The years of exile and the failure of Kurarian endeavours elicited different reactions from the patriots. One former activist threw in the towel and published a repudiation of all the tenets of Kurarian identity that he and his comrades had striven to establish and propagate: the golden past, cultural achievements, Kurarian heroes, the long history of struggle for liberation, and even their common language as the basis for certain rights. Above all, he argued, the Turarians were not enemies. Thus he came to be seen as one of the most prominent Kurarian traitors. But some of his former comrades remained undaunted by failure. They continued to carry the torch of Kurarian nationalism, tirelessly asserting their national identity, stating arguments for Kurarian rights and attempting to garner support for the Kurarian cause. Among their publicistic efforts to portray themselves as victims of the oppressive Turarians, a little-known novel stands out. The adaptation of an Occidentalian genre enabled a prominent Kurarian activist to reinvent Kurarian revolt as an inspiring drama of bravery and rectitude, a story replete with heroes, patriots, traitors and foes.

INTRODUCTION

There is something particularly elusive about failed nationalisms and the sense of identity and rights which engendered them. The suppressors of separatist threats to their territorial and ideological integrity are not likely to dwell on such a confrontation or document its history. If the Kurds had managed to forge a nation-state in the aftermath of World War I, or at least to achieve a measure of recognition and legal status, then their early leaders would have been revered, their struggles for self-assertion glorified, significant texts intensely studied and canonized. As it is, we do not possess a great body of knowledge about early nationalist leaders, and the extensive studies of the Kurdish movement have understandably concentrated on the larger picture, on documenting and interpreting developments, and locating reliable sources in order to establish the relevant social and political facts.[1] This study, however, is concerned less with how and why Kurdish nationalism did or did not "catch on" than with the efforts made by the Kurdish elite to construct a viable concept of Kurdish identity[2] around which a we-group could consolidate that, in turn, would support secular and religious leaders in their aspirations.

It has become commonplace to locate the matrix of nationalism in the imagination. National identity is invented and constructed in the mind. But national or social identities are little more than umbrella terms for an amorphous, many-layered, continually evolving yet tenacious phenomenon, which contains myriad codes for behaviour, judgment, loyalty and obligation. This explains the difficulty in negotiating transitions in self-definition, even in periods of identity-crisis, when alternatives to traditional identies are sought. The complexity also accounts for difficulties in assessing the make-up and potency of any national identity at a given time.

Scholars of nationalism point to the crucial distinction between ethnic awareness and national identity.[3] It is one thing for a group

---

[1] To name some of the most significant: Bruinessen (1978, 1991, 1992 a), Olson (1989), Behrendt (1993).

[2] Bruinessen (1992 a) elaborated on aspects of Kurdish identity in the tribal milieu as well as in early nationalism.

[3] The studies of Anderson (1983/1993), Gellner (1991), Hobsbawm (1983, 1992),

to be aware that objective criteria, such as language or religion, differentiate them from other groups, and quite another thing for members of this group to define their social identity primarily upon the basis of this distinction. The French model of nationalism, based on the democratic rights of all its citizens, was the model for Ottomanism, itself a precursor of national identity. Yet the dominant pattern in the late Ottoman Empire was the development of ethnic-based nationalism despite (or because of) the fact that religion and not ethnicity had been the decisive criterion for belonging and political participation until the Tanzimat era. For this reason we have concerned ourselves here with national identity based upon ethnic belonging.

Social identity—whether based on the tribe, the *umma* or the nation—implies boundaries and requires a willingness to sacrifice individual or family self-interest and even one's life should those boundaries be violated. The shift from the more or less tangible collectivities of family, clan and tribe to the ethnic group as the basis of social and moral significance requires a leap of the imagination, and it is this leap that identity-makers must chart. Their task is to construct a meaningful and persuasive image of the imagined community in order to project it as a transcendent entity to which a people may willingly transfer its devotion and allegiance. The imagined community must offer the promise of security, benefits and opportunities, and self-respect. Fundamental to the process of defining an ethnic identity and imbuing it with the aura of a moral imperative are the functions of inclusion and exclusion, crystallized in the opposition of one group to another. "We" is opposed by, and indeed conceived in opposition to, an inimical Other which negatively affects the development, welfare or historic mission of the we-group. The imagined community acquires contours as much through defining who it is **not** as who it **is**. The opposition facilitates a positive self-view, as weaknesses may be seen as the result of unjust treatment by the other. This in turn generates the legitimacy of nationalist claims. Alain Touraine has argued that an interest group is capable

---

Lemberg (1964), Hroch (1968, 1985) and Elwert (1989 a, 1989 b) have influenced the focus and assumptions of this study.—"Imagined community" is probably one of the most influential concepts in historical scholarship during the last two decades. Students of nationalism refer exclusively to Anderson when speaking of "imagined communities"; however, Lemberg used this very term in its German equivalent ("vorgestellte Gemeinschaft") twenty years before Anderson wrote his book.

of becoming a social movement only when the three principles of identity, opposition and totality (legitimacy) coexist and interconnect.[4] Only by liberating itself from the chains of the Other can the we-group accomplish its mission and achieve self-fulfillment.

While Touraine was not referring primarily to opposition on a conceptual level, this will be a major concern of the present study. The basic dichotomy between Kurds and Turks will gradually be grafted onto the Kurds' perception of themselves and their history. Patriotic thinkers have long appreciated the worth of prejudice, stereotypes and even delusion in creating conceptual dichotomies and polarities. Love of one's own heroes, as well as hatred of the Other are useful not only in generating patriotic fervour,[5] but in portraying the secular variants of the saints, sinners and demons in the dramaturgy of their struggle. Kurdish propagandists would increasingly employ binary opposites to present their appeal to "Occidentaly" for sympathy and support.

The scope of this study, as outlined in the preview, extends from the emergence of Kurdish nationalism around the turn of the century (including the 19th-century background), to its decline in the mid 1930's in Turkey. This decline was paralleled by a revival in Syria.[6] The focus is on the publicistic efforts of Kurdish nationalists to define, justify and propagate their objectives, especially in the various newspapers established for this purpose. Kurdish writers had to define and present the Kurds. Their job was to create textual representations which would at best both inspire an inner Kurdish identification and enhance the image of Kurds as they were perceived in the West. Kurds, like other Ottoman minorities before

[4] Touraine (1974), pp. 174–179.

[5] Cf. Herder's praise of prejudice as something capable of unifying a nation, making them stronger, happier, and more prosperous, cited in Giesen/Junge (1991), p. 299. Ernst Moritz Arndt (1769–1860), Professor in Greifswald, strongly advocated a national uprising against Napoleon. He commented on the value of hatred of other nations: "What is the harm to a Frenchman if a German calls him a bag of wind, a fool . . . let it (the prejudice of one nation against another, MS) stand as a charitable partition . . . Thus hatred remains a holy and protective delusion in the nation . . . so we do not end up as feeble images which resemble everything and nothing . . ." ("Über Volkshaß", in: Ernst-Moritz Arndt: *Über den Volkshaß und über den Gebrauch einer fremden Sprache*. Leipzig 1813. Cited after the reprint in Jeismann/Ritter (1993), pp. 333–334.

[6] I have not dealt with the important developments in British-mandate Iraq, but rather concentrated on the activities of those Kurdish nationalists who later emigrated to French-controlled Syria, retaining their focus on Turkish Kurdistan.

them, imported a European model but did not take it on lock, stock and barrel. Rather, they selected from the repertoire of national symbols and concepts such as the "Awakening", adding and discarding as prospects for success dictated. The nation had to be invented, but it could not be just any nation.

In his treatise on nationalism, Hobsbawm commented on the difficulty of assessing the extent to which patriotism is actually the supreme force motivating fighters for the nationalist cause, whose voices history has not recorded: "The real relations between proto-national identification and subsequent national or state patriotism must often remain obscure for this reason. We know what Nelson meant when he signalled his fleet on the eve of the battle of Trafalgar, that England expected every man to do his duty, but not what passed through the minds of Nelson's sailors on that day . . .".[7] But the implication that our written records enable us to know the minds of patriotic authors is perhaps misleading. Nationalist leaders, especially in the early phase of group-formation, are a diverse bunch, motivated by sundry reasons and varying greatly in their commitment. There are the idealists, opportunists, pragmatists, hangers-on. Certainly, all are deeply concerned about their uncertain futures, and dissatisfied with their prospects. Their publications range in motivation and intent from pedagogical/scholarly endeavours to self-aggrandizement or blatant propaganda. Some texts comprise perhaps all these elements, and most contain a hidden agenda. Whatever their motives or objectives, and regardless of historical inaccuracy or mendacity, the sources dealt with in this study were examined to illuminate the discourse which engendered various, often conflicting concepts and images of Kurdish identity.[8]

Part One deals first with factors relevant to traditional Kurdish self-definition at the time the national inventers took up their missions at the end of the 19th century. This involves a résumé of 19th-century resistance to Ottoman rule not only because the revolts

[7] Hobsbawm (1990), p. 78.

[8] The Kurdish language was a cultural marker but did not, until the mid 1930s become a medium for discourse among the writers examined in this study. Even then, Kurdish writers were not able to relinquish the support of other languages. Thus the texts dealt with here were written in everything from Ottoman Turkish to English, French and German.

illustrate patterns of allegiance, belief and opposition, but also because the revolts, and particularly their leaders, became crucial elements in the mythology of Kurdish liberation. Moreover, these revolts were almost literally the breeding ground for later nationalists. Some of the most prominent figures of the early Kurdish movement were the progeny of 19th-century revolt leaders. The following sections of Part One deal largely with the organizations and newspapers in which strategies and consensus were sought for staking Kurdish claims. This process, which involved associations, alliances and confrontations among Kurds from widely different backgrounds and diverging ideologies, is traced right up to and includes the Turkish War of Independence. Inevitably, the study has had to deal with the ticklish question of when nationalism begins to exist or whether we can even rightfully call the protagonists of the Kurdish Awakening nationalists.

Part Two deals with reactions to Turkish policies regarding the Kurds. While nationalism took its course in Turkey as well as in Iraq, Iran and Syria, these states increasingly regarded the Kurds as a burden. Initial attempts of emigré Kurds to establish a dialogue with Ankara gave way to strident propaganda. After the failure of a series of revolts organized from both within and outside Turkey, Kurdish nationalists narrowed their focus and embarked on a course of cultural nation-building which had been envisioned in the early Kurdish journals and was now rendered practicable and expedient with the support of French orientalists active in Syria. Several of the publications dealt with in Part Two will be familiar to researchers of Kurdish nationalism. I will be giving these texts a close reading, viewing them in their geo-political contexts and within the framework of what their authors were trying to do in terms of defining and promoting Kurdish identity and legitimacy and championing their goals. Finally, I analyze how the erosion of their personal and collective prospects affected the visions of some of the most persevering of Kurdish nationalists.

In Part Three, I treat a little-known novel co-authored by one of the most prominent Kurdish nationalists of his generation and mentor of the subsequent generation of Kurdish nationalist leaders: Kāmurān Bedir Khān. I will attempt to show that the novel reflected a rather successful, if highly problematic, borrowing from a western literary genre upon which the author was able to superimpose his own vision of Kurdish identity.

Kurdish nationalism had been effectively neutralized within Turkey by 1938. That it was to be reawakened from the 1950s onward is an almost completely different phenomenon and is not the subject of this study. Thus the use of the term "failed nationalism" at the beginning of this chapter.

PART ONE

"AWAKENING" THE KURDS

CHAPTER ONE

THE 19TH-CENTURY BACKGROUND: RELIGION AND TRIBALISM

Despite significant linguistic and religious differences Kurds saw themselves and were seen by others as a distinct group.[1] But the Kurds, in contrast to the Ottomans and Persians, never experienced political unity. This has been attributed to their tribal organization and the geographical fate of Kurdistan as a buffer zone between the rival Ottoman and Safavid Empires. By no means the only divisive element in 19th-century Kurdish society, tribalism was fundamental to political and economic organization and constituted an essential element of social identity. The majority of Kurds were nomads or semi-nomads who dominated the settled, non-tribal peasants whom they did not even consider to be Kurds. Although the boundaries between tribal groups were permeable, they provided the main criteria for inclusion into the we-group. Each member was bound to uphold the honour and avenge insult or injury to the group. Authority was vested in the *agha*, a clan as well as a tribal leader. He was able to retain his position only if his followers were satisfied that he could assure the protection and subsistence of the tribe; otherwise, tribal members might shift their allegiance to a more powerful leader. A strong *agha* had to deal swiftly and forcefully with competitors and create situations in which to demonstrate strength and thus discourage contestation of his dominance.[2] Such *aghas* wielded considerable power and achieved a high degree of devotion among their tribes.[3]

---

[1] Bruinessen (1992 a), pp. 23–25; Bruinessen (1992 b), pp. 34–38. Most of the Kurds adhere to Sunnite Islam. A minority are Shiʿites. A considerable number of Kurds are Alevi, a religious community in Turkey whose beliefs are quite distant from the teachings of Twelve Shiite-Islam. Furthermore, there are specific religious groups which are only to be found in Kurdistan, such as the Ahl-i Ḥaqq and the Yezidi. The latter in their rites combine Zoroastrian, Manichean, Jewish, Christian and Islamic elements. For the characteristics of Kurdish dialects cf.: "Kurds, Kurdistān", *EI* (2), vol. V; Kreyenbroek (1992), pp. 68–83.

[2] Bruinessen (1992 a), p. 78.

[3] Rich (1836), travelling at the beginning of the 19th century in Kurdistan, was astounded at the degree to which Kurds deferred to their tribal leaders, remarking

Kurdish contacts with the Ottomans date from the beginning of the 16th century, when İdrīs Bidlisī,[4] a high-ranking Kurdish advisor to the Ottomans, convinced Kurdish rulers to support Sultan Selīm against the Safavids. After the defeat of the Persians, several virtually independent, quasi-dynastic Kurdish principalities were established. These so-called emirates existed alongside tribal confederations. Rivalry amongst the emirs made it easy for the Ottomans to play the groups off against one another and thus prevent the rise of a strong, consolidating leadership. The emirates were awarded privileges such as the right to coin money and have the *khuṭba* read in their names, and dispensation from the obligation to pay tributes and recruit soldiers for the Ottoman forces. In return for virtual independence they were expected to recognize Ottoman sovereignty, keep order and patrol the border with Persia. Internally, the Kurdish emirates experienced in the 16th and 17th centuries economic and cultural growth, each striving to attain a high degree of cultural representation at their courts, with their rulers becoming patrons of the arts.[5]

At the beginning of the 19th century, Sultan Maḥmūd dispatched his new troops (*ʿAsākir-i manṣūre-i Muḥammedīye*) to impose central rule and consolidate his eastern provinces. The subjugation of Kurdistan had become crucial to the empire's inner security as it could provide a bulwark against Russian expansion. The emirs were eventually eliminated as counterparts to Ottoman authority, but in large-scale rebellions they provided massive resistance against what was perceived as encroachment.

Parallel to the interventions of the central government was the steady growth of Western influence in Kurdistan, as manifested in the establishment of consulates, missions, churches, schools and hospitals. Christians, and especially Armenians benefitted from the support of these institutions by acquiring an education, valuable commercial and political contacts with the West, and a heightened sense of the injustice of their position vis à vis the dominant Kurds. Kurds responded to the gains in status and wealth of the Armenians and their challenge to Kurdish domination with increased violence, thus

---

that they were willing to make any sacrifice, even to follow them into exile: pp. 86–87.

[4] "Bidlisī, İdrīs", *EI* (2) vol. I, pp. 1207–1208 (V.L. Ménage).

[5] This was the era in which the most acclaimed Kurdish poet, Aḥmad-i Khānī, composed his epic poem *Mem ū Zīn*, see below.

providing the Great Powers, especially Russia and England, with the opportunity to intervene in internal Ottoman affairs as protectors of the Christians. The Tanzimat granted equal rights to all Ottomans, thus cementing the loss of privileged identity for the Kurds. The reforms and intrusions of the central government and the mounting influence of the West were seen as different aspects of the same phenomenon, a victimization of Muslims.[6] The weakness of the government was manifested in its yielding to Western demands. The government, moreover, after destroying the very structures which had provided some modicum of law and order, failed to provide alternative protection. However, reaction and resistence to these identity-threatening changes crystallized not in outright enmity toward the Porte, but rather in animosity to the West and the Ottoman Christians. They were framed as the inimical Other, whose assertion of rights and status had damaged Kurdish prospects and dignity.

The course of the rebellion led by the *emir* of Botan, Bedir Khān, is illustrative of the strategies of consolidation and resistance powerful Kurdish leaders employed.[7] Bedir Khān had been named *emir* in 1821. He was able to establish and sustain rule by forming alliances with both Muslim and Nestorian tribal leaders, and by providing order, security and spiritual leadership in his region.[8] But his attempt to assert his strength vis-à-vis the Porte, by refusing to send troops to the Ottoman-Russian war, resulted in a military campaign led by the sultan's newly modernized troops. In 1838, the capital of Botan, Cizre, was besieged and Bedir Khān was forced to capitulate but not to forfeit his office. A year later, when İbrāhīm Pasha's troops defeated Ottoman forces, Bedir Khān seized the opportunity to regain his territory and extend his influence over most of Kurdistan. But he still recognized the sultan, and for a time the *emir* was tolerated.[9] What brought about his downfall, and the eventual exile of the Bedir Khāns from Botan, was related to the significant, wide-reaching changes to the balance of power in Kurdistan mentioned above.

---

[6] Bruinessen (1984), pp. 115–116.

[7] The best account of Bedir Khān's rise is in Bruinessen (1992 a), pp. 177–180; Behrendt (1993), pp. 166 seqq.

[8] Nikitine (1975), p. 193 who quotes an account by Agop Chahbaz. Cf. also Kutschera (1979), p. 14 who derives his assessment of spiritual leadership from the accounts of missionaries who met with the *emir*.

[9] According to Kutschera (1979), p. 15, Bedir Khān was at the height of his career from 1844–1848, when he coined money and had the *khuṭba* read in his name.

Christian missionaries had been particularly active in trying to convert the Nestorian Christians who, in turn, became hopeful that they might throw off the Muslim yoke. Even Austen Layard, who was critical of Kurdish tribal leaders and their treatment of Christians, was sympathetic regarding the fears of Kurds towards the Christians. In 1843 a confederation of Christian Nestorian tribes refused to pay tribute to the emir of Hakkari who asked for assistance from Bedir Khān. A massacre of Nestorians ensued which was widely publicized in the West. The French and English governments lodged severe complaints and demanded measures be taken. This finally forced the Ottoman government to exile the *emir* in 1847. The demise of the *emir* and the law and order he had ensured was perceived then to be as much a function of increased Christian influence as of the Ottoman will to curb the power of the Kurds. The ensuing fractionalization of power resulted in an increase in conflicts among the tribes, who were not to be united for several decades. After the defeat of the Ottomans in the war with Russia in 1878, two of Bedir Khān's sons, who had led Kurdish regiments in the war, returned to Botan to assert leadership. The elder, ʿOṯmān, proclaimed himself *pasha* and apparently profited from the memory of his father's rule. The majority of the tribes supported the *emir* who quickly asserted such prerogatives of his father as having the *khuṭba* read in his name. Bedir Khān rule this time lasted for less than a year.[10] That their attempt was not crowned with success did not deflect the energies of their brothers and nephews to sustain the Bedir Khān's aura. Some of them later tried to cast their ancestor in the role of the first Kurdish nationalist leader,[11] but there is nothing to suggest that the Bedir Khān rebellion represented a divergence from traditional efforts to resist central authority, or that a sense of Kurdishness inpired these activities.

The growth of Islamic mystic brotherhoods, in particular the Naḳşibendi and the Ḳādirīya, is related to the sense of insecurity engendered by the loss of traditional power structures and threats to subsistence and identity in Kurdistan. Neither the brotherhoods

---

[10] Bruinessen (1992 a), p. 181.

[11] Bedir Khān's rebellion is described in detail by Bedir Khān (1928 b). Kutschera (1979) calls Bedir Khān "the king of Kurdistan" (p. 13) and exaggerates his territorial strength when he refers to him as "the only Kurd since the legendary eras who imposed his authority over all of Kurdistan" (p. 16).

nor the political power of the sheykhs were new phenomena. Because of their Sunni orthodoxy, the Ottomans had favoured the Nakşibendi and allowed them to figure prominently in the consolidation of the realm. By the first decades of the 19th century, the Nakşibendi had developed a program to strengthen Islam and thus counter the superiority of the West. The Ottoman Empire would be rejuvenated by "rallying its Muslim citizens around the common goal of strength through unity in belief", by following the *sunna* and rejecting "bad innovations" (*bid'a*), forcing rulers to do the same. This program involved a campaign of international scope reaching from the Far East to North Africa.[12] Kurdistan was strongly influenced by Mevlana Khālid, himself a Kurd.[13] In the early 1820s, most of the tribal leaders Rich encountered during his travels were *murīd*s (disciples) of the local *sheykh*.[14]

It has been argued that one of the reasons for the rise in status of the brotherhoods was the fact that a power vacuum had opened with the fall of the *emir*s, who previously had been able to control the *agha*s. This situation enhanced the importance of *sheykh*s who, as leaders of the religious brotherhoods, were the only remaining representatives of an authority which transcended the individual tribes. *Sheykh*s could mediate in conflict situations between *agha*s, as the *sheykh*'s congregation was not identical to the membership of a tribe. The *sheykh*'s authority depended on his ability to forge alliances and on his charisma, which derived from magical and medicinal skills, the ability to intercede with the saints, descent from the prophet and, not least of all, from the economic power which many had been able to amass. It was logical that tribes and clans would consolidate around strong spiritual leaders to ward off threats which were largely perceived as directed against Islam. Membership in brotherhoods was an experience in an expanded social identity, as a *sheykh*'s following might include many tribes. Although Islam had long been the transcendental identity for Kurds, that identity was made more tangible and more emotional in the rituals of the mystic brotherhoods.[15]

---

[12] Mardin (1991), p. 130.
[13] Bruinessen (1984), p. 112.
[14] Rich (1836), pp. 140–141.
[15] Olson (1989), p. 3.

Şerif Mardin's study of the political dimensions of the Nakşibendi order, which was one of the two most popular *ṭarikats* in Kurdistan, indicates that the Nakşibendis offered "a body of concepts and a form of life" which would enable those who felt particularly threatened by the changes in their society to be integrated into a significant totality. The Nakşibendi could capitalize on the tradition of the "discourse of the unjust", which cast the marginalized elements of Ottoman society, who behaved according to the *şerīʿat* as the "devout just" against the powerful Ottoman elite which was known to operate according to non-*şerīʿat* standards.[16]

The most significant and widely discussed revolt of the 19th century was that of the Nakşibendi *sheykh* ʿUbaydullāh, who became the first Kurdish leader to mobilize a large number of tribes against the Sublime Porte, initiating a pattern of religious leadership that would continue well into the Kurdish nationalist movement of the 20th century.[17] It was indicative of the quality of Ottoman-Kurdish oppposition that the *sheykh*'s declared aim to establish an independent Kurdistan was justified by poor social conditions and the corruption and abuses of officials. ʿUbaydullāh and his followers, who had fought in the Turkish-Russian War,[18] seem to have been concerned, in the wake of the Treaty of Berlin, that the Porte under European pressure was about to grant Armenians and Nestorians independent states on Kurdish territory. Proclaiming his devotion to the sultan, he removed himself and his followers to Persian territory as the location of his envisioned independent state. It is not clear whether he did so with the approval and support of the sultan. But, in any case, the Kurdish League, launched by ʿUbaydullāh had Ottoman backing and was intended to counteract Armenian claims.[19]

In a letter to an American missionary that has been almost as widely quoted as Khānī's prologue to *Mem ū Zīn*, ʿUbaydullāh argued that the Kurds were a separate people, and could govern their affairs independently.[20] On the face of it this would seem to be a mani-

---

[16] Mardin (1991), pp. 134–137.

[17] On ʿUbaydullāh's revolt: Olson (1989), pp. 1–25. Olson bases his description mainly on Wadie Jwaideh (1960, which I was not able to consult). Behrendt (1993), pp. 214–226, has the most up-to-date account.

[18] Kutschera (1979), p. 20.

[19] Olson (1989), pp. 5–6.

[20] Olson (1989), p. 2.

festation of Kurdish national feeling. There are the contours of national identity: ethnic distinction and the desire for self rule. But it is significant that this statement was made in a letter to a foreigner and does not seem to have been meant for local consumption. Witnessing Armenian strategies, Kurdish leaders had seen the advantages of being recognized as a "nation" in order to achieve support abroad.[21] It is doubtful that ʿUbaydullāh's "nationalist" statements reflected a new concept of goals and self-definition or motivated the *sheykh*'s followers.

Although there is some indication that ʿUbaydullāh recognized and resented ʿAbdülḥamīd's exploitation of the Kurds in disposing of the Armenian threat, he did not challenge the authority of the sultan, whose popularity as caliph was undiminished.[22] There seems to have been a degree of image-splitting in the attitudes of Kurds towards the sultan. To the extent he was associated with the government, he might be perceived as weak and unsupportive. But Ottoman officials and Kurdish leaders' efforts to control administration and trade functioned as a sort of smoke-screen between the people and the sultan. This left the latter free to operate in the minds of the people simply as the caliph, the spiritual leader.

ʿAbdülḥamīd encouraged this image-splitting by focussing on Muslim unity to consolidate Kurdish allegiance to the empire. He often blamed the Porte for the implementation of the unpopular reform measures meant to alleviate injustices towards the Armenians, while he emphasized his role as caliph.[23] To this extent, the *Ḥijāz* railway, and its important function in facilitating pilgrimages to Mecca, served to cement his claim as spiritual leader of all Muslims. Claiming that Europe was carrying out a new crusade disguised as politics,[24] he could emphasize the role of Muslim unity in surviving the onslaught.

---

[21] Behrendt (1993), p. 217, appraising standard assessments of ʿUbaydullāh as the first true national leader, comes to the same conclusion. He shares Bruinessen's reservations about the text, which is known only in its English translation. Possibly, the "worldview of the translator" affected the nationalist tenor of the statement.

[22] Nikitine (1975), p. 189.

[23] Duguid (1973), p. 142.

[24] Ende (1984), p. 81: "Among the political and intellectual leaders in the Ottoman Empire in the last years of the 19th century it was common to view European policy of the time towards Islam in general and Turkey in particular, in a historical parallel to the crusades. Sultan ʿAbdülḥamīd II repeatedly expressed the view that Europe was carrying on a crusade against him and his empire under the cloak of politics".

Whereas Maḥmūd had tried to subjugate the Kurds through force and warfare, ʿAbdülḥamīd saw the Kurds as allies in the struggle against the advance of the great powers and the nationalism they fomented among the Christian minorities. The sultan established irregular cavalry units, the so-called *Ḥamīdīye*, who were recruited by the leaders of the tribes. They were educated at specially established schools, armed and placed outside the jurisdiction of Ottoman administration and regular military command. With these advantages, they could easily rise against their neighbors with impunity. Although the experience of serving in a completely Kurdish regiment doubtless had some positive effects on Kurdish unity,[25] later nationalist leaders and scholars were unanimous in their assessment that the establishment of the *Ḥamīdīye* reflected the old pattern of encouraging factionalism by playing off the Kurds against one another. The balance of power was tipped against all those who were not in alliance with the Sunni tribes who constituted the *Ḥamīdīye*, such as the Alevi, who were not included in the recruitment process.[26] *Ḥamīdīye* terrorization of the Armenians nourished the image abroad of Kurds as primitive, uncontrollable and brutal.[27] *Ḥamīdīye* rule was an obstacle to any efforts to impose order on the Kurdish provinces.[28]

Kurdistan, then, at the end of the 19th century, presented a picture of dissolution, fractionalization and tribal conflict. If there was any unifying tendency at all, any indication of a larger, "transcendental" identity, it was Muslim identity and loyalty to ʿAbdülḥamīd, the "Father of the Kurds".[29] There is no indication that the boundaries between the Kurds and other ethnic groups such as the Turks were significant. The boundaries between the tribes themselves were only surmounted by the antagonisms towards Christians—and this opposition had become more entrenched.[30] Christians were seen as

---

[25] See below for the participation of *Ḥamīdīye* leaders in the Saʿīd Revolt.

[26] Olson (1989), pp. 11–12. This had consequences for Kurdish solidarity in the early 20th century. Alevis supported, for the most part, Young Turks and the Turkish Republic. They did not take part in the Saʿīd revolt, see p. 90.

[27] See p. 24.

[28] See Bruinessen (1992 a), pp. 187–188, on one of the most famous *Ḥamīdīye* leaders, İbrāhīm Pasha, referred to as the "uncrowned king of Kurdistan". He was loyal to the sultan but one of the worst enemies of the provincial administration.

[29] Bruinessen (1992 a), p. 268.

[30] As Duguid (1973), p. 151, points out, by 1895 there was no distinction made between revolutionaries and other Armenians: enmity was generalized.

inimical to the Muslims, already having usurped Muslim privileges, as well as having demonstrated their disloyalty to the empire.

Muslim identity was both jeopardized and reinforced by the superiority of the Western powers and their widely perceived intention to feast on the empire once the "Sick Man of Europe" collapsed. ʿAbdülḥamīd had successfully channelled diffuse feelings of frustration, fear and aggression into enmity towards the Armenians, thus assuring that the Kurds remained firmly anchored in the Ottoman camp.

CHAPTER TWO

ḤAMIDIAN OPPOSITION

In the last quarter of the 19th century, numerous schools and institutions of higher education were established in the Ottoman Empire to meet the need and demand for secular education which was now seen as crucial for catching up with the West.[1] The devastating loss of territorial possessions as a result of the Russo-Turkish War had reinforced an awareness that the empire's strength was on the wane. Feelings of vulnerability, fear and self-loathing in the face of obvious European superiority and control engendered an identity crisis. Among the Western values and ideas absorbed by the graduates of the secular schools were the concepts of the nation and its concomitants: democracy, patriotism and the criteria for national differentiation. The well-proved model for aspiring nations, patterned after the Italian process from the Renaissance to the Risorgimento, made cultural revival a prerequisite for the "rebirth" of a nation. These concepts determined much of Muslim discourse on reform and on redefining Ottoman identity. Due to Ḥamidian censorship and bans on political discussion, "historical and cultural matters assumed a great importance in the newspapers and magazines. These subjects, particularly language and literature, gave rise to heated debates, which often served as a disguise for political controversy".[2]

Turks and Kurds were united in their opposition to ʿAbdülḥamīd, who was seen as the main obstacle in achieving reform,[3] but the preoccupation of the Turks with their language and culture prompted the Kurds to take an interest in their own. The small elite of Kurdish intellectuals originating primarily from notable families of the Kurdish provinces, had to acknowledge not only Western superiority, but also their own particularly negative image in Europe. In as much

[1] For the origins and development of Ottoman higher education from the middle of the 19th century onwards see the present author's unpublished *habilitation* thesis (University of Bamberg, 1994).

[2] Kushner (1977), pp. 14–15.

[3] The group of four who established the CUP in 1889 included two Kurds, ʿAbdullāh Cevdet and İsḥāḳ Sükūtī, see Hanioğlu (1995), passim.

as they were known at all,[4] they were considered wild, primitive and cruel, mainly as a result of their widely publicized repression of the Armenians.[5]

The Ottoman discourse on reform and identity increasingly became influenced by Western Orientalist views and Turkist ideas in the second half of the 19th century.[6] Although the majority of the Young Ottomans had sought an identity which embraced other ethnic and religious groups, from the beginning they had difficulty envisioning a non-Muslim identity. Soon they began to see the Turks as the most dependable of Ottomans and to focus on Turkish history, literature and language. This orientation and the absolute lack of interest in the Kurds underlined the vulnerability of Kurdish culture. The Kurdish language was not employed in writing and had been neglected as a cultural medium, and Kurdish history was unknown even to the Kurds themselves. Kurds who began to feel they should attend to Kurdish cultural needs did not see this additional focus as contradictory to their Ottoman identity as reformers. Even Ziya Gökalp, later to become the "Turkish Mazzini",[7] was apparently involved in this early cultural revival and is reported to have participated in compiling a Kurdish grammar and dictionary.[8] Nevertheless, there were isolated individuals who already propagated Kurdish separateness. The posthumously influential poet Hadji Ḳadirī Koyī, who was

[4] Kadri Cemil Paşa (1991), p. 36, relates the following anecdote: "On the day I moved into the pension . . . in Lausanne the landlady asked me in in front of the guests from more then ten different countries gathered at the dining table: 'Monsieur you come from İstanbul—are you a Turk or a Greek?' In my broken French I answered: 'Neither Turk nor Greek'. In answer to her question 'Then what nation do you belong to'? I answered: 'I am a Kurd'. Everyone at the table looked at me as if they had heard something very strange. Of course I was embarrassed. And I was hurt that I belonged to a nation that nobody knew. Fortunately there were two Russians present who helped me and were able to say something about the Kurds and Kurdistan. The next day I sat in the salon after breakfast. The landlady asked: 'You say you are Kurdish. Where is your country?' I opened the map lying in the living room and pointed to the city Diyarbakır where the name Kurdistan was written in large letters and said: 'This is where I come from'. The landlady had told her friend, Monsieur Jacques who was the editor of the newspaper *Gazette de Lausanne*, that she had a Kurdish guest. Monsieur Jacques had answered: 'I can't imagine a Kurd in a European salon'". Kadri Cemil attributed the mistaken notion that Kurds were a "wild mountain people" to Armenian propaganda.

[5] As late as 1944 an English officer asserted, "Kurds are generally known to the outside world as a race of bloodthirsty brigands", Burton (1944), p. 67.

[6] Kushner (1977), esp. chapter 3.

[7] Lemberg (1964), vol. 1, p. 270.

[8] Kadri Cemil Paşa (1991), pp. 29–30.

residing with the Bedir Khān family at the time of his death in 1897, railed against Ottoman leaders and sheykhs, encouraging the Kurds to liberate themselves from the yoke of the Turks. But as he recorded in his poems, no one would listen to his advice or warnings. "They dispute my wholesome words", preferring the "illusions of the sheykhs".[9] Edmonds uses the case of Hadji Ḳadirī Koyī to support his exaggerated argument that nationalism developed among the Kurds in the second half of the 19th century, "parallel with other subject races of the Ottoman Empire".[10]

---

[9] Fuad (1970), p. XXXVI.
[10] Edmonds (1971), p. 88.

CHAPTER THREE

KÜRDISTĀN

After the failed putsch against ʿAbdülḥamīd in 1896, many opponents of the regime went into exile, among them prominent Kurds such as ʿAbdülḳādir, the son of ʿUbaydullāh, and the sons of the *emir* of Botan. Miḳdād Midḥat Bedir Khān took up residence in Cairo, one of the centers of opposition to ʿAbdülḥamīd, and in 1898, he founded the first Kurdish newspaper, *Kürdistān*, with the subtitle "Newspaper in the Kurdish language for the purpose of awakening the Kurds and for encouraging the study of the arts".[1] The first three issues were published in Kurdish, but, beginning with the fourth issue, there were articles in Turkish. This shift reflected a crucial dilemma of the Kurds. The defining characteristic of the Kurds as opposed to other groups was language, but their language was rarely printed or taught and was not standardized. *Kürdistān* was written in the Kurmanjī dialect of Botan, which was not necessarily understood by educated Kurds speaking other Kurmanjī dialects.[2] The newspaper was to be distributed free in Kurdistan. While we might assume that many of the illiterate Kurds would have had access to a newspaper reader in the village café, it remains a matter of conjecture how many literate Kurds would have been able or motivated to

[1] No. 1 (30 Ḏūlḳaʿde 1315/9 Nisān 1314/April 22, 1898): "Kürdleri īḳāẓ ve taḥṣīl-i ṣanāʾīʿe teşvīḳ için şimdilik on beş günde bir neşr olunur Kürdçe ġazetedir." Beginning with no. 3 (28 Ḏūlḥicce 1315/7 Mayıs 1314/May 20, 1898) the title runs: "Kürdleri taḥṣīl-i ʿulūm ve fünūna teşvīḳ eder naṣāʾiḥ ve edebiyāt-i Kürdīyeyi ḥāvī on beş günde bir neşr olunur Kürdçe ġazetedir." Although in the preceding numbers there were articles in Turkish, only in no. 25 (6 Cumādelāḫire 1318/18 Eylül 1316/ Otober 1, 1900) is it added: ". . . ve Türkçe ġazetedir." *Kürdistān* was printed successively in Cairo, Geneva, London, Folkstone and again in Geneva. I have used the reprint by Kamāl Fuʾād (1972) (nrs. 10, 12, 17, 18 and 19 are missing in that reprint).

[2] Martin Hartmann who conducted studies on the Kurdish language at the turn of the century, interviewed an educated Kurd from Diyarbakır in Paris. Ferīd Bey, a scion of a notable family in Diyarbakır and nephew of a *Ḥamīdīye* officer, had spoken nothing but Kurmanjī before being sent to Istanbul to the *ʿAşiret Mektebi*. He was able to read and comprehend an issue of *Kürdistān* only with great difficulty, although his comprehension improved when it was read to him: Makas (1979), pp. 1–3.

overcome the difficulties presented by an unfamiliar dialect. According to the impressum the circulation numbered 2.000; the newspaper was free of charge. Later the publication was transferred to Geneva (starting with No. 6) and edited by Miḳdād's brother ʿAbdurraḥmān Bedir Khān,[3] who was a member of the Young Turk opposition and closely associated with the newspaper *ʿO̱tmānlı*, edited by ʿAbdullāh Cevdet and İsḥāḳ Süḳūtī, the two Kurds who had been co-founders of the Committee of Union and Progress (CUP).[4]

The issues of *Kürdistān* manifest an unabashed Kurdish self-awareness and attribute Kurdish suffering to a long history of Ottoman domination. Kurds are portrayed as the victims of bloodthirsty padishahs.[5] But this generalization, which placed blame squarely in Ottoman quarters, must be seen as reflecting the particular sentiments of the Bedir Khān family. They were a singular case, having been forced to live in exile after their father's defeat and thus feeling robbed of their rightful status. Through ʿAbdülḥamīd's policies in the Kurdish province they must have felt their province was being further alienated from their hereditary leadership.[6] It is reasonable to assume that national concepts and the role of leadership in propagating them offered the Bedir Khāns a prospect for regaining status. By belonging to and, to a certain extent, constituting the avant garde, they became the self-appointed awakeners, saviours and spokesmen of their people, thus extending—if in modified fashion—the myth of their father's services to his people. But we should not reductively view the Bedir Khāns' zeal in propagating Kurdish awareness as sheer opportunism. Certainly they had been transformed by a secular education and saw this as the only solution to Kurdish backwardness. Only with the skills acquired in a secular education could Kurds hope to participate in modern society. One of the first issues contains a petition in Turkish to ʿAbdülḥamīd to allow distribution of the paper in the Kurdish provinces.[7] The absence of a Kurdish

---

[3] He gives an account of his biography in *Kürdistān* no. 26 (22 Ramażān 1318/1 Kānūn-i evvel 1316/January 13th 1901), pp. 1–2.

[4] Hanioğlu (1995), passim.

[5] Ibrahim (1983), p. 179, note 3 translating a passage in Kurdish in *Kürdistān* no. 27 (22 Ḏūlḳaʿde 1318/28 Şubāṭ 1316/March 13, 1901).

[6] Ḥamīdīye Pasha İbrāhīm had erected a virtual kingdom in Botan: Bruinessen (1989), pp. 250–252.

[7] "Şevketlü ʿaẓīmetlü sulṭān ʿAbdülḥamīd-i ṯānī hażretlerine ʿarżu ḥāl-i ʿabidānemdir", no. 4 (12 Ḏūlḥicce 1316/21 Mayıs 1314/April 23, 1899), pp. 1–2; no. 5 (27 Muḥarrem

newspaper and the lack of education among the Kurds are cited as the reasons not only for Kurdish backwardness but also for foreign intervention in the eastern provinces.[8]

In time-honoured fashion, the editors of *Kürdistān* appeal to the nation to awaken from their sleep of ignorance.[9] They must recognize their backwardness, deprivation and vulnerability and they must change if they are to survive in the modern world. Aside from trying to instill notions of the necessity and value of education in their readers, the authors lay the foundation for creating a Kurdish national identity. Wishing to recreate the nation in their own enlightened image, they postulate the Kurds as a separate, distinct group with a heroic past. The authors, following in the footsteps of the Ottoman Turks, present the standard evidence for the existence and worth of a nation: an old history, great Kurdish leaders, foremost among them Saladin,[10] and monuments of cultural achievement such as *Mem ū Zīn*,[11] which exemplified the potential of a Kurdish people unhampered by foreign oppressors. The language, which was powerful enough to allow Aḥmad-i Khānī to become a great poet, could once again sustain a great culture. The Kurds could again become a nation able to hold its own with developed Western cultures. Thus offering a new self-definition, criteria by which the Kurds should assess themselves, and values by which to determine their goals, *Kürdistān* authors charted the course which they hoped would lead to a new identity based not on tribal or religious affiliation but on a shared culture and language.

In order to achieve a national revival it was paramount that the Kurds recognize the sultan's culpability in their present dilemma. The sultan's policies are demasked as self-serving and as neglecting

1316 [sic]/4 Ḥazīrān 1314/June 17, 1898) [the date in the original seems to be wrong], pp. 1–2. Cf. Hartmann (1898), p. 112: "Es (*Kürdistān*, MS) ist in der Türkei verboten, und jeder Kurde, in dessen Händen es angetroffen wird, wird schwer bestraft."

[8] *Kürdistān* no. 4, p. 2.

[9] See Strohmeier (2002, forthcoming).

[10] Ende (1984), pp. 79 sqq., demonstrates that it was the awakened interest in the crusades as a parallel to contemporary history which led to the discovery that Saladin, in contrast to other Muslim heroes, was highly admired in the West and thus was a likely figure to restore Muslim pride. Saladin's career as Muslim hero was already several decades old when the Kurds claimed him as their own. Nāmıḳ Kemāl published a Saladin biography in 1872.

[11] See the following chapter.

Kurdish needs. His use of the *Ḥamīdīye* troops is presented as a plot to subvert the Kurds by inciting them to violence against the Armenians, thus discrediting the Kurds in the eyes of the world. The authors frequently appeal to their compatriots to cease hostilities towards the Armenians, to realize that it is the sultan who is truly responsible for Kurdish suffering.[12] It is assumed that if the Kurds see ʿAbdülḥamīd as the inimical other, instead of identifying with his goals and values, they will awaken to their true interests. They will be able to shift their loyalty and orient their aims and expectations towards Kurdish solidarity.[13] Although the attempt to deconstruct ʿAbdülḥamīd's image as father of the Kurds implies the culpability of all Ottoman sultans in holding back the Kurds, this theme is not taken up again in this or later issues.

The aims of the publishers of *Kürdistān* were twofold: to postulate the Kurds as a separate group with a proud past and the potential to compete with other nations, and to diminish ʿAbdülḥamīd's great attraction for Kurdish leaders and the masses. It is possible that the Bedir Khāns would have liked to inveigh against the Muslim identity of the Kurds, but in order to appeal to their projected reader they rather invoked Koran verses and *ḥadīṯs*.[14] We must assume they realized that they could not gain support from tribal leaders or sheykhs by preaching an anti-religious identity. Nevertheless, religion played a minor role in the deliberations of the authors.

In the proclaimed efforts of the publishers to support the arts and crafts (*fünūn*), *Kürdistān* published poetry by Kurdish writers, among them Hadji Ḳadirī Koyī (approx. 1817–1897), a revolutionary poet who had attacked foreign rule, feudal lords and religious leaders who exploited people under the cover of religion.[15] In his poems, written in Sorani, the opposition to the Ottomans is direct and unqualified. He laments how little Kurds know of the world, thinking that "only the Turkish and the Persian sultans exist".[16] Ḳadirī Koyī advises the Kurds quietly to acquire cannons, rifles and mortars instead of hop-

---

[12] *Kürdistān* no. 27, p. 2: ". . . Kurds you are selling your honour . . .".

[13] "Kürdistānın vażʿīyet-i ḥażıra ve müstaḳbelesi", *Kürdistān* no. 29 (2 Receb 1319/1 Teşrīn-i evvel 1317/October 15, 1901), p. 3: "Ignorant people follow the shepherd like a flock of sheep".

[14] Ibrahim (1983), p. 180.

[15] Fuad (1970), p. XXXIII.

[16] Cf. also *Kürdistān* no. 25, p. 3: ". . . We are orphans in the world of civilization and politics . . ."

ing for intercession in today's world: "The arrow is the blessed coat of mail and the spear is protection on the battlefield."[17] In another poem he appeals to the Kurds to follow the example of the Bulgarians, Serbs, Greeks and Armenians who are independent because they fought against Ottoman rule. Ḳadirī Koyī eventually came to live in İstanbul with the Bedir Khāns, where he tutored and made family members familiar with *Mem ū Zīn*.

While we may assume that the Bedir Khāns were influenced by Ḳadirī Koyī's views, their agenda required that they create interest and support for exploring Kurdish history and language. Their most likely disciples would be drawn from the educated, urbanized Kurdish elite who had joined ranks with the opposition to ʿAbdülḥamīd, and were not of a mind to question their Ottoman loyalty. The authors confined themselves to forging stronger bonds between Kurds and their culture, trying to suggest an alternative, positive, future-oriented identity which offered hope for overcoming the perils and obstacles to their continued existence.

"Fatherland" (*vaṭan*) and "nation" (*millet*) are used at times to refer to the Ottoman Empire; at times to Kurdistan.[18] This implies that a clear distinction between "us" and "them" was lacking. If ʿAbdülḥamīd was the foe, then his elimination alone would solve the problem. Potentially divisive ethnic boundaries of the group are named but not developed. For this reason it would be anachronistic to find in early Kurdish newspapers and clubs indicators of a developed nationalism. Even if the model of Kurdish identity developed by the Bedir Khāns and carried on in the years following the Young Turk Revolution had been embraced, it would not have been a viable basis for a nationalist movement as it lacked the clear-cut notion of opposition.[19] But if we consider the three-phase model elaborated by Hroch in analyzing the development of national movements amongst smaller European nations, the newspaper *Kürdistān* belongs squarely in the first phase, the awakening of an interest and involvement in the language, history and culture of a people, usually on the part of intellectuals. This is followed by a second phase

[17] Fuad (1970), pp. XXXIII–XXXIV. Ibrahim (1983), p. 179.

[18] *Kürdistān* no. 7, p. 1: Kurdistan is called "real fatherland" (*vaṭan-i aṣlī*); no. 24, p. 3: Kurds are called a nation (*Kürd milleti*). The Kurdish word *welat* denotes Kurdistan: Ibrahim (1983), p. 181, note 3.

[19] Touraine (1974), pp. 174 sqq.

in which national interests appeal to a wider circle and the political program is formulated, culminating in the final phase: a mass movement.[20]

Many aspects of the Kurdish image portrayed by the authors of *Kürdistān* eventually became firmly entrenched in the self-definition of Kurdish nationalists, and have remained so to this day, especially when support for the Kurdish cause is being enlisted abroad. No single element has proved as enduring as Aḥmad-i Khānī's epic poem *Mem ū Zīn*, extracts of which were printed for the first time in *Kürdistān*.[21]

---

[20] Hroch (1968), pp. 24–25.
[21] Starting in no. 2 (14 D̲ūlDicce 1315/23 Nīsān 1314), p. 4.

CHAPTER FOUR

MEM Ū ZĪN

Mem ū Zīn constitutes the backbone of the argument that Kurds are a nation capable of attaining a high level of civilization, and possessing a language which can yield great literature. Nikitine referred to Khānī as the "Kurdish Firdousi".[1] The very existence of a great epic poem was fortunate for those early devotees of Kurdish language and literature. But the fact that the poem dated from the 17th century[2] and bore witness to an age-old concern with the Kurdish language and culture was a tremendous boon. The epic lends itself astonishingly well to the exigencies of national identity building because of its many-faceted appeal to diverse groups in Kurdish society. It is therefore not surprising that it is the most frequently-quoted text in the literature dealing with Kurdish nationalism,[3] and has become almost a "Declaration of Independence" in Kurdish history.

From the prologue, in which the poet informs his readers or listeners about his own assessment of the Kurdish situation and his poetic intentions, to the eponymous tale of the two lovers, a wide range of characters appear, symbolizing ideal and culpable behavior on a spiritual as well as material-social plane. On the level of the simple moral tale, the figures may easily be categorized as good and bad, heroes and traitors. The good characters embody what is noble in the Kurdish character and worthy of emulation; the negative characters represent what must be corrected or eliminated.[4] Their actions indicate paths to achieving various goals of self-realization. It is significant that all the characters are Kurdish, in contrast with

---

[1] Nikitine (1975), p. 281.

[2] Aḥmad-i Khānī was probably born in 1650–1 and may have died as late as 1707, see Shakely (1992), pp. 17 and 31.

[3] The following authors are only a few of those referring to *Mem ū Zīn* in the framework of the Kurdish nationalist argument: Edmonds (1971), Nikitine (1975), Bruinessen (1992 a), Ghassemlou (1965), Ibrahim (1983).

[4] Khānī's pedagogical inclinations can be surmised not only from the text itself but also from other writings, also in Kurdish with clear didactic intent, see Shakely (1992), pp. 34–39.

the various oral renderings of the fairy tale in which Mem, for example, might be the son of the King of Yemen. I assume that Nikitine[5] is not referring to Khānī's poem, since in the two available versions which I was able to consult, all the characters were Kurdish. Shakely also refers to Mem "in the old story" as having been the son of the King of Yemen but "Khani deprived him of his origins and kurdified him".[6]

Extracts of *Mem ū Zīn* were published in *Kürdistān* and other Kurdish newspapers established in İstanbul after the Young Turk Revolution.[7] However, from the very beginning, proponents of Kurdish nationalism have been almost exclusively interested in the part of the poem which later came to be known as the prologue (*dībacha*, from Persian *dībāče*) under the title "Derdē ma" (translated into Turkish as "Derdimiz", "our suffering").[8] This so-called introduction, but without the chapter heading, was published in the eigth issue of *Kürdistān*.[9] Celādet Bedir Khān wrote in 1933 in an open letter to Atatürk that his father, Emīn ʿĀli, brother of Midḥat and ʿAbdurraḥmān had tried to have *Mem ū Zīn* published in 1894 but that the committee in charge of granting permission censored large parts and so Emīn ʿĀli did not publish it.[10] It is easy to see why the sultan's censors would not have accepted such lines as those referring to Khānī's wish for a Kurdish king to "extract us from the hands of the vile"[11] and make them "our servants".[12]

---

[5] Nikitine (1975), p. 277.

[6] (1992), p. 97. See pp. 30, 34–35 on Khānī and the oral tradition.

[7] Starting in no. 2 (14 Ḏūlḥicce 1315/23 Nīsān 1314), p. 4. E.g., *Jīn* no. 12 (25 Şubāṭ 1335), pp. 14–15. Cf. the commentary of Memdūḥ Selīm Begi: "(Mem ū Zīn)'in ṭabʿı münāsebetiyle", *Jīn* no. 16 (10 Nīsān 1335), pp. 8–9. Also: "Mem ū Zīn'in ṭabʿı ḫitām buldu", *Jīn* no. 18 (8 Mayıs 1335). The foreword of the first printed version in bookform by Mukuslu Ḥamza can be found in *Jīn* No. 19 (21 Mayıs 1335), pp. 12–14.

[8] This chapter heading was inserted by Bozarslan (1968) in his edition and Turkish translation of *Mem ū Zīn*.

[9] (5 Receb 1316/18 Teşrīn-i ṯānī 1314/November 20, 1898), p. 4. It is interesting to note that the version in the critical edition of Rudenko (1962), p. 34, verse 232, and the one in *Kürdistān* differ in the respect that in *Kürdistān* a "Rūs" (Russian) is added. Surely, this is a modern addition which shows how flexibly, or rather manipulatively, texts like these were treated. Cf. also the complete version of the *dībacha* in Turkish in Sasuni (1986), pp. 48–50.—The prologue was also published, though without mentioning the "Rūs", by Ṣāliḥ Bedir Khān (in Kurdish): "Ḳaṣīdā Hażret-i Şeykh Aḥmad-i Khānī", *Rojē Kurd* no. 3 (11 Ramażān 1331/1 Ağustos 1329/August 14, 1913), pp. 27–29.

[10] Bedirxan (1992), p. 28.

[11] Meaning Turks and Persians, Shakely (1992), p. 125.

[12] Shakely (1992), p. 130.

But more important than the availability of the prologue is the assessment of the Kurdish situation, which could so effortlessly be applied to the contemporary situation of Kurds, while lending a prophetic aura and historical legitimacy to the appeals of early proponents of Kurdish nationalism. Lamenting the servitude and deprivation of the Kurds, Khānī appeals to them to recognize their faults and their virtues. They are the victims of their neighbors, but only because they are "always disunited, they are always rebellious and split".[13] If they were to unite under one authority, their zeal and bravery would enable them to drive out their oppressors and "we would obtain knowledge and wisdom".[14] Khānī sees the Kurds of his time as "deprived", "destitute" and "doomed",[15] but there had been a golden time in the past when they had been heroes: "Every one of their princes is like Hatam in generosity. Every one of their men is like Rustam in bravery".[16]

Aspiring nationalists could find not only eloquent statements of their own convictions in "Derdē ma", but also the inspiring image of the poet himself as a figure worthy of emulation. The prologue contains a well-developed self-portrayal of the man of letters cum patriot, a paragon of dedication and self-sacrifice: "I suffered for the sake of the people".[17] Hating those responsible for the suffering of the Kurds, and envisioning a future where the Kurds could be free and responsible for their own cultural development, the poet forgoes the rewards of fame and success by not writing in Arabic or Persian as convention dictated.[18] Disdaining the language of the rulers, he wrote in Kurdish so that people would not say "the Kurds are without knowledge, without origins".[19] The lines introducing the tale explain how the story of *Mem ū Zīn* is to be interpreted. The poet states he is using the story as a "pretext"[20] and leaves no doubt that the tale is to be taken as an allegory of the Kurdish situation, an appeal to Kurds to throw off their oppressors.

Armed with verses that so easily lent themselves to use as direct agitation for Kurdish identity and unity, and inspired by the poet

[13] Shakely (1992), p. 129.
[14] Shakely (1992), p. 130.
[15] Shakely (1992), p. 131.
[16] Shakely (1992), p. 128.
[17] Shakely (1992), p. 130.
[18] Nebez (1969), p. 8.
[19] Shakely (1992), p. 130.
[20] Shakely (1992), p. 136.

himself as prophet and patriot, those mobilizing for the acceptance and support for a Kurdish cause might have felt the introduction provided more ample and sophisticated munition than did the tale of *Mem ū Zīn*, especially since it derived from the Kurdish oral narrative tradition. Educated Kurds prior to 1919[21] would probably not have had access to Khānī's version; they would have been familiar with one of the oral versions sung by minstrels.[22] In Celādet Bedir Khān's open letter to Atatürk he claims[23] that *Mem ū Zīn* circulated in the *medreses* of Kurdistan.[24] He may have been equivocating Khānī's poem with the oral versions that, by all accounts, were familiar to all Kurds.[25] Oskar Mann, who studied the Mukrī Kurds, recorded extracts from the poem as narrated by a professionally-trained bard who made his living reciting poems of the epic tradition in wealthy homes and coffee-houses.[26] Educated Kurds would have felt that such products of the oral tradition were inferior to written works.

It is difficult to say when and to what extent Khānī's version of *Mem ū Zīn*[27] influenced the process of identification. But a perusal of the two versions of the poem available in English and German[28] suggests that the epic tale had remarkable potential for being incorporated into early 20th-century patterns of identity and affiliation,

[21] See Nebez (1969), pp. 9–10 on editions, and Shakely (1992), p. 8.

[22] Bruinessen (1992 a), pp. 81–85, spoke in the 1970s with people who still remembered the *divāns* of wealthy *aghas* who would provide musical entertainment.

[23] Bedirxan (1992), p. 28.

[24] Bruinessen (1992), pp. 35–36, also states that Kurdish students until the 20th century studied Kurdish authors, including Khānī, at the *medreses*.

[25] For different versions of the narrative compare Makas (1979), and the more modern tellings upon which Alan Ward (1961) and Lescot/Wentzel (1980) based their narratives.

[26] The author describes the song schools to which youths with fine voices were sent to learn the epic tradition from masters who themselves had learned the poems orally: Mann (1906), pp. XXVIII–XXIX.

[27] I was not able to get hold of the book of Michael Chyet: *"And a thornbush sprang up between them": Studies on Mem u Zin, a Kurdish romance*. Ph.D. thesis, University of California, 1991.

[28] Shakely (1992) and Nebez (1969). Strictly speaking, only the latter may be considered a "version" of the poem. Both books were published by Kurdish scholars and both base their studies on the edition by Rudenko (1962). Shakely's study, as the title suggests, primarily considers the nationalist message in Khānī's poem, and focusses on the prologue. Of the actual story, only the scene in which rebellion is discussed warrants his attention. However, his translations are useful. Nebez, on the other hand, disregards the prologue and provides a prose summary of the story in German.

while projecting a broadly inclusive and thus integrative image of Kurdish identity as well as generating strong sympathies.

The story takes place in Botan.[29] It is the feast of *newroz* and the two young sisters of the *emir* have disguised themselves as men in order to wander among the crowds in the streets and form an idea of the men they would like to marry. They watch as two girls (actually men disguised as women) collapse. Zīn and Siti, who now have to rush back to the castle, leave their rings with the "girls" to whom they have taken a fancy.

The men in disguise are actually Tajdīn, the son of a minister, and Mem, a secretary at the court. When they see the names of the girls on the rings they are wearing they realize that the two youths they had seen before losing consciousness must have been the princesses. Mem is then overcome with longing for Zīn, whose ring he bears. Tajdīn tries to persuade him that, having a reputation for valour, they should not betray a weakness. But Mem declares he has lost his strength and bravery and is consumed by love. Meanwhile, the sisters have learned that their rings now belong to the two youths.

Pitying Mem, Tajdīn speaks to his brothers and their influential friends who arrange Tajdīn's marriage to Siti. Their strategy is that soon thereafter Mem may ask for the hand of Zīn.[30] After the wedding, Tajdīn advises the *emir* to expel his gate-keeper Bakr, whom Tajdīn knows to be base and vile. Bakr tries to exact revenge on Tajdīn by telling the *emir* that Tajdīn intends to exploit his relationship with the *emir* in order to usurp his relations' position. The *emir*, who is fond of Tajdīn, is at first doubtful. As proof of Tajdīn's arrogance, Bakr relates that Tajdīn had promised his wife's sister, Zīn, to Mem. Bakr tricks Mem into disclosing his love for Zīn, which seems to corroborate Bakr's conspiracy theory. The *emir*, enraged, has Mem taken to prison and placed in chains. The suffering of the two lovers begins. They will not be reunited until shortly before their deaths.

Deprived of their rightful partners, Mem and Zīn gradually waste away, but through suffering their love is transformed into a mystical quest for pure spiritual love. Their desire to be united becomes

[29] Bedirxan had been the *emir* of Botan. This may explain the family's dedication to popularizing the work. Cf. Bruinessen (1992 b), p. 49.

[30] In Nebez' retelling of the story the reason for Mem being second in line is his poverty, which apparently provides obstacles to his marrying nobility, p. 21.

an eagerness to die and thus achieve union with God.[31] Meanwhile, Mem's friends and Zīn's sister wait helplessly for the *emir* to have a change of heart. Finally, Tajdīn's brother insists it is time to use violence to force the *emir* to liberate Mem: "We will either release our Mem with blow or all of us will sacrifice our heads, manfully".[32] But one last time they ask for Mem's freedom, this time threatening to take matters into their own hands if he is not released. The *emir*, fearing an uprising, leads them to believe he will fulfill their demands when in fact Bakr has persuaded him to kill Mem. But when the *emir* visits his sister, intending to use her in his plot to do away with Mem, he finds her bedridden. Shocked at her condition, he realizes the suffering he has caused and is filled with remorse over betraying his sister and Mem. A messenger's report that Mem is dying revives Zīn who announces that her brother's compassion and contrition have freed her soul to leave her body and fly to Mem's soul. She directs her brother to celebrate her funeral with a feast as grand as her sister's wedding, and bids him to help the lonely, poor and oppressed, poets and artists "who burn like a candle" in order to enlighten their fellow men.[33]

When Mem is told shortly thereafter that he should go to the *emir* who wishes to free him, he proudly refuses to bow before the prince, "to be a servant, slave or prisoner to anyone other than God".[34] The lovers are liberated and united in death[35] as the crowds mourn the loss of the long-suffering victims of deceit. Tajdīn kills Bakr to avenge Mem's suffering.

Mem is not heroic in the sense that he has supernatural origins, strength or courage. On the contrary, he is shown as "weak" in the face of love.[36] He is heroic in the sense that he transcends his own

---

[31] Khānī was apparently very influenced by the writing of Jelāl al-Dīn Rūmī as both Nikitine (1975), p. 282, and Shakely (1992), p. 51, point out. Even Nebez' prose summary suggests the proximity to Sufi thought and the allegorical aspect of Mem and Zīn's suffering.

[32] Shakely (1992), p. 139.

[33] Nebez (1969), p. 39.

[34] Nebez (1969), p. 41.

[35] This union in the grave accounts for references to the epic as the "Kurdish Romeo and Juliet". In Makas' version (1979) the lovers are buried separately and Mem's grave is reopened some time after burial to reveal the lovers lying together, p. 14.

[36] It is interesting that Mem, in what I have gleaned of the oral tradition, is stronger and heroic in a more physical sense as one would expect in a heroic epic.

humanity in his willingness to sacrifice his life for his love and honour. Mem has been widely interpreted as a symbol of Kurdistan enchained, and the story as showing the way to save the nation.[37] All the characters are Kurdish and emblematic of the troubles and strengths of Kurdistan. The love story operates on a spiritual level, representing the transcendental quest for unity with God. But equally important are earthly love, loyalty and responsibility. Tajdīn and his brother are portrayed as brave, honourable, and capable of sacrificing their lives to free their friend, but too gullible in relying on the *emir* to mete out justice. The *emir* is a basically good man who blindly allows Bakr to drive a wedge between him and his loyal people. Bakr betrays the *emir*'s trust. He is motivated by petty jealousy, revenge and rivalry, thus embodying the qualities that Khānī had listed in the prologue as preventing the unity and happiness of the Kurds. Intensely spiritual as well as worldly-critical, Mem and Zīn would seem to offer both Muslim and secular visionaries of a united Kurdish nation, a treasure trove of inspiring role models encompassing the poet as patriot, heroes willing to sacrifice their lives for lofty values, and a ruler who, though initially led astray, is enlightened by the sufferings of Mem and Zīn and may be expected now to pursue the lofty mission that Zīn articulated. Bakr is the enemy within, the traitor: disloyal and self-serving. Apart from him, Kurds are shown as noble individuals, united in one political entity, dependent on the loyalty and devotion of all the community to achieve well-being.

If Mem represents Kurdistan without love or freedom, the victim of injustice, then surely the author was implying that the Kurds must unite and rise against wrongdoers: "The world becomes subjugated for the human being by sword and goodness".[38] The Bedir Khāns were clearly more interested in the secular appeal of the poem than

---

In the version recorded by Makas, when Mem admits publicly his love for Zīn, the *emir* commands his men to attack Mem with their daggers. Mem reaches for his own dagger with such force that the handle breaks. His friend *Karataschdin* (the Tajdīn of Khānī's poem) the narrator reports, gazes on Mem with admiration. He had never before seen such a man: Makas (1979), p. 11.

[37] Nikitine (1975), p. 179. In Celādet Bedir Khān's open letter to Atatürk he stated that all the heroes in the poem were symbolic, and that Khānī was using them to show solutions for liberating Kurdistan. This 250–year-old concern with Kurdish nationalism refuted, in Celādet's view, Atatürk's contention that Kurdish nationalism was a new development, Bedirxan (1992), p. 21.

[38] Shakely (1992), p. 127.

in its Sufi content, although they may well have realized its potentially integrative force.

Khānī drew on two different fairy tales, primarily it seems from *Memē Alan.*[39] It would be tempting to attribute at least a part of the Bedir Khān enthusiasm for Khānī's poem to the meeting of the "great" and "little" traditions in *Mem ū Zīn.* The poet had drawn on elements of the rich oral tradition to create high culture. It would have been conceivable that intellectuals who had adhered in many respects to European notions of national culture would have imbibed 19th-century romanticization of the simple people. Herder considered folk songs the "archives of the nation", and the unadulterated folk personality the essence of national character.[40] In fact, this attitude was not shared by the Bedir Khāns, who focused on pointing out the high culture of which the Kurds were capable. Makas, who received extensive assistance and encouragement from ʿAbdurraḥmān Bedir Khān in deciphering a Kurmanjī folklore text, reported that Bedir Khān provided willing and helpful remarks but did not hide his disdain as a cultivated Kurd for folk poetry, recommending that Makas focus his attention on Khānī.[41] This disregard for folk culture may be interpreted as an indication of how far this first generation of "patriots" was from being conventional nationalists. "Nationalism usually conquers in the name of a putative folk culture. Its symbolism is drawn from the healthy, pristine, vigorous life of the peasants, of the *Volk* . . .".[42] It was only several decades later, in the second generation of awakeners, that the culture of the *Volk* assumed significance.[43]

Scholars have recorded different versions of the orally transmitted tale which differed significantly from Khānī's version. It is in the

[39] Mam, king of the Kurds. See notes in "Nachwort", Lescot-Wentzel (1980).

[40] Fink (1991), pp. 453–492, here p. 474.

[41] Makas was introduced to Bedir Khān by Martin Hartmann, during Bedir Khān's sojourn in Geneva, pp. 18–19 in "Ein Gedicht aus Gawar": "Je dois aussi vous dire que toutes ces poésies ne sont pas biens fameuses. Je trouve inutil, peut-être même nuisible pour vous de vous occuper de telles poésies, parce que ça pourrait vous mettre dans des grandes erreurs. Il vaut mieux s'occuper des poésies de bons poètes par exemple de . . .".

[42] Gellner (1991), p. 57.

[43] Kushner (1977), pp. 51–53: Under the influence of Vambery, Turkish Ottomans had begun in the 1880's to view peasants as the true bearers of uncorrupted Turkish culture. The Kurds did not adopt a similar attitude until much later, see part three of this study.

nature of oral narrative that the narrator, depending on his own education and experience embellishes the tale. Ward states, "Mam u Zin *is* Kurdish literature", but goes on to ask "*which*" and "*whose*" *Mem ū Zīn*. This difference was ignored by many later nationalists, who perhaps mistakenly assumed that Khānī was the original author of the fairy tale known throughout Kurdistan. But as Khānī's version had not been published and there were few manuscripts, Khānī's version must have been accessible to only a few literate Kurds.

Abstraction and simplification are common strategies of national identity builders. Just as the Kurds were encouraged to declare only **one** language, **one** religion, and **one** culture in order to qualify as the cohesive cultural group a nation was alleged to be, they were to have only **one** *Mem ū Zīn*.

CHAPTER FIVE

İSTANBUL—PROMULGATING THE CASE FOR KURDISH INTERESTS

1. *Kürd Teʿāvün ve Teraḳḳī Cemʿīyeti* and Its Periodical

The first Kurdish organization, the *Kürd Teʿāvün ve Teraḳḳī Cemʿīyeti* ("The Kurdish Society for Mutual Help and Progress") was founded in 1908. A partial list of the founders reveals the predominantly aristocratic and CUP-oriented background of most of the members. This latter factor explains why some of the founders had already received important positions in the new government. Sayyid ʿAbdülḳādir, the first president of the organization, also became president of the senate (*Meclis-i Aʿyān*). He had participated in his father ʿUbaydullāh's revolt and, in 1896, was involved in a plot of the "war office" of the CUP in İstanbul to assassinate the sultan, and was subsequently exiled to Mecca.[1] Both the Bedir Khāns and Bābāns, who had been closely involved with CUP activities, figure among the founders of the organization, e.g.: Emin ʿAlī Bedir Khān and Aḥmed Naʿīm Bābānzāde. Şerīf Pasha, later to be the controversial Kurdish representative at the peace conference in 1919 is also listed as one of the founding members.[2] Recognized as a legitimate oppositional voice during the crucial years of the Young Turks' struggle, Şerīf Pasha was the ambassador to Sweden and had, in the sultan's name, protested against Young Turk participation in a European peace conference. However, after the Young Turk takeover, Şerīf Pasha mediated between the Young Turks and the Germans.[3] Şerīf had tried to secure a position under the CUP; when this didn't work out he turned against them and, in the wake of CUP reaction to the putsch, he was sentenced to death and went into exile.[4] In addition to the members of notable families, we also find persons with more

---

[1] Hanioğlu (1995), pp. 84–5.
[2] Behrendt (1993), pp. 270 sqq. Tunaya (1984), pp. 404 sqq. Sekban (1933), p. 21.
[3] Hanioğlu (1995), pp. 129, 281, note 328.
[4] Behrendt (1993), pp. 275–6.

modest backgrounds, such as Şükrü Meḥmed Sekban, who entered the group as he later reports "for humanitarian reasons".[5]

It is safe to assume that this organization comprised Kurds from different backgrounds (although mostly aristocratic) with varying motivations and ideological orientations, from Western-minded to devout Muslims. It is doubtful that many Kurds of this period had already experienced a romantic self-awakening to the (primary) importance of their Kurdish identities.[6] For the most part, they were attracted by the possibility of their ethnic background assuming significance in the struggle to save the empire and to assure status for themselves. The ideals of the Young Turk Revolution seemed to herald an era of increased Kurdish participation in the political process. As Muslims, they had not been excluded per se from participation but, as a result of their low level of education and the attempts to strengthen and centralize Ottoman bureaucracy, the Kurds felt they were underrepresented in regional administration and desired positions. That the founding Kurds were so prominent and that they had assumed positions of importance in the government were factors which would have encouraged membership in the group. In the first edition of the newspaper *Kürd Teʿāvün ve Teraḳḳī Gazetesi*, there is a page announcing the election of ʿĀrif Pirinççīzāde from Diyarbakır to parliament. He is characterized as possessing "public spirit", and membership in the society of the same name as well as in the CUP in his electorate. Other members of parliament referred to were Maḥmūd Nedīm (Urfa) and Sheykh Ṣafvet.[7]

However, the fall of ʿAbdülḥamīd from power meant the loss of positions and privileges for many Kurds who had enjoyed his protection. We have no information on their membership in or support of the *Kürd Teʿāvün ve Teraḳḳī Cemʿīyeti*. We can only assume they would have broadened the spectrum of the "disaffected", i.e. those dissatisfied with their prospects and in search of advancement, leaders and patrons. One prominent example of this group was Şerīf Pasha.

Predictably, the society's charter contains nothing which is not consonant with CUP ideology. Proclaiming a constitution as the source of progress for state and religion, the charter emphasizes Ottoman identity and the necessity of enlightening the Kurds about

[5] Sekban (1923), p. 8.
[6] See Strohmeier (2002, forthcoming).
[7] Cf. Göldaş (1991), p. 39.

the true compatibility of constitutionalism. In short, by pledging to propagate the values of progress and change among their compatriots, the founders of the society were asserting their one indispensability for the CUP-government in their attempt to reform the empire. Harmony and co-existence with the Nestorians and Armenians are mentioned as goals, and the deep ties to the caliphate are stressed. The society which defined itself as a "caritative organization" (*cemʿīyet-i khayrīye*) also pledges to work towards eliminating dissension among tribes and clans as it stands in the way of progress. The founders of the society declared their intentions to compile textbooks, grammar books and dictionaries to facilitate education in Kurdish. But at the same time, they pledged to support Ottoman Turkish as the official language.[8] This statement of purpose may be regarded as a reassurance that education in the mother tongue would not be a prelude to separatism, as it had been in the course of Ottoman Christian nationalism.

In a political sense, this may not appear such a "radical program". These were more or less the goals that Kurds working closely with the CUP had espoused. The CUP seemed still to be the likeliest means to achieving progress and science which, in turn, were the keys to acquiring some sort of political, cultural and religious sovereignty for the Kurds. Certainly, Kurds of all persuasions felt this, even though some Muslim leaders had misgivings about CUP attitudes towards religion.[9] There is some truth in the assessments of some scholars that leaders of the society were "paternalistic", that they did not share the liberal ideas of the Young Turks,[10] but as Hanioğlu has pointed out, the Young Turks themselves often had only a very utilitarian regard and rhetorical support for constitution and parliament.[11] As in any political movement there was a struggle for power. And, in this respect, the charter is significant in delineating the role that the Kurds and only the Kurds could play in winning over to modernism the backward Kurds of the Eastern provinces.

---

[8] Cf. the *nizāmnāme*, reproduced in Tunaya I (1984), pp. 409, 413.

[9] Behrendt (1993), p. 271.

[10] Behrendt (1993), pp. 271–272, quoting Bruinessen and Nezan.

[11] Hanioğlu (1995), pp. 201, 211. Young Turk thought had been greatly influenced by Le Bon—translated by ʿAbdullāh Cevdet—who devalued parliaments as hazardous bodies. Especially military men in the CUP had been influenced by von der Goltz' book (*Das Volk in Waffen*) which espoused strong government and a superior ruling elite.

The first article of the first issue of *Kürd Teʿāvün ve Teraḳḳī Ġazetesi* paints the same dark and gloomy picture of the Kurds which we encountered in *Kürdistān*. The Kurds are portrayed as having spent so many years with "eyes closed" (*göz ḳapalılıḳ*), "tongues lame" (*dilleri bağlı ḳalmış*), "half butchered" (*nīm-bismil*); and their present condition is contrasted with that time when Kurdish culture had produced brilliant scholars. The aim of the society was to overcome the "terrible darkness" (*müdhiş ḳaranlıḳ*) and "miserable muteness" (*acıḳlı ebkemiyet*) by bewailing the past and smiling towards a bright future.[12] In other words, there was little worth preserving among the Kurds—they must be made over completely.

The newspaper reflected the diversity of background and ideology underlying this group's attempt to stake Kurdish claims. Following in the footsteps of Young Ottomans several decades earlier, İsmāʿīl Ḥaḳḳı Bābān[13] formulated a hierarchy of constitutive identities: the Kurds were first Muslims, then Ottomans; their Kurdish identity was subordinated to the other two.[14] He reflected the convictions of many Kurds that their Kurdish loyalties not override their allegiance to the caliphate and to the Ottoman state.[15] Asserting that Kurds had always been loyal and a "stronghold of Ottomanism", he added that Kurdishness (*Kürdlük*) and Ottomanism (*ʿO̱ṯmānlılıḳ*) belonged together. The Kurds had not changed their nationality (*milliyet*), or their material and spiritual identity. The term *milliyet* was used with a variety of meanings in the late 19th and early 20th centuries. Still, it seems almost daring when Bābān asserts the distinctiveness of a Kurdish identity.

---

[12] Süleymānīyeli M. Tevfīḳ: "Muḳaddime", *Kürd Teʿāvün ve Teraḳḳī Ġazetesi* no. 1, p. 1: ". . . mażīmiz için ağlaya ağlaya ve faḳaṭ istiḳbālimiz için güle güle . . .".—The subtitle of the newspaper reads: "Cemʿīyetin vāsıṭa-i neşr efkārıdır. Şimdilik haftada bir defʿa neşr olunacaḳ dīnī, ʿilmī, siyāsī, edebī, içtimāʿī ġazetedir". According to the impressum Süleymānīyelī Tevfīḳ was publisher and director, whereas Diyārbekirlī Aḥmed Cemīl acted as editor-in-chief. The first number appeared on 11 Ḏūlḳaʿde 1326/22 Teşrīn-i ṯānī 1324/December 5, 1908. Neither in İstanbul nor in Ankara is there a complete set of the newspaper. My estimation is that there are ca. ten issues of which no. 1 is found in *Millî Kütüphane* and no. 8 in *Atatürk Kitaplığı*, see *Eski Harfli Türkçe Süreli Yayınlar Toplu Kataloğu* (1987), p. 147. Only the first issue was available to me, therefore nos. 2 and 3 have been cited from the secondary literature.

[13] For his career, see *TDEA*, vol. I, p. 275.

[14] "Kürdler ve Kürdistān", no. 1, p. 3.

[15] Cf. the opinion of a writer in *İḳdām* 1896: "By religion (*diyānet*) we are Muslims, by social order (*heyet-i içtimāʿīye*) we are Ottomans, by nationality (*ḳavmiyet*) we are Turks", Kushner (1977), p. 25.

Bābān goes on to lament the backwardness of the Kurds, pointing out that education is the only way out of the Kurdish dilemma.[16] He emphasizes the language factor in education as an instrument of integration into the Ottoman family: "The basis of the liberation of a nation is not national liberation but education. The key to education is language. The gate to civilization will be opened by this key".[17] One can and perhaps must interpret this as meaning that the Kurdish language is not important so much as a symbol or marker of Kurdish culture and race, but as a tool for education. Such a view might alleviate CUP concerns that the language itself constituted a claim to nationhood. Bābān also expresses concern that Kurds know so little of their history and argues the importance of writing a history of the Kurds.

It has been said of these early proponents of Kurdish interests that they had become alienated from the "real Kurds" through their Western education and urban experience, which was intensified by the years in exile.[18] This was not true of Bedīʿüzzamān Mollā Saʿīd-i Kürdī. Of all the contributors of the newspaper he was, perhaps, the best informed about the actual conditions in Kurdistan. There can be no denying that he was personally dedicated to raising the standard of education, and had gone to Istanbul personally to plead with ʿAbdülḥamīd about the necessity of building schools,[19] but he differed from many of the Kurds in the ʿAbdullāh Cevdet or Bedir Khān camp as to the proper focus of education. Saʿīd-i Kürdī was one of the most prominent advocates of preserving a religious orientation in the face of Westernization. Convinced that Western superiority and the West's ability to dominate weaker states stemmed from their scientific advancements, he wanted education to focus, on the one hand, on technical-vocational subjects and, on the other, on acquiring religious knowledge.[20] It cannot be said that he was advocating the status quo in this respect. He was deeply critical of the education he had received in the seminaries of Eastern Turkey and fought against the storing up of useless precepts. Thus he persevered

[16] No. 1, pp. 3–4.
[17] "Kürdçe'ye dā'ir", no. 3, cited after Sasuni (1986), p. 143.
[18] Ibrahim (1983), p. 178, argues that while the Kurdish nationalist oriented intelligentsia were tribal leaders in origin, they became alienated from their roots by classifying ʿAbdülḥamīd as their main enemy.
[19] Mardin (1984), p. 204.
[20] *Kürd Teʿāvün ve Teraḳḳī Gazetesi* no. 2, cited after Sasuni (1986), p. 143.

in the tradition of *ʿulamāʾ* leading the masses in movements that protest against the practice of the unjust.[21]

Aḥmed Cemīl did not share the euphoria colouring many of the the calls for education. He was aware of the difficulty of educating the Kurds under the present conditions, and linked the prospects of raising the level of education of Kurds to social and economic change. The region could not be developed until the Kurds broke with their traditional lifestyles and became sedentary. He suggested that the Kurds must be forced to abandon their habits, and argued that both disputes among the tribes and their "vagrancy" were damaging for the area's agriculture; and that their own laws and vendettas (*müşāreket-i intiḳām*) could not be made to conform to the laws of the state. Certain administrative units would have to be established to deal with these problems. With a certain optimism, however, Cemīl refers to Kurdistan with its great and untapped riches as the "Ottoman America". But the region possessed more than just prospects for development. It had been home to the "first schoolhouse of wisdom" (*ilk dersḫāne-i ḥikmet*) in world civilization. However, the historical outline Cemīl goes on to provide curiously begins with Kurdistan under the Ottomans, omitting Saladin as well as the "glorious past" of the independent emirates.[22]

Hopes for economic and cultural progress were not fulfilled. In parliamentary debates Kurdish members of parliament expressed their disappointment that during the period of constitutionalism nothing had been done to change the "wretched situation" of the Kurdish provinces which no longer seemed destined to become the Ottoman America, but rather their "Siberia".[23] Frustation was most acute regarding the educational sector, where the need for better schooling and more teachers had been largely ignored: "If the Kurds are educated the government will win them over. Then they will render good services . . . We are not concerned about Arabic, Turkish

---

[21] Mardin's study (1989) sheds light on how the poverty of Saʿīd-i Kürdī's parents, Armenian growth, administrative chaos and his reading of the İstanbul press all influenced his views. See also his biography in Bruinessen (1992 a), pp. 257–259. Mardin (1991), pp. 133–137.

[22] "ʿOṯmānlı Amrīkāsı ve seʿādet-i müstaḳbele-i ʿaşāʾir", *Kürd Teʿāvün ve Teraḳḳī Ġazetesi* no. 1, pp. 4–5.

[23] *MMẒC*, devre 2, içtimāʿ senesi 1, cild 2, 41. inʿiḳād (July 14, 1328/1912), p. 463.

or Kurdish. The main point is that they are educated and that ignorance is being eliminated".[24]

In 1910, a society (*Kürd Neşr-i Maʿārif Cemʿīyeti*) was founded for the purpose of spreading education among the Kurds ". . . who, among the empire's children, are the most deprived of the mercy of education . . .".[25] A school was established in the Çemberlitaş district of İstanbul but it was forced to close less than a year later[26] as had already been the case with the *Kürd Teʿāvün ve Teraḳḳī Ġazetesi* in 1909.[27] Of course, these measures created disappointment in Kurdish circles.

2. *Hēvī, Rojē Kurd, Hetavē Kurd*

The phase in which the Kurds and other ethnic groups could organize and consolidate their following was brief.[28] However, the oppression of Kurdish societies was not absolute, a fact evidenced by the founding of *Hēvī* by Kurdish students in 1912. *Hēvī* became a sort of hotbed for Kurdish nationalists. Şükrü Meḥmed Sekban, author of the two texts which will be examined in the second part of this study, was both mentor and patron of *Hēvī*, financing the rent of the club premises.[29] The growth of Turkish nationalism had aroused resentment in many "awakened" Kurds.[30] An emotional attachment

[24] *MMẒC*, devre 3, içtimāʿ senesi 1, cild 2, 34. inʿiḳād (July 2, 1330/1914), p. 270.

[25] Article 2 of the charter, reproduced by Göldaş (1991), pp. 248, 285.

[26] According to Bruinessen (1978), p. 445, note 19, Khalīl Khayyalī, son of the prominent family of Modki, Miri Kātibzāde Cemīl, an urban notable from Diyarbakır, and Kurdīzāde Aḥmed Ramiz were the three co-founders of this society who established a school and a publishing house which published *Kürdistān*. Saʿīd-i Kürdī, already famous as a religious scholar, also assisted with the school. Ṯüreyyā claims that ʿAbdurraḥmān Bedir Khān was head of the school, see Behrendt (1993), p. 270. Cf. also Kadri Cemil Paşa (1991), p. 29.

[27] Tunaya (1984), p. 406. Behrendt (1993), p. 276.

[28] Many leading Kurds, foremost among them Emīn ʿĀlī Bedir Khān, his son Ṯüreyyā and Şerīf Pasha were forced to flee in the aftermath of the conservative counterrevolt in 1909 in which a Bedir Khān was implicated, Behrendt (1993), p. 276 quoting Tunaya.

[29] Kadri Cemil Paşa (1991), p. 34.

[30] Celādet tells an illuminating story about the way young Kurds came to perceive that growth. In 1910, Yūsuf Aḳçura and İsmāʿīl Gasprinskij appeared as speakers in İstanbul. "Gasprinskij Efendi gave a long speech in a Turkish which only with difficulty could be understood by İstanbul Turks. He spoke continually of Turks and of people who were not Turks. Inasmuch I and my friends could understand,

to their Kurdishness arose particularly, it would seem, among the young, who were largely unfettered by the exigencies of family and position and more vulnerable to lofty ideals, romantic self-definition, and the notion of a heroic mission.[31] Whereas *Kürd Teʿāvün ve Teraḳḳī Cemʿīyeti* had been more closely linked to the Turkish leadership, *Hēvī* was made up of independent and idealistic youths whose unresolved social standing allowed them to take a more radical stance. The beliefs of *Hēvī* members may be traced in *Rojē Kurd* and *Hetavē Kurd*, which followed it.

In the first editorial, *Rojē Kurd* and *Hēvī* are described as "two monuments of awakening" (*iki ābide-i intibāh*).[32] In "A dream comes true", Ṣāliḥ Bedir Khān utilizes the rhetoric of victimization. The Kurdish youth had decided to proceed with progress and education against the ubiquitous insults directed against the Kurds. They had been neglected, exploited, intrigued against, and now it was time for them to awaken. If the Kurds continued to sleep they would lose their right to live (*ḥaḳḳ-i ḥayāt*). The Kurdish youth, on the other hand, were in possession of the truth and were determined to awaken and thus save the Kurds from corruption.[33]

---

the meaning of his speech was: Everybody is a Turk; in Turkey there are only Turks and there ought not to exist another people than Turks. I don't know if it was mere accident that there were no Turkish students attending the lecture. Besides me, there was another Kurd, a Circassian, an Albanian, a Georgian and a Greek. When we met at school the next day, the lecture was our only topic of discussion. As young people, we had been confronted with the fast developing principle of equality and ideas of freedom in the second constitutional period. We could not accept Gasprinskij's opinion. We were dismayed and shocked . . .". In reaction to Gasprinskij's speech, Celādet wrote an article about Kurdish history and the Kurdish people: Bedirxan (1978), pp. 24–25; Bedirxan (1992), pp. 21–22. Dersimi (1992), pp. 35–38, who studied in İstanbul mentions that after the policy of Turkification of the Young Turks gained momentum, a stronger consciousness developed amongst the Kurds of İstanbul. In fact, as he puts it, an atmosphere of "distrust" (*itimatsızlık*) and "aversion" (*nefret*) on the side of non-Turks against the "Turkish state" grew. Manifestations of "nationality" took place between Kurds and Turks. When Turkish students wrote on the blackboard the slogans "Ne Mutlu Türküm Diyene" [It is very doubtful if such a phrase was already in use many years before it was propagated in the Turkish Republic] and "Yaşasın Türk" the Kurdish students replaced the word "Türk" with "Kürd".

[31] Kadri Cemil Paşa (1991), p. 40: "Hevi pursued the goal of awakening a national feeling and Kurdish thinking amongst the Kurdish nation and of propagating Kurdish culture".

[32] "Gāye, meslek", *Rojē Kurd* no. 1 (14 Receb 1331/6 Ḥazīrān 1331/June 19, 1913), pp. 10–11.

[33] "Khülyā ḥaḳīḳat oluyor", *Rojē Kurd* no. 2 (14 Şaʿbān 1331/6 Temmūz 1329/July 19, 1913), pp. 10–11.

But, occasionally, sheer pessimism overshadows appeals for activism. İsmāʿīl Ḥaḳḳī Bābān paints perhaps the bleakest picture of Kurdistan, contrasting the paths the Kurds tread with those of the "civilized nations" which have created highways for cars and trains but: ". . . The street of the Kurds is a naked, wild and solitary place. On it there may be found only rare footprints . . ." The only thing that can help is education. In the same article he warns that although the government will help, the Kurds themselves must become active.[34]

Şükrü Meḥmed Sekban, who was already 30 and an established doctor when he co-founded *Hēvī*, was closely affiliated with the group, a fact which partially may be due to his own underprivileged background and lack of a family or tribal network to ensure advancement. Also, as instructor at the military medical school, he had close connections to students at an institution with a history of radicalism. His continued involvement with the prominent members of *Kürd Teʿāvün ve Teraḳḳī Cemʿīyeti* as well as his close contact to the students enabled him to assume a function as mediator between the two groups. A member of *Hēvī* recounted a scene at a *Hēvī* meeting. The students had severely criticized Kurdish conformists for neglecting Kurdish interests. Their attack was also aimed at the Kurdish member of parliament, Fevzī Pirinççīzāde, who was present at the meeting. Fevzī replied that the students should concentrate on their studies and not get involved in politics. Sekban defended the students, saying that they were being driven to politics because their own political leaders had failed to pursue policies in the interests of Kurds. Fevzī is reported to have left the meeting in anger, perhaps at the audacity of the students in daring to criticize someone of his status, or at the implication that he, as a Kurd, was obliged to represent Kurdish interests as defined by budding nationalists. A short time thereafter, lawsuits were filed against several *Hēvī* leaders on the grounds that the club had not been legally established. It is not recorded whether this development had any connection to the incident with Fevzī.[35]

---

[34] "Kürdlerin teʿālīsi", *Rojē Kurd* no. 3 (11 Ramażān 1331/1 Ağustos 1329/August 14, 1913), pp. 2–4 (here:) 2: "Bütün aḳvām bu teraḳḳī ve tefyīż yollarını çiğneyerek ārabalara, şimendöferlere otomobillere müsāʿid şāhrāhlar vücūda getirdiler Kürdün yolu ise çıplaḳ bir vaḥşetzārdır. Üzerinde pek seyrek ayaḳ izlerinden başḳa bir şey görünmez . . . Bu ṭarīḳ-i mehcūr ve metrūkī nūr hidāyetiyle aydınlatacaḳ yegāne bir ḳuvvet var ise o da bütün aḳvāmı aḳṣa-i ʿümrāne īṣāl eden maʿārifdir . . .".

[35] Kadri Cemil Paşa (1991), pp. 42–43. He mentions that *Hēvī* had an official license.

The trials never took place because, at the outbreak of World War I, *Hēvī* members were drafted into military service.[36]

Whereas the authors of *Kürd Teʿāvün ve Teraḳḳī Ġazetesi* had stressed the primacy of Ottoman identity and avoided delineating Kurdishness, writers for *Rojē Kurd, Hēvī*'s mouthpiece, often explicitly avowed their Kurdish identity and the responsibilities it dictated. They endeavoured to explore this identity, but frequently expressed frustration at how little they had to work with. What defined a nation? The writers of *Rojē Kurd* obviously accepted the view that a nation was a group of people with a common language, culture and history. But what did aspiring young Kurds know of all this? Their language was a shambles, not fit for education or literature; their culture was backward, and their history was a mystery. Thus there is a plaintive tone to many of the articles which are interesting because they indicate not only how a few Kurdish youths saw themselves, but also how the prominent Kurds who were guiding them defined and framed goals and opposition. The only enemy to appear in these pages was the Kurds themselves in their ignorance.

The title page of the first issue of *Rojē Kurd* bears the likeness of Saladin, intimating their identification with this perhaps greatest model of military strength among Kurdish heroes. Interestingly enough, the image of the foe (as implied by Saladin, who saved Muslims from would-be Christian conquerors) would hardly have aroused the resentment of the Ottoman Turks. Saladin was a more acceptable leader and symbol to the Turks than some of the other Kurdish heroes whose biographies were published by Kurdish journals.[37] Another historical figure singled out for attention is İdrīs-i Bidlisī,[38] who could also hardly be deemed controversial as he was considered the architect of Turkish-Kurdish co-existence. The second issue of *Rojē Kurd* contains a portrait of Karīm Khān Zand, who as leader

---

[36] Memdūḥ Selīm Begi: "İki eṯer-i mebrūr (Kürd Ḳadınları Teʿālī Cemʿīyeti, Hēvī Ṭalebe Cemʿīyeti)", *Jīn* no. 20 (4 Ḥazīrān 1335/June 5, 1919), pp. 4–10, (here:) 8–10.

[37] On Saladin's popularity among the Turks see Ende (1984), pp. 85–88: "At the beginning of World War I Saladin had advanced to a popular symbolic figure in the Ottoman-Turkish self-image". Ende also discusses conflicting Arab and Kurdish claims on Saladin.—Cf. also Strohmeier (1991) on Saladin as eponymus of the late Ottoman Islamic university in Jerusalem named al-Kulliyya al-Ṣalāḥiyya.

[38] "Derd ve davā", no. 1, p. 8.

of a Kurdish dynasty which ruled Iran from 1752 to 1797, was also, as a Kurd in Persia, unlikely to be offensive.[39]

In one of the many articles about the necessity for Kurdish youth to take an active role, one anonymous author compares the 20th century to a flood which may be withstood only with "civilization" (*medeniyet*) and "knowledge" (*maʿrifet*). A nation could not save itself only with courage, virtue and honour alone. The Kurdish youth must take the likes of Saladin, Mollā Gorānī and İdrīs-i Bidlisī as models.[40] Other articles too speak of the importance of knowing and following model Kurds in the context of strengthening the initiative and feelings of the youth.[41] But more contemporary heroes are awarded attention as well. The third issue of *Rojē Kurd* bears the portrait of Ḥüseyin Kanʿān Bedir Khān Pasha, one of the sons of the Emir. In 1879 Ḥüseyin had attempted to regain control of Botan; in 1910 he stood for parliament but was shot.[42]

In the framework of improving education, the language question was a frequent topic. It was controversial as it involved a symbol of Islamic identity, almost a monument to Islamic civilization: the Arabic script. As another author phrased it, "the first task is (to establish, MS) elementary schools; the first problem the script".[43] The position taken on this issue was indicative of where one stood in the spectrum of identities ranging from conservative Islamic to superwesternized. It is not surprizing that ʿAbdullāh Cevdet, who had stated in a famous article, that Western civilization must be taken over completely,[44] advocated adopting new letters[45] in efforts to raise the

---

[39] While the late Kurdish nationalist Ghassemlou (1965, p. 37), who spoke of the era of Karīm Zand as "a splendid chapter in Kurdish history", compared Karīm Khān to Saladin as a Kurdish ruler of other nations, Nikitine (1975, p. 178) is more sober in assessing both leaders in terms of what they brought their peoples. "Vassals of one (Persian Shah, MS) or the other (Turkish Sultan, MS), they exhausted their energies in the service of a cause which was not their own". Needless to say, early 20th-century Kurdish nationalists did not promote the non-Kurdish aspirations of such leaders, but rather the fact that Kurdish leaders could be recognized as heroes.

[40] No. 1, p. 8.

[41] Ṣāliḥ Bedir Khān: "Khülyā ḥaḳīḳat oluyor", no. 2, p. 10.

[42] Behrendt (1993), pp. 201–202. Kutschera (1979), p. 20. Neither author states his sources or indicates why Ḥüseyin was killed.

[43] Bulġāristānlı Ṭoġan: "Milletinize ḳarşı vaẓīfeniz", *Rojē Kurd*, no. 2, pp. 2–5, (here:) 4.

[44] Cf. Lewis (1968), pp. 236–237.

[45] No. 1, p. 4. According to Hanioğlu (1981), p. 317, Cevdet advocated the introduction of the Latin script. Cevdet himself writes only of "appropriate letters" (*müsāʿid olan ḥarfler*).

literacy rate to 40 percent.[46] At the other end of the spectrum we find the "Society for Education and Reform of Letters" (*Taʿmīm-i Maʿārif ve İṣlāḥ-i Ḥurūf Cemʿīyeti*) arguing that though it was possible for Muslim peoples to learn a new script, it would not be appropriate. Since the Kurds are an important element in the Muslim community, Arabic letters must be used.[47]

İsmāʿīl Ḥaḳḳī Bābān, reiterating his emphasis on the Muslim identity of the Kurds, also recommended utilizing reformed Arabic letters to make Kurdish a written language. He argued that the Kurds should not be separated from the Oriental family of nations. It would be a "crime" to follow the Latinization the Albanians had pursued.[48] Although he attributes great significance to the study of the Kurdish language as a basis for liberation, he is careful to point out that liberation is meant not in a political sense but rather as a liberation from the chains of ignorance. Bābān stresses that language studies do not imply a distancing from the Turks and Arabs nor does codification of the language mean proclaiming nationality, which is "forbidden by the *şerīʿat*".[49] Obviously he wished to placate Turkish fears of such eventualities. It is important to remember that the Balkan Wars were being fought during this period, and Ottoman territory was being relinquished.

Rojē Kurd is a forum for varying opinions regarding the most immediate tasks facing Kurdish youth. Doubtless one reason the tone of these articles differs from that of the previous journal is that the articles are addressed primarily to the youth to whom the task of implementing reform would be left. Bulġāristānlı Ṭoġan[50] delineated the mission of the Kurdish youth in words which evoke some of the terms employed by contemporary scholars in describing what it is that nationalists do: "Your people must be born again today as must most of the Muslim peoples in the East . . . Be assured that this way you will not only reawaken the Kurdish people, but 'create' a Kurdish nation from nothing".[51] The disdain felt by the Kurdish educated

---

[46] "Bir khiṭāb", no. 1, p. 4.

[47] No. 2, pp. 13–16.

[48] "Kürdlerin teʿālīsi", no. 3, pp. 3–4: ". . . Kürd şarḳ ʿāʾilesinden ayrılamaz . . . Ārnāvūd lātīncīlerini taḳlīd etmek cināyetdir".

[49] "Müsülmānlıḳ ve Kürdlük", No. 2, pp. 5–7.

[50] We know nothing about this author. Possibly he is writing under a pseudonym.

[51] "Milletinize ḳarşı vaẓīfeniz", no. 2, pp. 2–3: "Bu gün milletiniz, ekṯer-i aḳvām-i şarḳīye-i islāmīye gibi, yeniden dünyāya getirilmeğe muḥtācdır . . . Emīn olunuz, bu ṣūretle Kürd milletini yeniden ḥayāta getirmek değil, hiç yoḳdan bir Kürd milleti ʿīʿmālʾ etmiş olursanız".

elite for their primitive compatriots is manifested in their desire to make them over completely according to their own values, a tendency we have witnessed from the beginning of Kurdish journalistic activity. But Bulġāristānlı Ṭoġan admonishes the Kurdish youth not to follow the example of their Turkish counterparts who "were removed from their nation", and looked down on them.[52]

One of the writers most prominent in promoting Kurdish identity in this period was ʿAbdullāh Cevdet, who had evolved from being an Ottomanist to a federalist. In the years following World War I, he voiced some opinions which seemed to favour some sort of separatism. But the reality of the Turkish Republic soon made such views obsolete.[53] In a speech addressing Kurdish youth he said:

> We live in an era in which nations are taking shape. Individuals who do not have a certain personality possess no social value. It is the same with nations. A people without personality commands no respect. They are nothing more than a big mass of human beings. The function which memory has for an individual corresponds to the role of history for peoples . . . If a people does not have a written and complete history, it is as if that people had never lived. Do the Kurds have a history? The likes of *Şerefnāme*[54] cannot give a people its historical honour or honourable history. Nor can it protect them. The century in which we live is no joke. This is the 20th century. A people which does not possess the history of its past and future is not its own master. Peoples and individuals who are not their own masters become the possession of others.[55]

Cevdet, like other Kurdish intellectuals desired a strenghtening of Kurdish historical consciousness. Rhetorically he asks Kurdish youth: "What do the Kurds want to be, or what don't they want to be? An element in the Ottoman Empire? Certainly, but what kind of

---

[52] Ibid.

[53] Hanioğlu (1981), pp. 315–321.

[54] This is the famous Persian language *Sharafnāme* of Sharaf al-Dīn Khān Bidlīsī (1543–at least 1599).

[55] "Bir khiṭāb", no. 1, pp. 3–4: "Milletlerin taʿayyün ve taşakhkhuṣ etdiği devirdeyiz. Muʿayyin ve mütemeyyiz bir şakhṣiyete mālik olmayan bir ferd hiç bir ḳıymet-i içtimāʿīyeyi ḥā'iz olmadığı gibi şakhṣiyetine mālik olmayan bir millet de ʿesāmīsi oḳunmaz'. Ḥayvān-i nāṭıḳ sürüsünden başḳa bir şey olmaz. Meleke-i ḥāfıẓa ferdlerde ne ise tārīkh milletler için odur . . . Bir milletin ki mażbūṭ ve mükemmel olaraḳ bir tārīkhi yoḳdur, o millet hiç yaşamamış gibidir. Kürdlerin tārīkhi var mı? Bir (Şerefnāme) ile bir millet şeref-i tārīkhīsini veyākhūd tārīkh-i şerefini taṣarruf ve muḥāfaẓa edemez. Yaşadığımız ʿaṣır, şaḳa değil, yirminci ʿaṣırdır. Māżīsinin tārīkhine, müstaḳbelinin tārīkhine mālik olmayan millet kendisine mālik değildir. Kendi kendisine mālik olmayan milletler ve ferdler memlūk olur, başḳalarının mālı olur".

element? A rotting and rotten element? Or a renewed and renewing, a vital and revitalizing one?".[56]

In an article entitled "The road to unity", Cevdet expresses regret that a Turkish friend had characterized *Rojē Kurd* as a separatist newspaper because it contained some Kurdish articles. Cevdet makes it clear that he advocates the unity of Turks and Kurds. However, he stresses that it must be a unity in which diversity is not lost. In order to characterize the relationship of the two peoples, he uses the terms "unity" (*tevḥīd*) and "individual development" (*tefrīd*). To this end, he quotes a passage from the Koran that God made human beings different in order to allow them to become one: "I do not wish to speak as a Turk or a Kurd, but rather as a free and free thinking citizen of Turkey. The best road to unity is development of the individual . . . God made human beings different in order to allow them to become one and a passage in the Koran reads: 'We have created them as peoples and branches, so that they get to know each other'. This means clearly that each element of the population must be given the space to develop their natural and ethnic inclinations in order to create mutual trust among all groups. The view that multinational states can only make their way towards unity via a single language, a single legal code and a lack of differentiation, is foolish and mistaken . . . The unity of nations is constituted by unity of interests . . . Our century is the era of nations. Even the most determined and resistant governments and states will be unable to prevent this development. We want the unity of nations (in the Ottoman Empire, MS). Thus we must desire the individual development of these nations . . .".[57] Cevdet suggests that unity and separation may be achieved along the lines of the Swiss model of a federative association of cantons.

Only three issues of *Rojē Kurd* were published; then it was forced to close by an "arbitrary act" of government, whereas *Hēvī* was able to continue its activities for some time.[58] Nothing is known of the

---

[56] "Bir khiṭāb", no. 1, p. 4: "Ne olmaḳ istiyorlar? Yāḫūd ne olmamaḳ istiyorlar? 'Oṯmānlı İmparatorluğunda bir 'unṣūr mu? 'Unṣūr faḳaṭ naṣıl 'unṣūr, çürüyen ve çürüten bir 'unṣūr mu yoḳsa müteceddid ve müceddid, ḥayy ve muḥyī bir 'unṣūr mu?"—The chemical parallel is not just a rhetorical device but probably betrays the man of science's view of the situation, cf. Hanioğlu (1995) on science and chemistry. See below a similar passage in Sekban's writings.

[57] "İttiḥād yolu", *Rojē Kurd*, no. 2, pp. 8–9.

[58] "Bir tārīkh-bir tes'īd", *Jīn* no. 24 (3 Eylül 1335/September 7, 1919), p. 8. Kadri Cemil Paşa, p. 41.

events surrounding the closure. Two months later the successor to *Rojē Kurd, Hetavē Kurd* ("Kurdish Sun") started publication, with ʿAbdülʿazīz Bābān as editor.[59] Despite the change in editorship, the authors and concerns remain largely the same, as demonstrated in a *Hēvī* declaration which rearticulates and justifies the organization's goals and its role in propagating the 'awakening'. Once again we encounter the familiar schema of the great nation which, although held back in its development, scorned by other nations, could, if united, finally overcome its miserable situation. "All nations which began to awaken did this by establishing organizations . . .". *Hēvī*'s aims were: to promote communication and solidarity among students, prevent discord among Kurdish leaders and work on the development of the "forgotten" Kurdish language and literature. In the struggle to attain "happiness" and "prosperity", religion, too, was an integral part.[60]

Mevlānzāde Rıfʿat underscores the fact that awakening (*iḥyā*) the Kurds depends on the Kurdish language, and consists of ". . . teaching them of their existence and their right to live . . ." as well as ". . . showing them the path to progress . . .". He leaves no doubt that the latter is irrevocably linked to a national orientation: "The nations which don't know their nationality and don't pursue the national ideal have in mankind remained behind and lifeless".[61]

But it was not only ignorant Kurds who needed to be taught. Educated Kurds also possessed an inadequate knowledge of Kurdish life. ʿAbdullāh Cevdet enumerates some of the many areas requiring investigation in order to determine practical policies in Kurdistan. Going beyond the common concerns with history, language and literature, he points to the need for information on demographics, the economy and land ownership among the Kurds, as compared with other nations in the Ottoman Empire. But lest the majority of the Kurdish youth dedicate themselves to academic projects, or use their education to achieve solely personal ambitions, Cevdet stressed that one of the crucial issues in implementing goals and eliminating the

[59] Issues 1 and 3 also contain the portraits of two members of the Bābānzāde family, ʿAbdürraḥmān and İsmāʿīl Ḥaḳḳī.

[60] "Kürd Ṭalebe Hēvī Cemʿīyetinin beyānnāmesidir", *Hetavē Kurd* no. 4–5 (27 Cemāẕiyilākhir 1332/10 Mayıs 1330/May 23, 1914), pp. 1–4.

[61] "Muḥterem Hetavē Kurd Gazetesi müʾessislerine", no. 2, pp. 2–3: "Millīyetini bilmeyen, millī ideal arḳasından ḳoşmayan milletler kütle-i beşer içinde pek geride, rūḥsuz olaraḳ ḳalmışlardır".

factors impeding success was the return of the Kurdish youth to Kurdistan: "If you would rather be the founders and teachers of elementary schools in Kurdish villages than *ḳaymaḳāms* and *müdīrs* elsewhere, only then, Kurdish youth, are you truly on the path which must be tread".[62]

Cevdet's focus on the social reality of the Kurds was reflected throughout the ten issues of *Hetavē Kurd* in articles on subjects as diverse as hygienic conditions among the tribes, the underdeveloped road system, agrarian conditions, assessments of the numbers of Kurdish speakers in certain regions, and the conditions experienced by Kurdish professional groups such as the porters (*ḥamāl*) of İstanbul. In an as yet halting fashion attention is directed towards material traditions. The front page of the second issue of *Hetavē Kurd* departs from the practice of depicting Kurdish heroes of old or contemporary patriots, featuring a photograph of a family with the suggestive caption: "A Kurdish family in Damascus, which has retained its nationality". The picture and caption imply that "nationality" is related to customs such as dress. Given the magnitude of ignorance about Kurdish society reflected in Cevdet's scholarly agenda, it is not surprising that this aspect of Kurdish society, despite its importance in European nationalist ideology, had not yet attracted great interest among the largely cosmopolitan educated elite. Nevertheless, letters to the editor and "reports from correspondents" (*Kürdistān mektūbları*) doubtless contributed to the readers' awareness of regional and group differences and stimulated a stronger and less abstract sense of belonging.

In contrast to Cevdet's call for the Kurdish youth to return to Kurdistan, Mevlānzāde Rıfʿat argues for a cautious approach to Kurdistan. He urges the Kurds to follow the example of their "racial brothers",[63] the Armenians, who had, in the context of their "national and social revolution", sent young people to the villages in Anatolia only after conferring with scholars in Europe: "Let us first determine

---

[62] "Kürd ġazetesi muḥarrirlerine", *Hetavē Kurd* no. 1 (23 D̲īlḳaʿde 1331/11 Teşrīn-i evvel 1329/October 24, 1913), p. 2: "Bir Kürd köyünde bir mekteb-i ibtidāʾī müessis ve muʿallimi olmayı lāʿalāttaʿyīn bir yerde ḳaymaḳām ve müdīr olmağa tercīḥ edeceğiniz zamān, ey Kürd gençleri, ve ancaḳ o zamān düşülmesi lāzım gelen yola düşmüş olacaḳsanız".

[63] This seems to be one of the earliest examples of racial argumentation, which was not common among the Kurds until after World War I, in particular after the Sheykh Saʿīd Revolt and the founding of *Khoybūn*, see pp. 95 sqq.

our goals and prepare ourselves carefully, and only then make our way to Kurdistan".[64] Other authors side with Cevdet regarding the necessity of transferring the struggle from the Ottoman capital to the countryside. As Aḥmed Rıfʿat Bābānzāde put it: "If we desire the progress of our nation then we must give up our promenades on the paved streets of İstanbul. Let us go rather to the most remote corners of Kurdistan and establish printing presses".[65]

Aside from young students, *Hetavē Kurd* targeted a group which traditionally had had a pervasive influence on simple people: the *ʿulamāʾ*. Applying the positions of such reform theologians as Muḥammad ʿAbduh and Saʿīd-i Nursī to the Kurdish issue, Necmeddīn Kerküklü harshly attacks the irrelevance of *ʿulamāʾ* teaching.[66] Kurdish scholars had not served the Kurds: "..Kurdish scholars! . . . I ask you as Kurds: Have you recited and interpreted *Ḳurʾān* verses and *ḥadīṯs*, which are useful to us as a group and awaken us? All I can say is no . . .". Kerküklü attributes many of the conflicts among the Kurds to a lack of patriotism (*muḥabbet-i ḳavmīye*), the sentiment which had enabled the Christian nations to achieve progress.[67] Addressing the Kurdish *ʿulamāʾ* as "Khoca efendiler", he establishes the moral imperative of serving the nation: "First, you are Kurds, second, you studied in Kurdistan. Has your work been dedicated to the Kurds, Kurdistan, the Kurdish language? To this question you cannot answer anything but no".[68] It was in the power of the scholars to initiate the "era of happiness and prosperity" by explaining to the people the meaning of "legitimate nationality" (*milliyet-i meşrūʿe*).[69]

The third issue of *Hetavē Kurd* is dedicated to the memory of the recently deceased İsmāʿīl Ḥaḳḳī Bābān (1876–1913). A lyrical obituary emphasizes the victimization of Kurds.[70] Bābān's death is depicted as a bitter loss for the Kurdish nation, and his deep spirituality is praised.[71] Bābān's article in *Kürd Teʿāvün ve Teraḳḳī Gazetesi* empha-

[64] "Muḥterem Hetavē Kurd Ġazetesi müʾessislerine", no. 2, pp. 2–3.
[65] "Kürd gençlerine", no. 3, pp. 18–19.
[66] Saʿīd-i Nursī had railed against the irrelevance of the teaching of Muslim scholars in *medreses* with arguments resembling ʿAbduh's, see Mardin (1984), pp. 200–201.
[67] No. 1, pp. 11–13.
[68] No. 2 (4 Muḥarrem 1332/21 Teşrīn-i ṯānī 1329/December 3, 1913), pp. 11–12.
[69] No. 1, p. 12.
[70] "Zavallı Kürdlük ve bir ufūl", pp. 2–3.
[71] Kerküklü Necmeddīn: "Bedbakht Kürdler", no. 3, pp. 7–9.

sizing the hierarchy of identities, reprinted in this issue, is somewhat incongruous, because, at least for radical *Hēvī* members, there had been a shift in the hierarchy of identities.

Although there was certainly a broader basis for the Kurdish movement at the beginning of World War I, even among the educated classes and especially among the Kurdish officers of the tribal regiments, there was no readiness to pursue emphatically Kurdish political goals. The loyalty of most Kurds remained pledged to the caliph first and, then, to their tribes. Ideals such as patriotism and nation were mere abstractions and had not taken root in their thinking.[72] Nonetheless, an expansion of Kurdish self-consciousness is manifested in the pages of the journals examined here. A consensus within a small group of Kurds (the awakeners) had arisen about the concept of a distinctly Kurdish way as opposed to the "conformist" course of action chosen by the Pirinççīzāde and their ilk. For the former, the Kurdish way seemed rightful. Doubtlessly, it was also an avenue for advancement. From 1898 to 1913, the Kurdish movement had expanded to include not only the Western-oriented urbanized Kurds, but also those of a religious orientation, struggling to impose their views, debating on the essence of the lowest common denominator. They all shared the view that the Kurds required a renaissance, and that education was the most essential ingredient in change. But they had differences as to the nature of their goals, depending on the world view and the social and economic positions of the various proponents of change. That education was seen as a panacea for the ills of Kurdish society was a result of the transformation experienced by these urbanized Kurds. They had learned through contact with Western ideas, and the experience of the effects of education in the rise of the Greeks, Armenians and Bulgarians. The optimism and fervour to which some had succumbed may be seen as the sort of illusion that nationalism fosters, but also may have been due to a certain alienation, surrounded as they were by likeminded compatriots and little realizing how outlandish their goals must have seemed to the Kurds in the remote eastern provinces of the Empire.

ʿAbdülḥamīd, as a specifically Kurdish foe, had been a source of strength, a useful foil in building a sense of Kurdishness. Indignation over the sultan's targeting and exploitation, his deliberate neglect of

[72] Kadri Cemil Paşa (1991), pp. 44–45. Bruinessen (1992 a), p. 269.

and his tyranny over the Kurds drew Kurdish notables, intellectuals and certain religious leaders together. ʿAbdülḥamīd was a legitimate enemy against whom these Kurds could rally. But with ʿAbdülḥamīd's exile, the coherence of Ottoman opposition dissolved. It became clear that the Young Turks were bent on consolidating the empire and understandably sensitive about ethnic concerns no matter how much these were professed to be secondary to Ottoman unity. The Ottoman Turks gradually occupied the void left by ʿAbdülḥamīd in the victim-oppressor paradigm, as Kurdish hopes of becoming the equal partners of the Turks faded.

Despite their affirmations of the priority of Ottoman identity over Kurdish, the authors of the newspaper articles demonstrate a certain distancing from the Turks. On the other hand, all Kurds were deeply if variously enmeshed in social, ideological, economic and personal relations with the Turks with whom they had shared the same education and the experience of political opposition. These bonds hampered the development of a self-assertive, robust and distinct Kurdish identity. The constant declarations of Ottoman identity, the assurances that the Kurds did not wish to be separate do not indicate the mere camouflaging of true Kurdish intentions. The Kurdish avantgarde well knew that even in their own midst, not to mention among the population of the Kurdish provinces, there was little acceptance of parting ways with the Turks; Kurds and Turks were united in their wish to save Ottoman lands from Western transgression. Moreover, the Kurds had no powerful allies abroad and, in the Kurdish homeland, the antagonism against the West and the Armenians was strong. Even as the Balkan provinces were being lost and the hopes of saving the empire were vanishing, the Kurds had to play the Ottoman card for as long as the empire—however imminent its demise—continued to exist. It would be anachronistic to speak of Kurdish nationalism before World War I. There was little more than a hint (e.g., Cevdet's suggestion of a federal system as in Switzerland) of political goals, constrained as advocates for Kurdish interests were by the common identity with Turks. The Kurds were ostensibly and probably for the most part consciously, limited to promoting language and cultural goals for their compatriots. Kurdish thinking since the *Ḥamidian* opposition was characterized by dualism. Wishing to be recognized as Kurds, they considered themselves loyal Ottomans. They wanted to be a group apart, and yet be united with the Turks.

To develop and proclaim a true program of opposition would have required declaring the Turks to be enemies. As Touraine noted, it is through defining who "we" are, in opposition to a foe, that what "we" want (legitimate rights) emerges.[73] Moreover, the largely negative self-portrayal of the Kurds in which they dwelled on their miserable situation was not an image to arouse a sense of common identity. What advocates of a Kurdish cause had nonetheless achieved was the assembly of a core group who shared the concept of distinctly Kurdish interests and culture. For this group, which comprised most of the Post World War I protagonists of Kurdish activism, Kurdishness had become a mission. They had been converted and "awakened".

---

[73] Touraine (1974), pp. 174–179.

CHAPTER SIX

POSTWAR MOBILIZATION

1. *Kürdistān Teʿālī Cemʿīyeti*

In the brief period between the signing of the armistice and Mustafa Kemal's successful harnessing of forces opposed to Allied occupation and control, Kurdish identity began to appeal to a broader spectrum of Kurdish society. Joining the prewar protagonists of the Kurdish cause were tribal chiefs, military leaders, Alevis and Zaza speakers, who established for the first time a truly representative Kurdish society, the *Kürdistan Teʿālī Cemʿīyeti* ("Society for the Elevation of Kurdistan").[1] In the context of Ottoman defeat, Allied occupation and partition, Kurdish identity appeared to offer the prospect of recognition and self-realization in whatever the new order might turn out to be.

Three factors stimulated interest in Kurdishness: initial Turkish encouragement, British support or at least sympathy, and the Wilson Principles. During the war Allied plans to partition the Ottoman Empire had become known. After the Mudros agreement, it was clear that the Allies, in particular Britain, favoured an Armenian state. However, Great Britain did not wish to tarnish the reputation it had won in the Mosul province during the war as a supporter of Kurdish interests. Encouraging Kurdish separatist aspirations was also a way of weakening Ottoman claims to Anatolia. The Istanbul government, on the other hand, quickly encouraged the building of Turkish-Kurdish groups to demand autonomy for the Kurds in order to weaken the Armenian claim to the six Eastern Provinces, which the Allies were already calling Armenia. Although Turkish support rather quickly ebbed, their initial encouragement and the fact that the British seemed to take Kurdish claims seriously, contributed to

[1] Göldaş (1991) has collected a considerable amount of information on the society, though his study is somewhat lacking in analysis and clarity. For a list of leading members, see Bruinessen (1989), pp. 400 sqq.

the feeling that there was a good case for aligning with Kurdish leaders.[2]

Point 12 of Woodrow Wilson's Fourteen Points proclaimed a "guarantee for the life" and "autonomous development" for the nationalities of the Ottoman Empire. For Kāmurān Bedir Khān, the Wilson principles meant that "every people should rule itself".[3] Clearly, if the Fourteen Points were to be applied, then the Kurds were justified in expecting anything from autonomy to independence.

That the *Kürd Teʿālī Cemʿīyeti* did not embark on a clear political course in pursuit of one of these aims was due less to conflicting goals among the various factions[4] than to uncertainty about the outcome of the peace process. What would be allotted to whom? What would remain of the sultanate-caliphate? But the Kurds were not inactive. Only weeks after the armistice the first post-war Kurdish journal appeared under the timely name *Jīn* ("Life"), to be followed soon after by another journal, *Kürdistān.* In Cairo, Ṯüreyyā Bedir Khān founded a branch of the society and others were organized throughout Kurdistan. Şerīf Pasha, who had spent the war years in Paris, had paved the way for assuming a role as Kurdish representative at the peace talks. Many, such as ʿAbdülḳādir, who had occupied influential posts before the war, were reintegrated into the government. Prominent Kurds had a foot in all the right doors, prepared to participate in whatever the coming order might bring.

2. *Jīn* and *Kürdistān*

With *Jīn* and *Kürdistān,* Kurdish authors embarked upon a ten-month period of intense publicistic activity. It appears that there were many educated men anxious to use the two Kurdish newspapers as a means to create or develop their Kurdish profiles. Evidence of patriotic engagement might lead to positions in whatever administrative arrangements would be made for Kurdistan. Considering the future careers

---

[2] See Olson (1989), pp. 22 sqq., for British and Turkish involvement in Kurdish nationalism.

[3] "Kürdistān için", *Jīn* no. 3 (20 Teşrīn-i ṯānī 1334/November 15, 1918), p. 5.

[4] ʿAbdülḳādir envisioned autonomy under the caliphate, while a more radical faction centered around the Bedir Khāns was in favour of separation.

of some of the writers, one can believe the ardour of their articles and assume they were genuinely dedicated to Kurdish nationalism.[5]

Possibly, in an effort to stem hackneyed references to the awakening, ʿAbdullāh Cevdet, writing under the pseudonym "A Kurd", titles his article in the first issue of *Jīn*, "The Kurds are not asleep". After praising Wilson's Fourteen Points (January 8, 1918), he comments on the progress of the 'awakening':

> "Kurds, is it possible to sleep in such a tumultuous era? I do not consider it necessary to shout: Hey, Kurd, awaken! Because if the Kurds are still asleep, that means they died long ago. The Kurds are awake and they will awaken the masters who have kept them asleep for centuries. They (the Kurds, MS) will repay evil with goodness. 'We are living in an era in which to sleep for an hour means the death of a nation'".[6]

If, in İḥsān Nūrī's words, Wilson's principles were a "bandage for the wounds of repressed nations"[7] the Kurds had to qualify for their bandage by proving they had been unjustly wounded—and this was particularly difficult considering the atrocities against the Armenians in which Kurds had been implicated. Several authors argue that the Armenians were not the only Ottoman nation to have suffered in the war, pointing not only to the deaths of Kurds but also to the immense numbers of refugees.[8] The suffering of the Kurds throughout history is repeatedly emphasized: "The Kurds are the most unjustly treated nation".[9]

The negative portrayal of the Armenians is surprising in view of pre-war declarations of solidarity and common race. But Armenian

---

[5] Among the authors writing for *Jīn* and *Kürdistān* were Kāmurān ʿAlī Bedir Khān, Memdūḥ Selīm and Iḥsān Nūrī.

[6] "Kürdler uyḳuda değil", no. 1 (7 Teşrīn-i ṯānī 1334/November 7, 1918), pp. 5–6: "Kürdler, böyle bir ʿaṣrın böyle bir ḳıyāmetinde uyumaḳ mümkün müdür? Ey Kürd uyan! diye bağırmaya ben lüzūm görmem. Zīrā eger Kürdler uyḳuda, ḥālā uyḳuda iseler çoḳdan ölmüşler demekdir. Kürd uyanıḳdır ve kendisini ʿaṣırlardan beri uyḳuya daʿvet etmiş ve uyḳuya ṭalmış olan khüdāvendleri de uyandıracaḳlardır. O kendisine sūʾi ḳaṣd etmiş olanlara ḥüsn-ü ḳaṣd ile muḳābele edecekdir. Biz 'bir ʿaṣırda yaşıyoruz ki bir sāʿat uyumaḳ, bir millet için ölmekdir'". Cf. also Siverekli Ḥilmī in his article "Kürd gençlerine", *Jīn* no. 8, pp. 7–8: ". . . Don't sleep . . ." and ". . . Finally we can liberate ourselves . . .".

[7] "Wilson prensibi ve Kürdler", *Jīn* no. 15 (30 Mart 1335/March 27, 1919), pp. 3–5.

[8] Memdūḥ Selīm Begi, "Bir ḥaḳīḳatı tenvīr", *Kürdistān* no. 8 (28 Şaʿbān 1337/29 Mayıs 1335/May 1919), pp. 100–101.

[9] Meḥmed ʿOṯmān Bedir Khān: "Kürdlük ve Kürdistānı yaşatabilmek", *Kürdistān* no. 8, p. 98.

claims to key centers in Kurdistan called for repudiations which assumed various forms.[10] One month after the Armenians had outlined the contours of independent Armenia, Şerīf Pasha submitted his own 13-page "Memorandum on the Claims of the Kurdish People" in which he characterized "the Armenian" as demanding "more than he is entitled to", due to the fact that he is "impelled by his commercial and grasping nature".[11] As another writer pointed out, the Armenians had always looked down on the Kurds. The Armenians had once been the "shepherds leading a herd of oxen"[12] (meaning the Kurds, MS), but the situation had changed according to the ratio of the population. Kāmurān Bedir Khān bases his claim that the Kurds are numerically superior to the Armenians in Kurdistan on the "thoughts of objective European scholars".[13]

The refugee problem is perhaps the single most frequently addressed "current" topic. During the war, large numbers of Kurds had fled or been driven away from their homes. Their fate was crucial to all parties. Those favouring an Armenian state cannot have been in favour of expediting their return although the Armenians were unsuccessful in attempts to prevail on the Allies to prevent the return of Turkish and Kurdish refugees to the Eastern provinces. As the displacement of the refugees weakened Kurdish claims to numerical supremacy in Kurdistan, it is not surprising that one member of *Kürdistān Teʿālī Cemʿīyeti* claimed that the refugee problem was the most important issue facing the Kurds. The Kurds had been introduced to the importance of statistics, and many of the articles, aside from dealing with the desolate situation of the refugees, provide numerical support for Kurdish claims.[14] Meetings were held with Seyyid ʿAbdülḳādir, then president of the Senate (*Meclis-i Aʿyān*), to

[10] See Behrendt (1993), p. 310, for an Armenian memorandum submitted to the peace conference in February 1919.

[11] *Memorandum on the Claims of the Kurd People* (1919), p. 12, cited after Küchler (1978), p. 449.

[12] Ibnürreşīd: "Vażʿīyet-i ʿumūmīye-i Ekrāda bir naẓar", *Kürdistān* no. 8, pp. 92–97, here: 93–94.

[13] "Kürdistān ve Kürdler", *Jīn* no. 9 (16 Kānūn-i ṯānī 1335/January 13, 1919), pp. 6–9; in particular he mentions the book by Paul Imbert: *la renovation de l'Empire ottoman: Affaires de Turquie*. Paris 1909.

[14] Ḥakkārīlī ʿAbdürraḥīm Raḥmī: "Kürd mühācirleri ne ḥālde?", *Jīn* no. 8 (9 Kānūn-i ṯānī 1335/January 6, 1919), p. 4. "Kürd mühācirlerinden ne ḳalmış", *Jīn* no. 11 (15 Şubāṭ 1335/February 9, 1919), pp. 7–8. Cf. the article by Ibnürreşīd in *Kürdistān* no. 8, pp. 92–97.

regulate the return of "600.000 Kurds to their homeland".[15] Disregarding problematical refugee numbers, ʿAbdürraḥīm Raḥmī arrived at the following conclusion: ". . . They call our area Kurdistan. Aside from a few officials, there are no Turks. If there are no Turks, then what about the Armenians and others? The Armenians constitute only 5 percent of the population and 2 percent the others. If this is so, then there is no other nation in Kurdistan besides the Kurds. Accordingly, Kurdistan belongs to the Kurds. Aside from the Kurds, no one else has a claim to it".[16]

But who exactly were the Kurds? Şerīf Pasha's memorandum[17] portrayed the Kurds as a separate people, a nation with claims to a nation state. One crucial function of the Kurdish journals was to flesh out the distinctiveness of the Kurds and to justify their political claims. Equally important was the development of Kurdish group-awareness by reducing the boundary-drawing which created oppositions amongst the Kurds. Thus, articles in the journals range from emotionally inflated calls for unity[18] to discussions about the "Society for the Elevation of Kurdish Women"[19] and current events. Information on the history, language, literature and geography of Kurdistan as well as attention to particular groups (*ḥamāl*s, tribes) and practical tips for Kurdish students abroad might appeal to a broad spectrum of Kurdish society—certainly the letters to the editor indicate this was the case. Religion is very much in evidence throughout the journal. İbrāhīm Ḥaydarīzāde, who subsequently was named *sheykhülislām*, stressed the loyalty of the Kurds to the caliphate.[20] Mevlānā Khālid, founder of the Nakşibendī order in Kurdistan, is treated as

---

[15] *Kürdistān* no. 8, p. 1.

[16] *Jīn* no. 6 (25 Kānūn-i evvel 1334/December 21, 1918), pp. 14–15. The original is in Kurdish. I have translated it from the Turkish version given by Göldaş (whose information on pages und numbers are wrong) (1991), pp. 137–138.

[17] It was published on March 22, 1919. Oddly enough, it was not printed in Turkish until June 1919 in *Kürdistān* no. 9 (11 Ḥazīrān 1335/June 12, 1919), pp. 109 sqq. There seems to have been no Kurdish version of the memorandum.

[18] Ḳāḍīzāde M. Şevḳī in *Jīn* no. 4 (28 Teşrīn-i ṯānī 1334/November 23, 1918), p. 16: ". . . Let us unite in memory of our ancestors and not sacrifice our beautiful fatherland for the sake of leadership positions and base interests . . ." (according to the Turkish translation given by Göldaş, 1991, p. 83).

[19] Memdūḥ Selīm Begi: "İki eṯer-i mebrūr (Kürd Ḳadınları Teʿālī Cemʿīyeti, Hēvī Ṭalebe Cemʿīyeti)", *Jīn* no. 20 (4 Ḥazīrān 1335), pp. 8–10. Cf. also *Jīn* no. 25 (2 Teşrīn-i evvel 1335/October 7, 1919), pp. 14–15.

[20] "Bir ḥasbiḥāl", *Jīn* no. 1 (7 Teşrīn-i ṯānī 1334/November 7, 1918), pp. 3–5. Cf. *Jīn* no. 2 (14 Teşrīn-i ṯānī 1334/November 16, 1918), p. 1.

one of the "great Kurdish figures". The author opens his article with the statement: "Faith is the only force which can set an entire nation in motion with the will to pursue a goal".[21]

In at least one case a prominent Kurd seems to have been wooed by the editors of *Jīn*, who published a *ghazel* in Turkish by Süleymān Naẓīf.[22] Three months later, however, an author complains about Naẓīf and accuses him of being neither Kurd nor Turk in his "dull articles".[23] Naẓīf was an example of a Kurd who remained indifferent to the possible political implications of his ethnic identity.[24]

The attempt to establish the broadest possible criteria for inclusion mandated reducing or denying the validity of factors which mitigated against unity among the Kurds. In the context of the frequently discussed need to standardize the Kurdish language, one author addresses the opinion that the dialects prevented Kurds from uniting on the basis of language. In answer to the question, "Can there be a common language for the Kurds?" the author provides an affirmative answer. Those who maintained dialects were an obstacle, he accuses of "superficial thinking". On the contrary, he holds, dialects were a "blessing" as they enriched the "treasury of words" (*khazīne-i luġāt*).[25]

A language-factor potentially more divisive than dialects was the problem presented by Turkish speakers among the Kurds. Kurdī-yi Bitlīsī argues that not everyone who spoke Turkish was a Turk. In Bitlis, for example, Turkish was spoken—but did that mean the population was Turkish? On the contrary, maintained the author, Kurdistan was inhabited by Kurds who spoke Kurdish at home, and had not begun to speak Turkish until the *Tanzimat* period, when the government forced the Turkish language on the Kurds. Such policies

---

[21] Süleymānīyelī M. Nejād Tevfīḳ: "Ḥażret-i Mevlānā Khālid", *Jīn* no. 10 (2 Şubāṭ 1335/February 1919), pp. 1–5: "Bir milleti ṭoplu olaraḳ bir ġāye peşinde istekle ḳoşdurabilecek ḳuvvet ancaḳ dīndir".

[22] "Gazel", *Jīn* no. 11 (15 Şubāṭ 1335/February 14, 1919), pp. 6–7.

[23] Berzencīzāde ʿAbdülvāḥid: "Gönül ister ki . . .", *Kürdistān* no. 8 (21 Mayıs 1335/May 29, 1919), pp. 99–100.

[24] He published an unfavourable account of Şerīf Pasha in which he referred in a pun (Şerīf Pasha was called in French "Beau Chérīf", in Ottoman this is transcribed as "boş ḥerīf") to the latter as "Boş Ḥerīf" (No place. İkinci ṭabʿ, 1910)—which may well have caused irritation in Kurdish activist circles. Cf. on Naẓīf: Karakaş (1988), pp. 211–212.

[25] Kurdī-yi Bitlīsī: "Kürdçeye dāʾir", *Jīn* no. 14 (21 Mārt 1335/March 18, 1919), pp. 10–14, here: pp. 13–14.

as making proficiency in Turkish a requirement for government employment had amounted to a catastrophe for Kurdistan.[26]

Whereas earlier Kurdish publications had avoided dealing with the divisive aspects of Kurdish society, in the pages of *Jīn* and *Kürdistān* they are frequently addressed, if only summarily. Yamlekīzade, for example, explained that the Shīʿa and Sunna division had prevented progress among the Kurds.[27] In a letter to *Jīn* a youth complains that urban Kurds were ambivalent about their Kurdish identity. They hesitated to call themselves Kurds or to speak Kurdish, and they had departed from Kurdish ways. Even though Kurdish was spoken in the marketplace, city-dwellers spoke Turkish, to avoid "insults". Villagers, on the other hand, had become used to insults. According to the writer, such behaviour had led to great material and spiritual discrepancies between villagers and city-dwellers. These differences had to be reduced so that "both personalities" (*şakhṣīyet*) might be united.[28] In a later issue of the journal, another author from the same area takes issue with the view that urban Kurds are indifferent to their Kurdish identity. Conceding that there were, naturally, differences between villagers and city-dwellers, he maintains, nevertheless, that communication and interaction between the cities and villages had assured that those Kurds in the cities were not isolated from other Kurds.[29] In both texts the implicit assumption is that the simple people are more truly Kurdish than urban Kurds. This is a far cry from the view of the early protagonists concerning a Kurdish cultural revival. No longer regarded merely as the targets of an educational, cultural make over, rural Kurds are increasingly viewed as members of the Kurdish nation in undisputed possession of a sacred and fleeting good: Kurdish tradition and culture. While it would be a mistake to overestimate the numbers of Kurdish leaders who adopted this view, it undoubtedly gained currency as educated Kurds absorbed

---

[26] In support of his statement he quotes a Russian general who remarked that only 500 Turks lived in the entire province of Bitlis: "Kürdistāndaki şehirler sekenesi Türk müdür?", *Jīn* no. 6 (25 Kānūn-i evvel 1334/December 18, 1918), pp. 1–9.

[27] "Kürd ne idi, neler ister", *Jīn* no. 5 (12 Kānūn-i evvel 1334/December 8, 1918), pp. 1–3.

[28] Bir Kürd genci: "Jīn ġazetesine", *Jīn* no. 11 (15 Şubāṭ 1335/February 14, 1919), pp. 15–16.

[29] Sivereklī Ḥilmī: "Şehirlīler ve köylüler", *Jīn* no. 13 (10 Mārt 1335/March 7, 1919), pp. 13–15.

the concepts and notions surrounding the ideology of nations. In the context of standardizing Kurdish, one author even talks of focusing on the culture of the simple people. Their language, especially that of "old women", he considered "pure" and thus a suitable model for codification.[30]

Kurdish authors increasingly draw on the work of European scholars as proof of their historical and linguistic uniqueness. The article on "Kurdistan" from the *Encyclopaedia Britannica* is translated into Turkish and printed in several installments. However, the editor comments that the numbers cited in the article are incorrect: There were not 2,5 million Kurds, but rather 5 million.[31] Kurdī-yi Bitlīsī translated a chapter on the Kurds from a book about Turkey.[32] The passage relates to the ancient history of the Kurds as reflected in the names Kyrtii and Karduchi, thereby illustrating the continuity of Kurdish history. Mythology, too, could be employed as evidence of Kurdish distinctness. Kurdī-yi Bitlīsī relates the legend of Żoḥāk to prove that the Kurds are Iranians.[33]

Despite some new perspectives and in spite of the impending partitioning, the authors of *Jīn* and *Kürdistān* still pursue an agenda by and large laid down in the pages of the first Kurdish journal, *Kürdistān*: 1) decrying the dismal circumstances of the Kurds and asserting the need to awaken them; 2) referring back to a venerable history and culture which provide the main argument for 3) substantiating the distinctiveness of Kurds and the righteousness of their political claims.

The image and the reality of the Kurds are again, as in the pages of earlier journals the object of lamentation, self-pity, shame and anger: "Today every nation has knowledge and culture. Only we have none. And that is the reason we are scorned. We are religious, but we do not know the commandments of our religion. We are brave, but we employ our bravery in killing one another. We are generous, but we do not spend our money on religious purposes,

---

[30] Kurdī-yi Bitlīsī: "Kürdçeye dā'ir", *Jīn* no. 15 (30 Mārt 1335/March 27, 1919), pp. 11–16, here: 14. Kurdī-yi Bitlīsī is a *nom de plume* of Khalīl Khayyālī, see Malmîsanij (1991), p. 111.

[31] *Jīn* no. 10 (2 Şubāṭ 1335), pp. 6–9; no. 11 (15 Şubāṭ 1335), pp. 3–6; no. 12 (25 Şubāṭ 1335), pp. 1–4.

[32] "Kürdlere dā'ir", *Jīn* no. 13 (10 Mārt 1335/March 7, 1919), pp. 10–13. Author: Henri Mathieu, title: *La Turquie et ses différents peuples*. Paris 1857.

[33] "Kürdler münāsebetiyle Zoḥāk efsānesi", *Jīn* no. 1 (7 Teşrīn-i ṯānī 1334/November 1918), pp. 7–11.

but (rather) on dances and bribes, on aghas and sheykhs".[34] Education is still stressed as necessary to redress the neglect of Kurdish history, literature and social organization. In January 1919, elections were held to select the executive board of the *Kürd Taʿmīm-i Maʿārif ve Neşriyāt Cemʿīyeti* (Kurdish Society for the expansion of education and publications).[35] The aim of the society was to spread education in order to "equip our nation with future-oriented and science-based modern abilities, without which one can hardly imagine our continued existence or further political efforts." The society recognized that only a language and history which conformed to modern standards could qualify as "identity papers" (*varaḳe-i hüvīyet*) entitling a people to modern nationhood. This society immediately assumed editorship of *Jīn*.[36]

Perhaps the most lasting contribution made by the society was the first complete edition of *Mem ū Zīn*. In his preface to the poem, Müküslü Ḥamzā elaborated on the significance of literature in assuring the survival of a people ruled by another. A nation which develops its literature obtains the right "to rule in the palace of words" ("... *söz sarayında salṭanat sürmeye* ..."). Literature, according to Ḥamzā, enables a people to acquire the sympathy of other nations. He cites the example of the "little Greek nation" which, by cultivating its literature under Ottoman domination, had been able to find many supporters who eventually helped the Greeks liberate themselves from Ottoman rule.[37]

The Kurds were more than ever aware of the necessity of passing what was perceived as a "general test", in which the "pitiable" nations, i.e. those without nationhood, would have to "demonstrate their abilities" in order to be allowed to "acquire prosperity, security and the privileges of rights and powers".[38] Recognition and sup-

---

[34] Ārvāsīzāde Meḥmed Şefīḳ: *Jīn* no. 2 (14 Teşrīn-i ṯānī 1334/November 9, 1918), p. 15, cited after the Turkish translation given by Göldaş (1991), p. 88.

[35] *Jīn* no. 7 (2 Kānūn-i ṯānī 1334/January 1919), p. 16.

[36] "Kürd Taʿmīm-i Maʿārif Cemʿīyeti beyānnāmesi", *Jīn* no. 10 (2 Şubāṭ 1335/ February 1919), pp. 10–16, here: 10, 14.

[37] The foreword of the publication of *Mem ū Zīn* (the original was not available to the author) is supplied by Bayrak (1994), pp. 326–328. The Kurdish version is to be found in *Jīn* no. 19 (21 Mayıs 1335/May 20, 1919), pp. 12–14. Given the allusion to Greek independence, it is ironic that the poem appears in May 1919 almost simultaneously with the Greek invasion of İzmir.

[38] Meḥmed ʿOṯmān Bedir Khān: "Kürdlük ve Kürdistānı yaşatabilmek", *Kürdistān* no. 8, p. 98: "Bedbakht milletlere açılan bu imtiḥān-i ʿumūmīde ehlīyet göstere-

port from the West were conceived as fundamental for survival, cultural revival and the achievement of political goals.

3. *Hēvī*

One facet of the self-promotion perpetrated by some Kurds involved documenting their own early role in representing Kurdish interests. Several articles draw attention to the pre-war activities of *Hēvī*. Commenting on the reestablishment of the student group, Memdūḥ Selīm, himself a former member (in any case, a contributor to *Rojē Kurd*), noted that many of the members had been lost in the war after being forced to submit to the "heavy chains of an ill-considered militarism". In a scarcely veiled critique he contrasts the young Hēvī members with older Kurdish leaders. Unlike the great and dignified men who, out of fear and prudence, had been content to doze in their comfortable corners, the *Hēvī* group dared to hope and declare their dissatisfaction. When the government had been unsuccessful in its efforts to bribe *Hēvī* into complicity, the police had picked them up and thrown them into prison. Memdūḥ Selīm quotes one of the speakers (ʿAbdullāh Cevdet?) at the celebration of the reestablishment of *Hēvī*: "Our youth has shown that they have liberated themselves from the Oriental spirit and mentality . . . They have not, as Orientals do, destroyed something already in existence, but rather, by setting their edifice on a basis which already existed demonstrated their faculties of continuity, resistance and will".[39] Although it is not clear which accomplishments of *Hēvī* were being referred to, the conviction and bravery of its members is a recurring theme.

A declaration of *Hēvī* published in *Jīn* describes the pre-war group as a "handful of youths, the children of a deprived nation, who met in the dark corners of İstanbul, walking on a dark, difficult and dangerous road, carrying a trembling torch which bore the name Hope . . .". Their patience and endurance had been rewarded with deprecation, scorn, prison and death, but they had remained dedicated

bilecek olan milletler iḳtidārları haḳḳları dākhilinde bir imtiyāza, emīn bir ḥayāt ve saʿādeṯe nāʾil olacaḳlardır".

[39] "İki eṯer-i mebrūr (Kürd Ḳadınları Teʿālī Cemʿīyeti, Hēvī Ṭalebe Cemʿīyeti)", *Jīn* no. 20 (4 Ḥazīrān 1335/June 1919), pp. 8–9.

to the honour of the nation. The society declares its aims to be cultural: establishing contacts with the youths of Kurdistan, creating a network for Kurdish students in Europe, fighting for Kurdish tradition, honour and ideals.[40]

In retrospect, it is almost ludicrous that groups were so intensely and dramatically concerned with writing a Kurdish history book and developing the Kurdish language during this politically crucial period, but we must remember that for many of these writers and members of organizations it was a question of creating public profiles, jobs for themselves, underscoring their patriotic eminence, and attempting to inspire youth with their fervour.

Nevertheless, we do have some records indicating that the meetings of Kurdish societies were concerned with political as well as cultural issues. At a meeting attended by a large number of Kurdish intellectuals and youth, dissatisfaction was articulated with the government's failure to appoint Kurds to administer their own areas and to return refugees to their homes. One speaker assessed the Kurdish situation as follows: If Kurds did not immediately claim their rights on the basis of the Wilson Points, their rights would not be recognized and the Kurds would again be repressed and neglected. A delegation had already visited representatives of the four allied powers and presented a memorandum containing Kurdish suggestions for administering Kurdistan. Stressing that the return of refugees was the most important aim of the society, they expressed a lack of confidence in the government, since nothing had been undertaken. The government was accused of repeating the same mistakes the CUP had made in relation to Albania and the Arab provinces. Emphasizing ties to other Islamic nations and trust in England, the foundation of Kurdistan (*Kürdistān'ın te'essüsü*) was demanded. It is striking that even in the context of criticism of the government and the call for Kurdish administration, the terms autonomy and independence are not mentioned.[41]

In the end, the cultural and publishing activities of the *Kürdistān Te'ālī Cem'īyeti* had little if any impact on the processes which were to seal Kurdistan's fate. One reason for this is that despite the size

[40] "Kürd Ṭalebe Hēvī Cem'īyeti beyānnāmesi", *Jīn* no. 21 (18 Ḥazīrān 1335/June 19, 1919), pp. 12–13; no. 22 (2 Temmūz 1335/July 3, 1919), pp. 11–13.

[41] Memdūḥ Selīm Begi: "Kürd Ḳulübünde bir muṣāḥabe", *Jīn* no. 21 (18 Ḥazīrān 1335/June 19, 1919), pp. 1–7.

and varied composition of its membership, no figure emerged who represented or in any way controlled the vast human resources of Kurdistan. Certainly, ʿAbdülḳādir would have been a likely candidate for this role. His charisma, religious leadership and political influence recommended him. However, he had spent much of his life in exile and his political life in İstanbul was closely associated with the government. Thus, as the standing of the latter declined, ʿAbdülḳādir's career also was implicated. Şerīf Pasha, on the other hand, had few qualities to endear him as a Kurdish leader of the masses. It is not even certain that a majority of the "Society" was satisfied with the former diplomat.[42] Berzencīzāde ʿAbdülvāḥid defends Şerīf Pasha against the accusation that he was working on behalf of Armenian interests. In the same article, the author touches upon the very subject which continued to obstruct consensus-building, clear perspective, strategy, and goals: "One wishes that each Kurd in his surroundings might be well-acquainted with his enemies, those who juggle with his fate and render his future something to be scorned".[43] The author seems to imply that neither Şerīf Pasha nor the Armenians were working against the Kurds as much as did those who pursued the goal of ". . . Turkifying the Kurds outwardly . . .", but ". . . in reality were turning the life of an innocent nation into a toy".[44] But although the author points to the necessity of recognizing the enemy, he can only allude to the enemy's identity. Kurds could not—for tactical, religious and ideological reasons—vilify the Turks as their opponents, not even when they were openly calling for an independent state, especially not if this involved alliance with the infidel. But as independence-oriented Kurds realized, some sort of acceptance of the Armenian claims was a prerequisite to attracting Allied good will, something on which Kurdish aspirations depended.

Although Şerīf Pasha's memorandum to the peace conference contained anti-Armenian rhetoric, the accompanying map outlined the borders of a truncated Kurdistan which allowed space for an independent Armenia.[45] A complete repudiation of Armenian rights meant forfeiting statehood of their own. It is probable that this containment of Kurdish claims had sparked controversy in Kurdish circles.

---

[42] Alakom (1995, pp. 77–97) has studied Şerīf Pasha's "Kurdish mission" in detail.
[43] "Gönül ister ki! . . .", *Kürdistān* no. 8, p. 99.
[44] Ibid.
[45] See Behrendt (1993), p. 327 and note 41 on Şerīf's map.

The anti-Armenian tone of many of the articles and the assertion of exclusive claims to Kurdish provinces make it seem unlikely that Şerīf Pasha spoke for most of the educated Kurds in İstanbul. By June they had access to the memorandum in the journal *Kürdistān* in Turkish, but the map was published only in the English version. Many Kurds hoped to pose as Armenian "friends" until the signing of the peace treaty, and then prevent the return of the Armenians to the Eastern provinces.[46] Whatever strategic intricacies were behind the officially pursued courses of action, any concessions to Armenian expansion were unthinkable to Kurds who would be affected. In addition to forfeiting lands, they feared Armenian vengeance after the losses and suffering which the Kurds had assisted in inflicting on them.

The Ottoman government, obviously aware of the drift of the negotiations regarding the Eastern Provinces, embarked upon a campaign against nationalist Kurds. In an article published in the summer of 1919, Kurdish nationalist leaders were accused of playing into the hands of the Armenians. Those Kurds desiring independence "had not the slightest attachment to the Kurds . . . if they had, they would have returned to Kurdistan and dedicated themselves to raising the standard of education of the Kurdish people, who were so ignorant and backward".[47] At the same time, the government was active in the Kurdish provinces, encouraging Kurdish tribal leaders to reject the goal of independence under a foreign mandate.[48]

Şerīf Pasha's memorandum of March 1919, condemning the acquisitiveness of "the Armenian", had alluded to the presence of "somewhat fierce" and "warlike" *Ḥamīdīye* troops in these areas. Doubtless, he wished to suggest that the Kurds would not peacefully relinquish their homeland. But the agreement signed by Şerīf Pasha and the chief Armenian representative, Boghos Nubar, eight months later stated that "our two nations, both Aryan, have the same interests and pursue a common goal, namely their liberation and independence . . .".[49] Both parties agreed to leave the determination of exact

[46] Dersimi's account of the Koçgiri revolt which he, as a *Kürdistān Teʿālī Cemʿīyeti* member helped to instigate, indicates that this society must have been exploring military options much earlier: Olson (1989), pp. 26–51.

[47] Kutschera (1979), p. 28, quoting from French foreign ministry documents.

[48] Ibid.

[49] Behrendt (1993), p. 435, quoting from text in Hovanissian.

borders to the peace conference, although they must have known the American Harbord commission had informed the Kemalists that they had found Anatolia to be Turkish.[50] The agreement provided the framework for the relevant clauses in the Treaty of Sèvres.

The pro-Western faction could accept the definition of the Kurds as propagated by Şerīf Pasha, and also the consequences: Armenian control of some Kurdish lands and a British protectorate. Pro-Western Kurds had long advocated co-existence with the Armenians. The terms of the agreement represented for them a reasonable compromise. But to those with a primarily religious identity and a long-standing hatred of the Armenians, the agreement was tantamount to betrayal. The agreement was published in Ottoman newspapers in February, 1920, spawning immediate protests against Şerīf Pasha and the *Kürdistān Teʿālī Cemʿīyeti*. One group of well-known Kurds condemned a peace agreement with the enemies of Islam at a time when "the blood of 500,000 martyrs had not yet dried".[51] ʿAbdülḳādir tried to assuage both Turks and Kurds by stating that the treaty was not directed against Turkey: "The Turks are our coreligionists and our brothers".[52] He argued that the Kurds desired not separation but rather autonomy.[53] ʿAbdülḳādir further emphasized, "It is absolutely false that the Kurds wish to separate from Turkey. I myself am not an advocate of separatist ideas . . . Only the unity of Muslims can assure their progress and their improvement."[54] ʿAbdülḳādir's plea for autonomy rather than independence incurrred the wrath of both the Ottoman government and the radical groups of the *Kürdistān Teʿālī Cemʿīyeti*. In parliament, demands were made to expel ʿAbdülḳādir on grounds of "violating the oath of fidelity he had taken towards the fatherland, the nation and the sovereign" and, after a closed meeting of parliament, he was forced to retract his statements.[55]

Kurdish nationalists, including the *Hēvī* group, left *Kürdistān Teʿālī Cemʿīyeti* to form the *Kürd Teşkilāt-i İçtimāʿīye Cemʿīyeti* ("Kurdish Society for Social Organization") which was led by Emīn ʿĀlī Bedir Khān.

[50] Behrendt (1993), p. 330.
[51] Behrendt (1993), p. 331. Cf. Göldaş (1991), p. 33.
[52] Kutschera (1979), p. 30.
[53] Göldaş (1991), pp. 282–283, reproduces a Latinized version of the declaration of ʿAbdülḳādir in *Iḳdām*, 27 February 1920. Behrendt (1993), p. 331, has the German translation.
[54] Kutschera (1979), p. 31, quoting from another interview with ʿAbdülḳādir.
[55] Kutschera (1979), p. 31.

One of their most important contributions was the creation of the first Kurdish flag.[56] Any semblance of Kurdish unity was gone and, perhaps even more important, the Kurdish leader with the greatest status and integrative potential had been, in official circles at least, discredited, though he continued to enjoy the support of the majority of Kurds living in İstanbul.[57]

The inability of the *Kürdistān Teʿālī Cemʿīyeti* to put forth and sustain either an integrative (and uncompromised) figure or a consensus-based statement of goals, drove Kurdish leaders, especially in areas acutely threatened by Armenian claims, into the arms of the Kemalists. From the outset of Mustafa Kemal's activities in Anatolia from mid-1919, he had succeeded in luring the Kurds away from that society. As the hero of the Dardanelles, he had considerable initial appeal which increased as he was perceived to command real strength and to provide an alternative to the partitioning of the empire. It was not difficult to cast himself as a hero-leader (*ghāzī*) fighting against the infidels. The Kurds had no one to counter this latter-day Saladin. Kurdish leaders such as Şerīf Pasha appeared to be traitors willing to sign away the fatherland to the Armenian enemies.[58] Mustafa Kemal was the integrative figure able to consolidate widely divergent groups, and to strengthen existing emotional bonds which could be stretched to sustain brotherhood, loyalty, and an alliance against the common enemy. The caliphate provided the link between the Turks and the Kurds and, indeed, between conflicting groups of Turks.

---

[56] Göldaş (1991), pp. 195–208 has the most information on the society. Cf. also Bruinessen (1989), p. 506, who provides a list of members, including the Bedir Khāns, Sekbān, Memdūḥ Selīm, ʿAbdullāh Cevdet, Şükrü and Ḥikmet Bābān and others. See also Kadri Cemil Paşa (1991), pp. 60–62.

[57] Bruinessen (1992 a), p. 278. Emin ʿĀlī Bedir Khān, in an interview in *Boğaz* (January 9, 1920), had stated even before the turmoil over ʿAbdülḳādir's remarks, that there were two currents among the Kurds: "We all accept the Sultan as the Caliph of all Muslims. But the stronger of the two Kurdish groups wishes to completely separate from Turkey . . . The other group is opportunistic and fears that Europe will abandon the Kurds to their fate . . . but they are a minority", from Bletch Chirguh [Pseudonym for Ṯüreyyā Bedir Khān according to Behrendt (1993, p. 10), for Celādet Bedir Khān according to Bayrak (1994, p. 57)], *La question kurde* (not available to the author), cited from Bayrak (1994), p. 85.

[58] See Olson (1989), p. 29, on Kemal's talk with ʿAlişan Bey, one of the organizers of the Koçgiri revolt, in which the former called ʿAbdülḳādir an instrument of the pro-British Istanbul government and a servant of the British.

The War of Independence was promoted as a *jihād* in defense of the caliphate and Muslim unity, and against foreign Christian invaders. Kemāl professed to be representing the interests of the sultan-caliph until he could be freed from foreign control. In the declaration drawn up at the Erzurum Congress in late July and early August 1919 the unity and indivisibility of the six eastern provinces were emphasized; they were "an integral whole which cannot be separated from each other or from Ottoman territory for any reason".[59] Point three of the declaration establishes the intention. "As all occupation and interference will be considered undertaken on behalf of establishing Greek and Armenian states, the principle of united defense and resistance is resolved". Neither Arabs, Turks nor Kurds are mentioned in this declaration, as the strategy is to appeal to Muslim brotherhood. The word "Turkish" was avoided in this and other nationalist declarations, thus dispelling any suspicions that Kemal's nationalists might be continuing a CUP brand of Turkish nationalism. "The Society to Defend the Rights of Eastern Anatolia" (*Şarḳī Anadolu Müdāfaʿa-i Ḥuḳūḳ Cemʿīyeti*) was defined in point nine as "the union of societies born out of the sufferings and calamities experienced by our land".[60]

In addition to offering a unique blend of military hero and religious champion, Kemāl had become a man with power and resources to confer on others. Kurdish notables and tribal leaders were invited to the congresses, were represented proportionally in the first national assembly and were promised the same rights in an independent Turkey.[61] When the provisions of Sèvres became known, Kemāl

[59] Shaw and Shaw (1977), p. 344.

[60] Shaw and Shaw (1977), p. 345.—Cf. Behrendt (1993), p. 321: "All of those Muslims living in this territory are true brothers who are imbued with the mutual willingness to sacrifice for one another, while respecting one another's racial and social situation" (based on the translation in Jäschke [1933]). Behrendt does not distinguish, as does Shaw, between the proclamation at Erzurum and the actual national pact, which was not signed in Istanbul until February 17, a month before parliament was dissolved. In the passage quoted above, it is interesting that this appears in Shaw as part of the national pact, but in a different context, namely: areas inhabited by Arab majorities would conduct a plebiscite—in this context Shaw writes: "All such territories inhabited by an Ottoman Muslim majority, united in race and in aspirations, are imbued with feelings of mutual respect, concern and devotion, and form an indivisible whole".

[61] Bruinessen (1992 a), p. 279. Bruinessen (1984), p. 140.

promised the Kurds the same.[62] Even as late as February 1922, a bill was introduced in parliament to give Kurdistan autonomy,[63] an indicator of how Kemāl managed to stretch his appeal to the point when resistance was no longer possible.

In the autumn of 1920, the Kurds took part in the campaign to defeat the Armenians which ended with the Armenians' renouncing all claims to Ottoman Armenia. Olson argues that the nationalist forces were largely successful because of Kurdish participation. Ironically, they were ultimately preventing the realization of their plans for a Kurdish homeland, whether autonomous or independent, as they no longer held the position of a valuable bulwark against the Armenians.

Kurdish leaders in İstanbul were cognizant of these developments and it is in this context that their involvement in the Koçgiri revolt must be seen. Shortly after the signing of Sèvres in August 1920, members of the *Kürd Teşkilāt-i İçtimāʿīye Cemʿīyeti* (*KTİC*) with which *Hēvī* and the *Kürd Millī Fırḳası*[64] had merged, participated in the Koçgiri revolt which was crushed by nationalist troops in April 1921.[65] Kemalists, largely by exploiting sectarian and religious differences, were able to persuade various tribes not to join the revolt.[66] Too, one must keep in mind that the revolt was organized and led by the more radical members of *KTİC*. They had already dissociated themselves from ʿAbdülḳādir, who doubtless still had the support of those religious Sunni Kurds who had not already been lured away by Kemāl. As the war against the Greek invaders was underway, the rebellion could well be depicted as treasonous. The lack of coor-

---

[62] But as Olson (1989, p. 26) points out, Kurdish willingness to participate in the campaign to repel the Armenians was at least partly in order to ensure that Article 64 of the Treaty of Sèvres could be implemented to Kurdish advantage.

[63] Olson (1989), p. 166.

[64] Another group which was founded (1919) in the process of the splitting up of *Kürdistān Teʿālī Cemʿīyeti*: Göldaş (1991), p. 193. Kadri Cemil Paşa (1991), p. 62.

[65] Dersimi, who has written the only account of the revolt, and was one of its main organizers, claims that, from the beginning, he had been against autonomy, and thus had approached the Bedir Khāns and others promoting Kurdish independence when he came to İstanbul. For this reason, I have referred to Dersimi's *KTİC* connection although Olson does not distinguish between *Kürdistān Teʿālī Cemʿīyeti* and *KTİC* (though it seems likely that one should do so after mid-March).

[66] According to Bruinessen (1992 a), p. 278, some Sunni Kurds saw it as an Alevi uprising. Olson (1989), p. 35, points out that Sunni tribes, however, did participate in the revolt.

dination and unity between tribal chiefs and nationalist leaders became apparent when the former demanded autonomy while the latter agitated for independence.[67]

With the establishment of the Turkish Republic, one by one the reasons for the solidarity and loyalty of nationalist Kurds were eliminated. The main link between the Turks and the Kurds, the caliphate, was abolished. The Turks reneged on promises to return Kurdish refugees to their homes. The Kurds were passed over when positions in the administration of the eastern provinces were established, while elections in Kurdistan were manipulated. More important, the Kurdish language was not allowed in schools, courts or in the administration. Thus, even Kurds who had never been prone to espousing nationalist ideas and who had suppported Kemāl were disappointed and embittered about the Janus-faced behaviour of Musṭafā Kemāl. An old Kurdish peasant, asked about his opinion of Kemāl, responded with a question: "Which one do you mean, for there are two Mustafa Kemals. One of them visited one tribal leader after another during his campaign and asked for their help in protecting the caliphate and sultanate, the sultan himself and religion as well as in fighting against the infidels. The other (Kemāl), after the War of Independence, deposed the sultan, closed the Koran schools and no longer showed us and our religion any respect. Which one do you mean?"[68]

The Treaty of Sèvres remained a dead letter. The Allies changed their attitude towards the Turks as a result of Kemāl's success and their own desire to extricate themselves from further conflict. Furthermore, the United States and Britain began to focus on their own interests in the oil fields of Mosul. Kurds were not represented at the Lausanne proceedings where the Turkish position on Kurdish issues became apparent. The British had less interest in the Kurds outside the Mosul area, and were not interested in a Kurdish state. It was decided that an international commission would deal with the situation and conduct a referendum. Thus, a very small hope still existed that at least some part of Kurdistan might finally enjoy cultural and political rights. But the illusion that Turkish nationalists would lend support to Kurdish aspirations no longer existed.

---

[67] Olson (1989), p. 34, quoting Dersimi.
[68] Beşikçi (1970), p. 299.

Many of the Kurds who had been active in the movement to achieve Kurdish rights and to cultivate Kurdish culture had been associated with the Allies. They fled to Europe,[69] Syria and Iraq to nurse their wounds and contemplate the future. They were not to take up the banner of Kurdish nationalism until the birth of *Khoybūn* in 1927.

[69] E.g., Kāmurān and Celādet Bedir Khān who both studied in Germany. Kāmurān finished his Law Doctorate at the University of Leipzig. His dissertation at the university library in Leipzig is reported as "missing" (most probably it burned in World War II). Celādet spent most of the years 1922–1925 in Munich. Unfortunately, his diaries from this period do not inform us about Kurdish politics, Bedirhan (1995). See further Nikitine: "Badrkhānī", *EI* (2), vol. I, p. 871. Elphinston (1952), pp. 91–94. Behrendt (1993), pp. 343–344, footnote 48.

PART TWO

THE KURDISH QUESTION IN THE TURKISH REPUBLIC

CHAPTER ONE

ŞÜKRÜ MEḤMED SEKBAN: THE PATRIOT

Among those who had staked their positions and resources on the chance of increasing Kurdish leverage and been catapulted into exile by the events of 1920–22, was the physician Şükrü Meḥmed Sekban. He had supported the Kurdish nationalist movement from its inception and was widely considered one of its most prominent activists.[1] The son of an army officer, Meḥmed Agha from Erġanī Maʿden, Sekbān was born in 1881, the same year as Musṭafā Kemāl, later Atatürk. He attended elementary and middle school in his home town and Hozat (Kızılkilise) and continued his studies at the high school in Diyarbakır. He studied at the Military Medical School (*ʿAskerī Ṭıbbīye*) in İstanbul where he was a classmate of Tevfik Sağlam[2] and graduated with the rank of captain in 1903. Subsequently, he interned at Gülkhāne hospital, and from 1905 to 1907, worked as a specialist in skin diseases at the military hospital in Edirne. In 1908, he rejoined the staff at the Military Medical School, and became a teacher there. After 1908, Sekban became active in Kurdish circles. We first see his name in connection with *KTTC* and then again as mentor of *Hēvī* in 1912. By his own account, he became interested in the Kurdish movement due to the same humanitarian concerns which had led him to take up medicine.[3] He used his influence as a doctor to arouse nationalist feeling among the lower strata of Istanbul's Kurdish community.[4] Although not a member of a notable

[1] For his membership in KTC see Tunaya II 186, Göldaş (1991), pp. 22 sqq.; in KTTC: Tunaya I, p. 404; in *Hēvī*: Kadri Cemil Paşa (1991), p. 34; in KTIC: Göldaş (1991), p. 196.

[2] Sekban is mentioned in Kazancıgil (1991), vol. 2, p. 93 and footnote 197. The date of death given here is 1962. Cf. Hatemi/Kazancıgil (1991), p. 57. The most detailed—if only comprising a few lines—information on Sekban's life and career may be found in the forewords of the two Turkish translations of his *La Question Kurde*: Sekban (1970), p. 7 and Sekban (1979), pp. 13 sqq. Also Ạnter (1990), pp. 74–76, has some impressionistic information on Sekban.

[3] Sekban (1923), p. 8.

[4] His office was located in the Saʿīd Paşa Khān opposite Galatasaray, *Jīn* no. 11 (15 Şubaṭ 1335/February 1919), p. 17. Dersimi related that Sekban encouraged him to agitate among the Kurds of İstanbul, Dersimi (1992), p. 42.

family, he had become a leader, as he later maintained, because of his abilities as an orator.[5] Sekban seems to have had close ties to both the aristocratic, secularly oriented leaders who had first articulated a Kurdish identity, and the students, who were perhaps most affected by nationalist feeling. He spent part of the year 1919 in Baghdad, but returned to İstanbul and practiced medicine. Compromised by his contacts with the Allies,[6] he must have deemed it unwise, perhaps even dangerous, to remain in Turkey. However, we do not know exactly when Sekban went into exile.

Just two months after the signing of the Treaty of Lausanne (July 24, 1923), Sekban published an open letter in Turkish under the title "What do the Kurds want from the Turks?".[7] In the main the letter, circulated as a pamphlet, dealt with what Turkish policy towards the Kurds should and should not be. It is the first official statement by a Kurdish leader about the new situation, particularly in regard to the Turkish policy of assimilation aimed at eliminating all sources of disloyalty.

In this letter, Sekban maintains that the Turkish government has four options in dealing with the Kurdish question. It can: 1) neglect the Kurds as had the Ottomans; 2) Turkify the Kurds; 3) wipe them out or deport them; or 4) recognize the Kurds as a nation (*millet*)[8] and allow them to conduct education in their mother tongue, which was the "holy right" of every nation.[9] Sekban employs a number of arguments—in none too orderly a fashion—in order to demonstrate that assimilation was unnecessary, unreasonable, unethical and impossible. His first argument, and indeed the crux of what is undoubtedly a rather frantic plea for clemency, hinges on the basic loyalty of the Kurds. As proof of this, he cites the reaction of the Kurds to their own temporary victory in the Sèvres agreement. Although Sèvres (August 10, 1920) had held out the prospect of an independent state, the Kurds had never desired separation from Turkey:

---

[5] Sekban (1933), p. 20.

[6] There is at least one record of Sekban approaching an American commission on behalf of Kurdish interests. Cf. Kadri Cemil Paşa (1991), p. 57.

[7] This open letter is dated September 14, 1923. On p. 31 there is a postscript under the date of December 18, 1923. In my copy no place of publication is given, but Sekban remarks in Sekban (1933), p. 25, that the letter was printed in Cairo. A latinized version of the letter can be found in Bayrak (1994), pp. 26–39.

[8] Sekban (1923), p. 14.

[9] Sekban (1923), p. 25.

"On the day the treaty was signed and the political rights of the Kurds were officially recognized, we remained with the Turks in painful mourning".[10] The image conjured up by the author illustrates Sekban's strategy of subsuming his own more radical stance into the general position of Ottoman Kurds, thereby postulating Kurdish loyalty. The image of mutual sorrow is a rather poignant reminder of the dilemma of conflicting identities faced by the Kurds and their unwillingness to define themselves on the basis of ethnic distinctions and rights in opposition to the Turks at the very historical moment when it most behooved them to do so. However, Sekban and the Kurdish nationalists with whom he was most closely associated had not shared this ambivalence. They had accepted the opposition inherent in demanding political rights and had acted accordingly, siding with the Allies against the Turks. But in maintaining that Kurds and Turks had always coexisted for "geographical, economic and religious reasons",[11] he implicitly disclaims his own former and present political aspirations. He argues furthermore that the Turks will benefit if they promote Kurdish development, since the Kurds could then more effectively support the Turks in the defense of their land against external enemies.

Drawing on historical precedents as well as his own experience, he contends that the Turks quite simply will not be able to assimilate the Kurds. During a period of medical service in Yemen, Sekban had realized that a people could not be civilized by a foreign culture.[12] In other words, the Republican aim of achieving modernization throughout the land would be lost on the Kurds. He professes innocently that he would welcome assimilation if it were a viable alternative to Kurdish development:

> If I thought . . . as our respected friend Żiyā Gökalp does, that the Turks could assimilate the Kurds, then I would be extraordinarily happy. But the Kurds could not be assimilated 300 or 400 years ago by the sword, nor will the weak Turkish culture and civilization be able to assimilate the Kurds. If it were possible to assimilate a foreign race then the Germans would have succeeded in accomplishing this with the Poles.[13]

[10] Sekban (1923), p. 12. There are many references to Kurdish loyalty, cf. Sekban (1923), p. 6 and 9.
[11] Sekban (1923), p. 24.
[12] Sekban (1923), p. 18.
[13] Sekban (1923), p. 15.

Citing the failure of the Germans to impose their language, culture and identity on the Poles, he asks dramatically: "If Germany, with its scientific power and superior culture, could not assimilate the Poles . . . . how can the Turks, especially in the era of nationalism, hope to assimilate Kurdish peasants to whom every national bond is foreign? . . . What a sweet daydream Turkification of the Kurds is. If it were possible, then even Şükrü Meḥmed, who has until now had scruples about killing a bug, would become a glowing and staunch advocate of such a policy".[14]

His tone, often sarcastic, veers towards pathos as he makes his final argument against assimilation: "Is it a crime or a dream when the Kurds demand what is right and great and sacred to the Turks?"[15] The Turks had achieved national independence but "we Kurds only wished to control our national language and the fruits of our work".[16] He insisted that the Kurds had never wanted separation and that the national pact had provided the basis of co-existence when it stated that "all territories inhabited by Ottoman-Muslim majorities are unified in religion, race and efforts, filled with the spirit of mutual respect and form a whole which cannot be partitioned".[17]

The pamphlet is anything but a straightforward appeal for consideration of Kurdish needs and interests, for education in the mother tongue and self-administration—as the title would lead us to expect. A preliminary reading yields the impression that there is little new or of interest to historians herein. This is probably the reason the document has been largely ignored by both scholars and loyal chroniclers of Kurdish nationalism. However, the open letter is not only the first statement made by a Kurdish political leader after the debacle (from their point of view) of Turkish national victory; it is, moreover, the first Kurdish reaction to Turkish policies of assimilation. Admittedly, the letter is not remarkable for the refinement or cogency of its argumentation. The reader intent on deriving some indication of the goals and strategies of the activist Sekban or what had remained of the Kurdish movement is left with more questions than answers. The tone and tenor of the 30-page "brochure" oscillate

[14] Sekban (1923), pp. 15 sqq.
[15] Sekban (1923), p. 23.
[16] Sekban (1923), p. 22.
[17] Sekban (1923), pp. 24 sqq. This citation corresponds to article 1 of the national pact (*miṯāḳ-i millī*). Cf. Shaw/Shaw (1977), p. 348.

from emotional, plaintive, ironic, apologetic and conciliatory to matter-of-fact, revealing a high level of ambivalence vis-à-vis the addressee and many of the subjects the author broaches as well as his own situation. This ambivalence makes it difficult to assess clearly the motivation and intentions of the author. But the resulting opacity does not diminish the suggestive and expressive value of the text as a document reflecting a brief phase in the history of Kurdish nationalism. It is a document suffused with tension and perplexity neither of which state should be surprising considering the recent traumatic events and the uncertainty as to how the political situation would develop.

In the passages quoted above, various elements stand out as being not quite appropriate to the occasion. Let us examine, for example, Sekban's claim that he would support, indeed advocate, assimilation if only it were possible.[18] We might suppose that this is a rhetorical device to set up a line of argumentation. His use of Yemen as an example, however, would be quite ludicrous to anyone with knowledge of the situation, since the Ottomans had never pursued assimilation policies—not even in areas which were much closer, and certainly not on the outskirts of the empire, where controls of any sort diminished. Neither had there been an attempt to assimilate the Kurds, although Kurdish nationalist writers were wont to equate 19th-century centralization policies with assimilation. The very concept of assimilation was foreign to the Ottoman administration which sought rather to control or neutralize groups threatening government authority. The comparison with Yemen leads one to wonder if Sekban really understood what was meant by a policy of assimilation, or whether he merely equated it with repression.

His next historical "evidence", the reference to Poland, is certainly more pertinent, as the German government had, indeed, following the Russian example, pursued a policy of Germanization. Sekban's reference to Poland was both timely and understandable. First of all, the Poles, like the Kurds, were dispersed throughout three partitioned sections, under Russian, German and Austrian control, respectively. Their national movement was almost as old as their partition and was a cause célèbre especially when, during World War I, the Poles fought with the Allies against Germany. But it was wishful

[18] Sekban (1923), pp. 15 sqq.

thinking to consider anything apart from the partitioning of Poland into three parts as similar to the situation of Kurds. However, Sekban wished to use the parallel to point out the dangers of repression, suggesting the Turkish nationalists should be leary of imitating the Germans, whose severe repression of the Poles in the years prior to World War I had resulted in nothing less than the loss of Poland. But if he is indeed trying to placate the Turks, to assure them of the non-separatist aims of Kurds, as so many of his remarks would suggest,[19] then it is not seemly to raise the specter of territorial loss, which is exactly what the Turkish nationalists wished to avoid. Nor was it diplomatic to disparage Turkish culture, claiming it too weak to assimilate the Kurds. Calling assimilation, as he does a few lines later, in summary, "a sweet daydream" seems to ascribe naiveté to those planning it, and implies a certain harmlessness, as if he were not aware of the violence and destruction which the enforcement of such policies incurred. Sekban's sarcasm was not likely to endear him to his professed or implied readers.

The letter is addressed to Sekban's "old friend"[20] Fevzī Pirinççīzāde, the same Kurdish notable and member of parliament who had been criticized by the *Hēvī* group some 11 years earlier. The author claims that he decided to publish the letter only after repeatedly failing to establish communication with the addressee.[21] He appeals to Pirinççīzāde to use his influence as "doyen"[22] of the Kurdish parliamentarians to better the situation of the Kurds, insinuating it is Fevzī's responsibility to do so. The Pirinççīzādes, one of the two important families in Diyarbakır,[23] had readily sided with Atatürk in the War of Independence and been rewarded for their solidarity. Fevzī was the elected representative from his city to the National Assembly from 1920–1927 and Minister of Public Works from 1922–25.[24]

---

[19] Sekban (1923), pp. 11, 23 sqq., most clearly in "Kürd, Türk birdir. Kürd, Türk demekdir": p. 27.

[20] Sekban (1923), p. 4.

[21] Sekban (1923), pp. 3 sqq., 31.

[22] Sekban (1923), p. 28.

[23] The other being the Cemīlpaşazāde, who while nationalist in orientation, did not become involved in the Sa'īd Revolt, cf. Bruinessen (1992 a), p. 295.

[24] Fevzī Pirinççīzāde, later Pirinççioğlu, was born in Diyarbakır in 1879 and died in İstanbul in 1933. He is said to have been a relative of Ziya Gökalp's mother. Fevzī was a graduate of a high school (*i'dādīye*) and worked as a civil servant. He was elected vice-president of the Republican People's Party in parliament in 1924, cf. Tunçay (1981), pp. 90 sqq.—The tradition of political leadership was continued by Fevzi's son Vefik (1909–1984). From 1961–1969, he was deputy for Diyarbakır

The letter is, in the main, a request that Fevzī make the contents of the letter (the arguments against assimilation) accessible to his fellow Kurdish parliamentarians,[25] and use his influence with Atatürk, to whom there is a long encomium in the last pages of the letter. However, if this was his aim, the discourse relating to Fevzī is at times inappropriate. At the beginning of the letter he invites Fevzī to make himself comfortable in an armchair or chaise-longue, light a cigar and have the letter read to him.[26] The image evoked of the letter's recipient is unmistakably that of the opportunist who enjoys security, comfort and power while those who have righteously fought for Kurdish interests have been forced to flee, giving up their homes and sources of livelihood. Why ask Fevzī to do something for the Kurds? There was not the shadow of a doubt that Pirinççīzāde and others of his ilk attributed no more significance to their Kurdish background than did Ziya Gökalp, the most prominent proponent of assimilation. Unaffected by appeals for national revival, unmoved by accounts of past greatness and the suffering to which their repressed brethren had been subjected, such Kurds had persistently refused to be "awakened". As a result of their "opportunistic" alliances, they attained positions, power and security. Such persons are problematic for any political movement which postulates the legitimacy and moral necessity of its aims. The canon of ethnic nationalism ordains the allegiance of each member to the ethnic group. Identity, loyalty and responsibility are not matters of choice: they exist *a priori*. Those who deny their ethnic identity by simply ignoring it or choosing to locate the focus of identity elsewhere must be condemned as traitors. If one postulates the nation on the basis of ethnic identity, there can be no granting of dispensation. The success of Pirinççīzādes and others who do not recognize the moral imperative of their Kurdishness weakens the appeal of Kurdish nationalism. But it is interesting that Sekban does not call Fevzī a traitor: he only implies it, perhaps hoping after all that Fevzī might yet be moved to honour his ethnic obligations to some small extent.

Appealing to Fevzī places Sekban in the paradoxical situation of seeking support from those who had betrayed their compatriots by

---

resp. Kahramanmaraş and acted as minister in 1963/64: Bayrak (1992), pp. 144 sqq.; *CDTA* 10, pp. 2699, 2714.

[25] Sekban (1923), p. 30.

[26] Sekban (1923), p. 4.

sacrificing Kurdish nationalist goals on the altar of Turkish nationalism. But as a past (and presently would-be leader) he must put distance between himself and the traitors. Perhaps his ironic stance towards his reader should be understood as an attempt to bolster his own moral superiority; it is a statement to other Kurdish protagonists that he, Sekban, is clearly not sitting comfortably in an armchair.

Kurdish leaders in exile may have had some—however vague—knowledge of the founding of *Azadī*, a clandestine organization established mainly by military leaders.[27] Sekban's letter must also be seen in this light: one of the primary aims of the letter may have been the desire to reassert a claim to leadership of whatever Kurdish movement was to evolve. On the other hand, it is quite possible that Sekban was asked by other exile leaders to sound out the possibility of establishing some channel of communication with the powers that be, and this is why he played down the polarity between the exiled Kurds and Turkish leaders.

The very events which had precipitated the flight of Kurdish activists into exile had restored to them the old dilemma which had marked the conceptualization and articulation of Turkish-Kurdish relations from the first stirrings of collective Kurdish self-consciousness: how to postulate the legitimacy and rightfulness of a Kurdish identity and demands without the framework of a clear opposition. Without a morally reprehensible enemy on whom to project the blame for their suffering, how could a strong sense of Kurdish righteousness develop to provide the impetus necessary for a nationalist movement? Clearly, to those who felt betrayed, such as military officers, tribal chiefs and members of the first national assembly who had received pledges from Atatürk, the Turks represented an inimical other; the making of their (Turkish) nation was to depend on the unmaking of any plans the Kurds had had for their own nation.

[27] Since T̲üreyyā Bedir Khān (1928) did not mention İḥsān Nūrī and other officers, Behrendt concludes that T̲üreyyā did not know anything about the leaders of the Saʿīd Revolt other than the sheykh himself. Only after establishing contact with İḥsān Nūrī, did T̲üreyyā in his influential *La question kurde* (1930) report that the officers of *Azadī* had led the revolt. I find it difficult to believe that Kurds in Syria were not aware of *Azadī* in 1928 since Nūrī had defected in September of 1924. Bruinessen (1989), p. 381, states that Memdūḥ Selīm, one of the founding members of *Khoybūn*, had had contacts to *Azadī* (this is not mentioned in the English translation) (Bruinessen 1992 a).

But as long as Atatürk was viewed by most as the *ghāzī*-hero, the liberator of Muslims from the invading Christians, clearly delineated Kurdish-Turkish opposition could not be articulated. Once again, Kurdish intellectuals were forced to retreat from the position of a clearly-defined Kurdish identity. Sekban's ambivalence, when he on the one hand refers to the Kurds as a "separate race" from the Turks but, on the other hand, maintains "Kürd Türk birdir" ("Kurds and Turks are one"), is an accurate reflection of the constraints placed on Kurdish nationalist discourse by the victory of the Turkish nationalists.

CHAPTER TWO

AZADĪ AND THE SHEYKH SAʿĪD REVOLT

Well before the exiled nationalist leaders were able to reassemble, revolt was under way in large areas of Turkish Kurdistan, a revolt its leaders envisioned as spreading and culminating in an independent state of Kurdistan. When it finally broke out in February of 1925, fighting was led primarily by the Nakşibendī Sheykh Saʿīd from Piran because many of the military and political leaders who had been involved in planning the revolt had been imprisoned or forced to flee.

As early as 1921, when many Kurds had already joined forces with the Turkish nationalists, Khalid Jibran Bey was agitating in the Kurdish provinces for Kurdish national aims.[1] Khalid Bey exemplifies a nationalist career which contrasts with those Kurdish intellectuals who had been involved in the Ḥamidian opposition. As the son of a powerful Kurdish *agha*, Khalid was educated in the tribal military school (*ʿAşiret Mektebi*) in İstanbul, becoming first the leader of a *Ḥamīdīye* regiment and, subsequently, an officer in the regular Ottoman army. However, by the end of World War I, Khalid Bey appears to have been receptive to the idea of Kurdish independence, although he fought loyally with the Ottoman army throughout the war. One of Bruinessen's informants states that a member of the Bedir Khān clan, then in Russia, had contacted the leaders of several Kurdish tribes, including the Jibrans, about receiving Russian assistance in establishing an independent state in return for fighting against the Turkish military. Sheykh Saʿīd, a relative by marriage to Khālid Bey, persuaded him to accept Bedir Khān's offer. The plans came to naught and Khalid eventually participated in the offensive on the Eastern front which resulted in a virtual ethnic cleansing of Armenians in the area. Bruinessen relates the anecdote to indicate the considerable power the sheykhs still possessed in mediating between tribes;

[1] Khalid was active first in Dersim then in Erzurum where he had been sent by the Kemalist movement, suspicious of his activities in Dersim, see Olson (1989), pp. 27–28.

the Jibrans would only accept Bedir Khān's offer if their rivals, the Khormek also accepted. But the anecdote also illustrates not only that Kurdish nationalism could be appealing enough to outweigh Ottoman loyalties, but that tribal factionalism inhibited the growth of any identification with a general Kurdish cause. Another anecdote has Khalid Bey experiencing a sort of epiphany upon the Ottoman victory on the Eastern front. By ridding the area of Armenians, the Kurds had unwittingly forfeited their historical status and value to the Turks as counterweights to the Armenians.

The clandestine organization *Azadī* was established by 1923 at the latest, and probably earlier.[2] Although there was an İstanbul chapter headed by ʿAbdülḳādir,[3] *Azadī*'s headquarters and focus of activities was located inside Kurdistan, centered around Erzurum.[4] Among the other prominent *Azadī* members were military men, who such as İḥsān Nūrī, were instrumental in fomenting support. Somewhat longer than Khalid Bey, Nūrī had kept one foot in the Turkish camp as an officer of the Turkish army until the ill-conceived mutiny of September 1924, which was intended to launch the great revolt. According to his own accounts, Nūrī had participated in the Eastern front offensive in Batum and Çürüksu. A *Hēvī* member in 1912, he returned to İstanbul after World War I,[5] where he made contact with "Zedki Bey Bitlisi",[6] the editor of *Jīn*, and wrote several articles for the journal. Parallel to his Kurdish activities he became the chairman of the İstanbul officers' committee which supported Mustafa Kemal. Nūrī opposed foreign occupation and the pro-British Ferīd Pasha government.[7] Since Nūrī had been a *Hēvī* member, we can assume that he had long harboured Kurdish national leanings. His

[2] Olson (1989), p. 28.

[3] Although he does not seem to have been involved closely in the revolt, ʿAbdülḳādir was sentenced to death after trial by an Independence Tribunal (*İstiklāl maḥkemesi*). In this instance, the verdict must be seen as a settling of accounts with those who had collaborated with the Allies or supported the old regime against the Kemalists.

[4] Bruinessen (1992 a), p. 280.

[5] According to Olson (1989), p. 46, Nūrī had been arrested, court-martialed and sent to Bitlis in 1919 for mutinying against his superiors, an incident not referred to in Nūrī's biographical notices.

[6] This is what İḥsān Nūrī calls him. Perhaps he meant Kurdī-yi Bitlīsī. In the newspaper, however, a certain Ḥamza (identical with no. 72 in Göldaş [1991], p. 42?) is mentioned as editor in chief; from no. 21 Memdūḥ [Selīm Begi] acted as editor in chief.

[7] See his *La Revolte de l'Agri Dagh* (1986).

initial support for Kemal indicates that for a time he felt Kurdish interests would be best served by participating in the Ottoman resistance to Allied control.

Another of the founding members of *Azadī*, Yūsuf Żiyā Bey, of the princely family of Bitlis, had also preferred association with the Kemalists, becoming a member of the first national assembly. He used his campaign for reelection in 1923 as an opportunity to obtain support for Kurdish nationalist goals. Many *Azadī* members, then, had been able to retain largely military positions under the Kemalists, not having been compromised by pro-Western activities as had so many of the heretofore prominent nationalists now in exile. While perhaps encouraged by pledges to protect Kurdish interests they were not content to passively await the realization of their goals. It is significant that the first *Azadī* congress must have taken place in summer 1923, i.e. before the 1924 secularization laws which would prove so useful to agitation against the Turkish government. But there were already indications that Kemalism was not going to provide the Kurds with satisfactory concessions; proponents of Kurdish interests were not among the members of the newly elected national assembly. Thus Kurdish nationalism may have begun to appear to be the only avenue for advancement.

As the group operated clandestinely, there are very few documents indicating how, exactly, they agitated for support. In view of the scant material available, it seems likely that there were two phases in mobilizing: prior to the summer congress, when military and tribal leaders were addressed, and a subsequent mass mobilization. The images of Kurdishness used to appeal for support varied accordingly.

The eponymous leader of the "nationalist revolt in religious garb"[8] was a fervent nationalist as well as a religious man. A call to rebellion sent out in March 1924, which is attributed to Saʿīd, is written in the then current nationalist mode.[9] Whereas in this call, religion is mentioned only very briefly, once mass mobilizing began in earnest, Sheykh Saʿīd exploited his religious authority and the religious iden-

[8] Both Bruinessen (1992 a) and Olson (1989), who have published detailed studies of the revolt, concluded that the motivation of the leaders was nationalist although the mode of mobilizing remained traditional. These alliances along tribal lines, especially those delineated by religious and linguistic differences, limited solidarity, see Olson's discussion p. 35.

[9] See Küchler (1978), pp. 176–178.

tity of his followers by issuing *fetvās* and campaigning against the Turkish nationalists as religious enemies. How is this discrepancy to be explained? The "call" was written prior to the first *Azadī* congress, which was attended by nationalists. Since Sheykh Saʿīd emerged as a leader at this congress,[10] we can view his summons in the context of his aspirations to leadership of a largely military, secularly-educated group. That would explain his conception of battle in the name of political ideals rather than in the name of religion.[11]

The Kurds are addressed as a nation whose obligation it is to deliver itself from the oppressive rule of the Turks: "You, the Kurdish nation! Good and evil lie in our hands. Only by virtue of our deeds will we be liberated and go from darkness to light. We have long lived under the despotism of the Turks. If we continue to wait for their mercy we will die rotten and decayed".[12]

The summons begins with a condemnation of Turkish rule in terms reminiscent of the Kurdish nationalist journals:

> The Turks, the Ottomans, have unfortunately gradually enslaved us over 400 years in the name of religion and the Islamic caliphate. They have led us into darkness and ignorance . . . (omission in the text given by Küchler, MS) these Turks who came to us as nomads and by dint of their cunning and deception managed to settle down. They occupied our land and destroyed it. Kurdistan was never such a ruin as today . . . our land was never so neglected. No Kurd, no believer, can accept this situation. We are all obliged to liberate ourselves from this bitter and unhappy life. For this reason, we may not deviate from the path of justice and truth.

The familiar image is evoked of a time when Kurds, free, had enjoyed a civilization which was destroyed by Turks whose heritage and origins are belittled. The Turks tried to teach the Kurds "hatred, laziness and indolence and plundering. They have never tried to teach us fine things, mutual love, tolerance, science and art. They have continually shown us the way to a nomadic life . . .".[13]

The Turks, responsible for Kurdish suffering, are portrayed as dishonest, disloyal and cruel. They have called on the Kurds in their hour of need, but never given them what was rightfully theirs: "They

---

[10] Bruinessen (1984), p. 153.

[11] It is also possible that Saʿīd's "right hand man", a notorious anti-cleric, penned the call. See Bruinessen (1989), p. 431, on Fehmī Bilāl Efendi.

[12] Küchler (1978), p. 177.

[13] Küchler (1978), p. 177.

have not only not kept their word—they have—as far as they could—plunged their swords into the breasts of Kurds".[14] The inevitable concern with the Kurdish image is also in evidence: "We must expose the (seemingly, MS) benevolent Turks and show how destructive, brutal and bloodthirsty they are . . . Let us strive for an honourable life; let us make a common sacrifice for freedom and happiness—let us obtain a good reputation for our nation. We must show the world that we are against rule by force, against rightlessness, and injustice and that we will resist it".[15]

Küchler, who quotes this text at some length, finds it persuasive due to the large number of "symbols which are particularly relevant for the Kurds". But the only instance I can find of a specifically Kurdish image is the evocation of the revered Aḥmad-i Khānī: "From the time of *Mem ū Zīn* until today, we have not organized our lives; we have not made the spirits of our ancestors happy. We have not fulfilled the wishes of Aḥmad-i Khānī. That is why we live in misery and make our enemies glad".[16] Aside from the reference to Khānī, which is so brief that it indicates most readers were familiar with the prologue, specifically Kurdish images are absent. Instead, the emphasis is on abstract values such as justice, truth, civil rights, freedom and brotherhood, with frequent exhortations to face the Turks with courage and not to fear death: "Your hands may not tremble in war. Do not fear death . . . Rather than live a meaningless life with the tyrant, we should prefer to die on the mutual path to justice and freedom. To be a martyr is sweeter than such a life".[17] Despite the reference to martyrdom, Kurdish soldiers are clearly being asked to fight and die not in *jihād*, but in a war of liberation.

No mention is made of Kurdish religion or of the Kurdish language as sacred values which had been violated, possibly because both issues were potentially divisive. Saʿīd was a Zaza speaker hoping to appeal to Kurmanjī speakers as well. Most if not all of the members of *Azadī* were Sunni Muslims who had not backed the Koçgiri rebellion, which had been supported mainly by Alevis.[18] Nor

[14] Küchler (1978), p. 178.
[15] Küchler (1978), p. 177.
[16] Küchler (1978), p. 178.
[17] Küchler (1978), p. 177.
[18] Some of the Alevis were Zaza speakers; others Kurmanjī, see Bruinessen (1984), p. 145. Despite Sheykh Saʿīd's efforts, Alevis refused to join forces. They preferred a secular to a Sunni Kurdistan, Olson (1989), p. 94.

are specific grievances outlined apart from the Kemalists' not having kept their promises.[19]

The only surviving document concerning *Azadī*'s view of itself, grievances and aims is a report made by British officers who interviewed a group of the hapless would-be insurgents around İḥsān Nūrī. Due to a misunderstanding, Nūrī and other officers had prematurely begun a mutiny in Beytüşşebap in September 1924. Upon realizing their mistake, they fled to Iraq and were interviewed there by the British. They gave mainly political, economical and cultural reasons for the impending revolt but also the abolition of the caliphate "which has broken one of the few remaining bonds between the Turks and Kurds".[20] The *Azadī* officers presented themselves as having been wronged by the Turks in terms of political discrimination (manipulation of elections), social discrimination (ill-treated in the army, poor prospects for advancement), cultural rights (Kurdish not allowed in schools) and economical exploitation (villages were plundered, no services provided for taxes). Nowhere is there any indication that religious concerns were paramount or even of minor significance.[21] Aside from independence, they did not seem to have formulated further goals: "When pressed . . . about leaders they offered the name Bedir Khān".[22]

Thus, for a large number of the participants nationalism, religion and tribe were inextricably intertwined in an expanding notion of identity based largely on their enmity with the Turks. They could accept the dichotomy of Turk versus Kurd, as it now represented their jeopardized future vis-à-vis the Turkish government's intentions, and see their revolt as a *jihād*. Kurdish leaders had closely witnessed how the War of Independence had been framed as a religious war, only to be followed by a rejection of their religious values, and the breaking of promises to the Kurds.

In 1925, when the important military leaders, including Khalid Jibran, had been arrested or had fled, Sheykh Saʿīd traveled around,

[19] According to Bruinessen (1984), p. 153, he also hoped that Turkish opposition to Kemalists might be supportive.

[20] Olson (1989), p. 44.

[21] However, according to Bruinessen (1984), pp. 143–144, they were seeking British assistance and may have accordingly articulated their grievances and goals so as to appeal to the British.

[22] Bruinessen (1992 a), p. 283. Olson (1989), pp. 41–51. But it is also known that only a short time later Saʿīd spoke of placing Kurdistan under the nominal leadership of a member of the caliph's family.

mainly through areas inhabited by Zaza-speaking tribes loyal to him, holding inflammatory talks[23] and issueing *fetvās* condemning the Ankara government for destroying religion.[24] This played into the hands of Turkish politicians at the time (and later), who were eager to reduce the revolt to religious resistance against modernism.[25] The revolt, doomed to failure by the limited support—many Kurdish leaders continued to support Kemāl or preferred to remain neutral—illustrates that the Kurdish national identity was not yet a widely-embraced "moral imperative". And yet, the Saʿīd Rebellion is a watershed in the development of Kurdish national identity. At the trial of the Independence Tribunal, Sheykh Saʿīd allegedly spoke of a process of self-discovery: "First I was an Arab, then a Turk and now I have become a Kurd".[26] We may interpret this statement as referring first to his descent from the prophet Muḥammad (*sayyid*); second, to his loyalty to the Sultan/Caliph. He had become a Kurd by virtue of his opposition to Kemalist Turkey. In the rhetoric of the urban intellectuals who had aimed for a Kurdish revival, the Kurds had been envisioned as a people to be "remade". In the Saʿīd Rebellion, the romantic, cultural view—the reference to Khānī—is present but marginal. Here is a people fighting for the rights that the recently-signed Treaty of Sèvres had guaranteed, against an enemy who intended to deprive them of these rights.

---

[23] Bruinessen (1984), p. 155.
[24] Olson (1989), pp. 93–95.
[25] Ṯüreyyā Bedir Khān (1928 a) argues that the government portrayed the religious character of the revolt in its dispatches to Europe, so as to prevent any indignation in regard to injustice towards minorities. But in Turkey, where the danger of religious solidarity loomed large, the revolt was labelled separatist; its organizers traitors. But a British intelligence source quoted in a report from 2 March 1925 predicted that ". . . for the satisfaction of public opinion in Europe, since the government will not be able to admit its negligence, the explanation that the revolt was due to foreign intrigue and the forces of reaction, will serve very well for dissemination . . . And by these means we can smother or threaten all the centers of reaction . . .", Olson (1989), pp. 89–90.
[26] Bayrak (1993), p. 325.

CHAPTER THREE

A LETTER TO İNÖNÜ

It must have been obvious to the exiled leaders that their leadership had been seriously challenged by the Saʿīd Revolt. This would explain the ambiguity and anonymity of the open letter to İsmet İnönü a year after the revolt.[1] In this publication, the first published assessment of the revolt by Kurdish leaders, the authors implicitly support the revolt by charging the Turkish government with full responsibility for the bloodshed; the Kurds who fought could not be blamed as they had fought out of "idealistic motives" (*mefkūre-i ḳudsīye*), not out of "personal ambitions" (*iḥtirāṣāt-i şakhṣīye*). But, at the same time, the authors dissociate themselves from the religious character of the revolt and stress their loyalty to the Republic. They describe themselves as Kurdish nationalists, but also as "supporters of the Republic and modernism" and "opponents of clericalism".[2]

The main aim of the letter appears to be to appeal for Turkish leniency, assuring the government that if autonomy were granted the problems with the Kurds would cease. The only way for Turkish nationalists to achieve consolidation and coexistence with the Kurds is to recognize the principles of the civilized world in the 20th century: nation and freedom. Furthermore, the authors point out that this demonstrate Turkish political maturity to their friends and foes alike.[3]

The anonymity of the letter suggests that there was yet no consensus regarding the path of continued resistance or the goals of autonomy or independence. While insisting on the guilt of the Turks, they are still envisioned as "brothers" and not referred to as "enemies" or oppressors. The tone of the letter suggests appeasement as much as condemnation. The authors were very likely probing and did not want to exclude either the possibility of cooperating with the Turkish government to improve the Kurdish situation, or of

[1] Text in Bayrak (1993), pp. 493–500.
[2] Bayrak (1993), p. 499.
[3] Bayrak (1993), pp. 496–499.

aligning themselves with the forces which had spawned the Saʿīd Revolt. The letter differs very little from Sekban's earlier open letter in terms of defining Turkish-Kurdish relations, and may well have been penned by the same author. Kurds and Turks are said to be "brother nations" who are condemned to live together; Kurds, however, would never accept being assimilated by the Turks.[4] For this reason, the authors suggest prophetically that it is time to find a solution not just for the problems of the 20th century but for the centuries to come, since Kurdistan would "become the incubator of violent hatred" and "the source of enemy invasions and aggressions" if Turkish policies continue.[5]

[4] Bayrak (1993), p. 496.
[5] Bayrak (1993), pp. 499–500.

CHAPTER FOUR

KHOYBŪN AND THE ARARAT REVOLT

Khoybūn, founded in Bhamdoun/Lebanon[1] just one year after the publication of the letter to İnönü, quickly shed the conciliatory tones, the rhetoric of alliance and brotherhood, and proclaimed as its goal the independence of Turkish Kurdistan. There was reason to hope that the League of Nations' intentions regarding regional autonomy for the Kurds in Iraq would be realized. *Khoybūn* represented the effort to unite all the disparate, scattered groups which had emigrated after the war or had somehow managed to flee into the mountains after the Saʿīd Rebellion, as well as Kurds in the area now under British Mandate, and Kurds from Iran. From the beginning, there were good contacts to Dashnak, the Armenian resistance group with whose help the Kurds hoped to bring the Kurdish question before the League of Nations.[2] The Armenians wanted to gain support for their claims in Turkey by assisting a war which could be presented as heroic resistance to Turkish oppression. Kurdish writers, in particular Ṯüreyyā Bedir Khān, profited from Armenian expertise in conducting propaganda campaigns. His pamphlets comprise the first full-fledged Kurdish national propaganda, replete with a fully developed image of the Kurds both as victims and heroic warriors intent on securing their rights from the Turks. Both Sekban and Celādet Bedir Khān are listed as the first chairmen of *Khoybūn*. It was indicative of the factiousness of that organization that members had to swear a "brotherhood oath" in which they pledged not to use their weapons against one another for two years.[3]

The nationalistic efforts of *Khoybūn* were aimed at overcoming the deep divisions between tribal and urban society by propagating a common Kurdish cultural heritage. Part of this heritage was the oral tradition of tales and myths, which are dealt with in part three of

---

[1] The executive committee resided in Aleppo until it was dispersed by the French authorities in 1928, doubtless due to Turkish protests: Kutschera (1979), p. 90.

[2] Ibrahim (1983), p. 670.

[3] Sasuni (1986), p. 184.

this study. Like the Armenian Dashnaks, who were organizing education in the Armenian language in Aleppo, *Khoybūn* also undertook to open schools. Despite some success, two of the *Khoybūn* principles met with severe resistance from tribal leaders: the alleged brotherhood of Armenians and Kurds and the concept of armed resistance under the command of a centralized military organization.[4]

Many *Khoybūn* members were very recent converts to Kurdish nationalism. "General" Ḥusayn Pasha of the Ḥaydaran tribe, who was promoted as one of the "most influential leaders of the Kurds"[5] was, according to İḥsān Nūrī, very powerful and very rich. He had refused to rescue Khalid Bey from his Bitlis imprisonment and had tried to prevent the flight of Sheykh Saʿīd's son and brother.[6] In the eyes of Nūrī, Ḥusayn Pasha was responsible for the death of at least one prominent *Azadī* member. Apparently this did not make him suspect to other *Khoybūn* members, who had had little if any connection to the Saʿīd Revolt. Despite inner rivalries and serious social and ideological differences, this organization represented the first attempt by intellectual, military, religious and tribal leaders to coordinate their resistance.[7]

Khoybūn dispatched İḥsān Nūrī as military commander of the revolt to be conducted in Ararat. His task was to transform "popular, spontaneous resistance" into an organized movement,[8] while *Khoybūn* mem-

[4] Fuccaro (1997), p. 310.

[5] Bedir Khān (1928 b), p. 54.

[6] Nouri (1986), p. 118.

[7] Bruinessen (1992 a), pp. 101–105, has an interesting discussion on the Hevērkan confederation, a group of tribes which had supported the Emir of Botan, Bedir Khān. By 1925, however, the tribes were considered loyal to the Ottoman government. Hajo, the leader of the tribes, answered the government's call to fight against the Saʿīd Revolt, but he avoided getting too close to the rebels so as not to be considered a traitor. In May 1926, Hajo led his own badly organized revolt and found it necessary to retreat to Syria. There he became the favoured spokesman on Kurdish affairs with the French Mandate administration. One of the most dynamic members of *Khoybūn*, he organized diversionary attacks in southeastern Turkey in order to engage government troops during the revolt at Ararat. It was probably on one of these forays that Celādet Bedir Khān accompanied him into Turkey. Cf. Nikitine (1975), p. 285. Fuccaro (1997, pp. 321–3) has an interesting and detailed account of Hajo's leadership career in *Khoybūn*.

[8] Nūrī's *La revolte de l'Agri Dagh* is the French version of an English translation. The original was said to have been written in Sorani. Nūrī, author of a Kurdish history in Farsi, was living in Teheran when contacted by a Kurdish students' group in Europe, at whose behest he attended a meeting in West Berlin in 1962. There he met the Kurdish leader Ismet Cherif Vanly, who called him the "old lion of

bers would conduct propaganda on behalf of the group and provide military support by recruiting from the tribal milieu. *Khoybūn* faced predictable difficulties in recruiting tribes for the nationalist cause. Moreover, the border controls by the French Government were stepped up, as they became alarmed by the anti-Kemalism of the Kurds.[9] The Ararat region[10] had been in revolt for some time under the leadership of Haski Tello, a leader of tribes who assumed, in accordance with the *Khoybūn* plan, the governorship of the Republic of Ararat, proclaimed in 1928. Whereas Nūrī had been one of the instigators of the Saʿīd Revolt, Haski Tello had actively opposed it. Nūrī described his mission as threefold: 1) to form a center of liberation, a task he decribed as "making a fortress of Agri Dagh"; 2) to proclaim the government of Kurdistan; 3) to organize a revolutionary army divided into small units, each with a different task, unified under one leadership. Meanwhile, *Khoybūn* members outside Turkey[11] would draw public attention to the Kurdish resistance and Turkish aggression and atrocities, hoping to "shake the political and economic credibility of Turkey".[12]

Religious rhetoric does not appear to have been significant in the Ararat Revolt although, according to Nūrī, sheykhs and aghas were still crucial leaders.[13] By this time, the Turkish government's policy of deporting Kurds to the western coast had delivered a number of Kurds who had, until then, been pro-Turkish, to the Kurdish

Ararat". Although some interesting details may be gleaned from his memoirs, they do not provide an accurate historical account of events, as the editors of the book are quick to point out in the introduction. Too much time had elapsed between the revolt and Nūrī's writing in the late 1960's. To refresh his memory of events, he consulted the notes of a Turkish officer, "Zohdi Goyven" (Zühdü Güven?). Nūrī's flight into Iran was interpreted as abandoning his army prematurely (Kutschera 1979, pp. 100–101) and, although he offered assistance in the efforts to maintain the Kurdish Republic of Mahabad in 1946, he was ignored. His memoirs presented the opportunity to reinstate himself as the self-sacrificing leader of a historic struggle.

[9] Fuccaro (1997), p. 310.

[10] This was roughly the same area which had been promised to Armenia by the Treaty of Sèvres.

[11] According to Uzun's literary biography of Memdūḥ Selīm, the latter spent two years at Ararat. Uzun draws heavily on Iḥsān Nūrī's memoirs for his account of Selīm's time with the rebels. Uzun has Selīm working on the newspaper *Ağrı*, published by the rebels, but Nūrī does not mention that Selīm was at Ararat.

[12] Nouri (1986), pp. 44–45.

[13] Kutschera (1979), p. 97, mentions that Saʿīd's son was involved in fighting in 1929.

nationalist camp. Among these was Bro Haski Tello, who had led troops first against the Russians and then against the Armenians at Ararat, later liberating the town of Bayazıd for the Ottomans and marrying the daughter of a Turkish governor. He had never supported Kurdish separatism until, according to Nūrī, Turkish troops came to deport him and his family: "It seems that Bro Haski Tello had not realized that for the Turkish government, since he was a Kurd, whether he had served or opposed the government, remained the same thing".[14]

In his memoirs Nūrī concedes that it had been a mistake to create only one center of resistance. This had made the Kurdish forces more vulnerable to superior Turkish military power. The Kurds had furthermore assumed that Iran would remain neutral, but once Turkish troops had entered Iran pursuing Turkish Kurds, Iran came to an agreement with the Turkish government, thus closing the borders as a supply and escape route in 1930,[15] roughly the period during which Nūrī fled to Iran with his wife.[16] There is not a great deal of reliable information on this revolt from which we might be able to reconstruct the notion of identity espoused by the Kurds. But if Vanly's assessment is correct that Nūrī had remained "a prisoner to the images of what he had seen at Ararat", and was not in tune with the changes in nationalist thought in the ensuing decades,[17] then his memoirs were written in a sort of time warp. Thus his memoirs warrant our attention as they convey the mentality of Kurdish leaders at the time. Nūrī employs the nationalist rhetoric of eternal resistance which suggests that the present and other recent revolts are manifestations of age-old aspirations. Those Kurds who refused to follow the dictates of their Kurdish identities did so at their peril. Either the Turkish government (as in the case of Haski Tello), public opinion or divine strategies ensured that traitors would be punished in this life or the next, and bring shame to their families and tribes. In devoting many pages to the fates of several promi-

[14] Nouri (1986), pp. 74–78. In his account, Tello's flight to the mountains and his first encounters with Turkish troops marked the beginning of Ararat resistance.

[15] See quote from the Tehran newspaper, *Irān*, dated July 10, 1930, reproduced in Nouri (1986), pp. 179–181.

[16] Although he recounts how he steadfastly refused all offers to escape "until the last drop of blood was shed" (Nouri 1986, pp. 61–63).

[17] Nouri (1986), p. 28.

nent Kurdish traitors, he shows how, more often than not, it was the Turks themselves who failed to honour Kurds who were loyal to the Turks. This latter theme also appears in the two writings of Ṯüreyyā Bedir Khān published in 1928 and intended to rally international support and sympathy for the revolt in progress.

CHAPTER FIVE

ṮÜREYYĀ BEDIR KHĀN

1. *Imagining the Enemy and the Continuity of Revolt*

Although Kāmurān Bedir Khān would eventually emerge as a sort of Kurdish ambassador-at-large, in 1928 it was clearly Ṯüreyyā,[1] the eldest of Emīn ʿĀlī Bedir Khān's sons, to whom this responsibility fell.[2] Having penned the only widely circulated texts published in the name of *Khoybūn*, which presented the Kurdish case for revolt, he also spent some time in the United States trying to drum up support for the Kurds. Widely quoted in academic and journalistic writing, Ṯüreyyā Bedir Khān's three publications established his reputation as the first propagandist of Kurdish nationalism. Because of their polemical, propagandistic nature, these texts must be evaluated critically as sources for historical research.[3] But as the aim of this study has not been to probe the veracity of Kurdish nationalist claims and argumentation, but rather to focus on the progress of Kurdish identity-

---

[1] For Ṯüreyyā's *vita* see *EI*, s.v. "Badrkhānī". He was the older brother of Kāmurān and Celādet and lived mainly in Cairo. Ṯüreyyā was a co-founder of *Khoybūn*. To appease the Ankara government, the French Mandate authorities "invited" Ṯüreyyā to leave Syrian territory in 1930 on the occasion of the Ararat Revolt. This may explain his use of the pseudonym Bletch Chirguh. Ṯüreyyā went to Paris, where he remained until his death in 1938: Rondot (1939), p. 114. In a French document from 1931, reproduced in Alakom (1998, p. 156), Ṯüreyyā is listed as president of the Detroit chapter of *Khoybūn*.

[2] Bruinessen (1989), p. 399, referring to a Foreign Office report from 1919, related that Ṯüreyyā had requested that the territories which had been under the dominion of his grandfather be returned to him. Bruinessen comments that the letter conveys the impression that Ṯüreyyā considered the land his private property rather than an independent state. One may assume that the two ambitious younger brothers accepted his prerogative as he had cared for their ailing father and supported them financially during their studies in Germany, see Bedirhan (1995), pp. 26, 35.

[3] Behrendt (1993) has shown with regard to Ṯüreyyā's publication (under the pseudonym Bletch Chirguh): *La question kurde. Ses origines et ses causes* (1930), that several enduring myths of Kurdish nationalism derive from inaccurancies in Ṯüreyyā's writing. Some scholars suspect Celādet, rather than Ṯüreyyā behind the pseudonym, but I agree with Behrendt (1993, p. 10) that Ṯüreyyā is the more likely author.

building as manifested in nationalist writing, we must regard Ṯüreyyā's publications as being of seminal importance.

From the very beginning, creating a viable Kurdish identity was simultaneously an inwardly and outwardly directed endeavor. The early advocates of Kurdish interests were aware of their late start. They attempted to compress several steps into one: developing language and historical research, educating their compatriots, awakening them to the Kurdish national identity and interests, all the while undertaking to improve the image of the Kurds held in the West. The Bedir Khān clan and many of the intellectuals involved in the Kurdish movement had always displayed an acute preoccupation with the "civilized world" and the long path the Kurds would have to traverse in order to be accepted by this superior world. Underlying this concern was the much articulated fear that the backward Kurds would not be able to catch up with the Western world, and might indeed be consumed by it should the demise of the sick man of Europe suddenly lay the empire open to foreign takeover. The early nationalists saw the greatest enemy of the Kurds in their ignorance and indifference; education was perceived as the weapon with which they would liberate themselves from backwardness and take their place in the modern world. Thus the predominant image of contemporary Kurds was negative; their attitudes and life style were seen as the roots of difficulties. The "civilized" world was evoked as a world apart, an ideal to be aspired to.

Les Massacres Kurdes en Turquie and *The Case of Kurdistan against Turkey*[4] represent a radical departure from this portrayal of the Kurdish situation. Gone is the backward Kurd and, in his place, is the Kurdish nation, valiantly defending itself against its age-old enemy, the Turks, who have committed countless atrocities in order to annihilate the Kurds. It is certainly not a novelty that an insurgent group conduct propaganda against the perceived enemy but, just two years earlier, in the open letter to İnönü, authors were still straddling the fence between "us" and "them", between justified revolt and ultimate loyalty. Chided for being at fault for the bloodshed of the Saʿīd Rebellion, the Turks had nonetheless appeared in the İnönü letter as brothers to the Kurds. To my knowledge, *Les Massacres* and *The Case* are the

[4] Hereafter referred to respectively as *Les Massacres* and *The Case*.

first attempt to present the Kurdish case to a Western public, in terms of a clearly defined opposition and legitimacy derived from Turkish injustice.[5] Distinct, unequivocal and pervasive enmity has replaced the reproachful but appeasing tone of earlier publications. The Turkish foe assumes almost mythical dimensions, depicted as a monster with a primeval drive to destroy other races.

Not only is the Kurd no longer portrayed as backward; his membership in the "civilized" world and his right to acceptance and assistance are presupposed. Had not the governments of the West fought the war to aid "weak nations"? If now they did nothing to help the Kurds then it might well be assumed that they and the League of Nations were interested only in aiding the strong.[6] The implication is that the Kurds are morally superior to the "civilized" governments who tolerate Turkish violations of internationally recognized rights and crimes against the Kurds. The author points out that Kemāl had been able to rely on French neutrality to isolate the Kurds.[7] Due to Turkish censure and the failure of the "civilized" governments to inform their citizens, the public has been led to believe that there was no longer a Kurdish question:

> The aim of the work is to make a résumé of the history of the Kurdish question which they (the Turks, MS) are trying to extinguish with blood and iron, (and) to follow the events which have condemned the Kurdish nation to death, from their origin until today . . . we want to establish once and for all the right of this nation to life, and to bring to light the real barbaric and egotistical causes of these massacres.[8]

The timing of the publication was significant. *Khoybūn* had only existed for a year, but already İḥsān Nūrī, the designated military leader of impending revolt was at Ararat and the Republic had been proclaimed. *Les Massacres* was an attempt to predispose the Western public to view the revolt sympathetically and, at the very least, remain neutral in the conflict. For this it was necessary to detract from the prestige and acceptance that the Turkish Republic enjoyed as a result of its well-publicized and well-received modernization policies. This

---

[5] On the other hand, Ṯüreyyā's writing also reflects the focus on developing a national identity on the basis of a shared heritage. Certainly, the common experience of victimization was a powerful element in this endeavour.

[6] Bedir Khān (1928 a), p. 39.

[7] Bedir Khān (1928 a), p. 15.

[8] Bedir Khān (1928 a), pp. 3–4.

in part explains why a great deal more effort was expended towards unmasking the Turk and revealing his "true nature" than towards portraying the Kurds in a positive light. But it is also true that a definite image of the enemy had been lacking in the Kurdish arsenal thus far and that this had inhibited the clear delineation of a Kurdish identity. The Armenian nationalists, cooperating with *Khoybūn*, shared their reservoir of resentment and mobilization strategies acquired over decades of agitating within their ethnic group and in Europe. These were directed mainly towards focussing on an inimical other who could be blamed for any humiliation and losses.

As Haarmann remarked, "Derogatory stereotypes are generated and applied by a given group in order to provide a psychological release in its dealings with another group which is feared and felt to be superior in certain respects".[9] Ṯüreyyā by no means invented the "evil Turk". Centuries of Turkish military prowess, exploits and rule had generated a plethora of negative stereotypes which Kurdish activists, once it became expedient to frame the Turks as enemies, could draw from. Ṯüreyyā could resort to the ". . . cruel and despotic power addict, who because of his innate character is devoid of any cultural refinement",[10] as the Turk had appeared in Arab history-writing, or to similar fears reflected in European prejudices regarding the Turk. These had been mobilized to the advantage of Ottoman minorities first by the Greeks and more recently and perhaps more systematically by Armenian nationalists. The processes of liberalization and modernization taking place in Turkey since the Young Turk Revolution and the establishment of the Turkish Republic had partially obliterated these collective memories in the West: *Les Massacres* sets out to reactivate them.

The very title of *Les Massacres* evokes memories of late 19th- and early 20th-century conflicts with Christians which took the form of highly publicized riots and killings. These had been exploited in the Western press to evince sympathy from the European public and to legitimize European and Russian interference in Ottoman affairs. Armenian nationalists in particular represented the events in Ottoman Turkey as wanton brutality. The Kurdish question itself had been a creation of the Sublime Porte in order to establish a bulwark in the

[9] Haarmann (1988), p. 178.
[10] Haarmann (1988), p. 176.

eastern provinces against Armenian (and thus Russian) territorial claims by calling for a Kurdish homeland.

In establishing the framework of oppression, Ṯüreyyā redefines the Kurdish question as the age-old attempt of the Kurds to defend themselves against Turkish efforts at extermination. The main thrust of his argument is aimed at establishing the historical continuity of Turkish aggression against all minorities—a continuity which can only be accounted for by the racial disposition of the Turks. In other words, the Turks, descendents of Attila and Jingiz Khān,[11] are an unchanging entity, barbaric and evil by nature. Only Western nations had been duped by the appearance of modernity in the 19th-century reform period and by the Young Turks and later the Turkish nationalists. Ṯüreyyā claims there was an enormous discrepancy between the appearance of Westernization and the hidden, inner reality at the onset of Young Turk rule: "The world public opinion believed for a moment that the Mongolian race was going to give the world a civilized government. But these disciples of Touran, disguised as civilizers were, in reality, preparing the most barbaric and bloody projects".[12]

The Turks are portrayed as having pursued throughout the whole of their co-existence with the Kurds and other races the aims of extermination and assimilation; the latter term being considered synonymous with the former. By locating themselves in the ranks of all nations wronged by the Turks, the Kurds strengthened their own claims of victimization. They could only profit from a transferral of sympathy and residual guilt regarding the Armenians to the Kurdish cause. From the beginning of Kurdish publishing activities, authors had exhorted their fellow Kurds to desist from attacking the Armenians and realize that the Armenians were not their enemies. In *Les Massacres*, the Kurdish self-definition is expanded to include the Armenians as a "sister nation",[13] a fellow "Aryan nation differing from the Kurds only in religion".[14] The Kurds and Armenians were seen to have shared the same fate at the hands of the Turks: deportation and massacres. Association with the Armenians could temper the prejudices against the Kurds as being brutal and uncontrollable, percep-

---

[11] Bedir Khān (1928 a), p. 37.
[12] Bedir Khān (1928 a), p. 4.
[13] Bedir Khān (1928 a), p. 7.
[14] Bedir Khān (1928 a), p. 14.

tions which had largely resulted from Kurdish involvement in Armenian persecution.

The author comments that the nationalism of the Young Turks differed from that understood by the civilized world. The Young Turks wanted "to create a Turkey in which non-Turks would not have a place in the sun" and to this aim they devised "projects of assimilation and extermination" depending on the ability of the subject nations to be assimilated. In comparison with the Arabs, for example, the Turks were too inferior in terms of "history, language, science and literature" to attempt to assimilate them. The Circassians, on the other hand, a race which had "throughout the centuries embellished and civilized the Tartar physique of the Mongolian race", were "recompensed" for their loyalty and services by "assassination or assimilation".[15]

Kurdish history is retold in a projection of the present conflict onto the entirety of history, a technique common among nationalist writers anxious to fix the date of awakening as early as possible, thereby imbuing their struggle with the venerability of time and emphasizing the magnitude of the wrongdoing. Turkish perfidy is traced to the earliest agreement between Turks and Kurds by which the Kurds had agreed to submission with the stipulation that their institutions and independence be preserved:[16]

> The Kurdish nation which had until this moment enjoyed the benefits of an advanced civilization, scientific, economic, industrial and other institutions lost, little by little, all of its grandeur and sank back into the darkest night . . . From the day he set foot in the Kurdish fatherland, the Turk[17] has only committed barbaric aggressions against the language, nationality, culture and faith of the Kurd. In order to lower Kurds to his level, the Turk took care to close all the doors to progress and instruction.[18]

Thus the drive to assimilate the Kurds is seen as being rooted in the constant aggressions which themselves were a result of the Turkish character. It goes without saying that the very idea of assimilation was foreign to the Ottomans. The idea of an ethnic Turkish nation

[15] Bedir Khān (1928 a), pp. 6–8.
[16] Bedir Khān (1928 a), p. 16.
[17] "Turk" and all derivative words in Ṯüreyyā's text are written with small letters, "Kurd" with capital letters, a convention I will not reproduce here.
[18] Bedir Khān (1928 a), p. 8.

does not appear until the Young Turk era. But Ṯüreyyā saw the will to assimilate as having been latent until, during World War I, the Turks saw their chance to assimilate the Kurds "to make disappear without exterminating a multitude . . . of robust, healthy, intelligent, brave human beings and amalgamate them to the Turkish race which was already contaminated by avarice, malaria, tuberculosis . . .".[19]

The author's concern with image correction focuses on exposing the alleged reality behind the civilized appearance of the Turkish nation. An image of Kurds emerges less by association with other victims, particularly the Armenians, than by contrast to the Turks. Several clusters of attributes are used to characterize the two nations and their relations. These clusters organized around five main binary oppositions are: civilized/barbaric, healthy/sick, Aryan/Mongolian, victimized/tyrannical, and idealistic/hypocritical and self-serving, whereby the first and positive characterization is attributed to the Kurds.

A contradiction inherent in the self-portrayal of a group willing to use violence in order to achieve nationhood, is that it must demonstrate that its acts of aggression constitute self-defense, rising from its victimization and oppression by an unjust ruler. But a victim is weak and does not *per se* inspire sympathy. The dilemma is resolved in many cases by delving into the comparison of the inferiority-superiority of the two nations which is closely related to the civilized/barbaric paradigm. Although İsmet Pasha had stated at Lausanne that Turks and Kurds were equal, he is quoted here as claiming sometime later that the "Turkish nation is above all other nations. Those who do not admit this superiority are in a state of battle with us".[20] Bedir Khān reasons from this:

> In order to become the equal of the Turk we must become Turks. In as much as we wish to remain Kurds, tyranny and death await us. How to imagine the possibility of Turkifying us! Wouldn't it be necessary at least for the nation wanting to assimilate us to be our superior in race, civilization, culture and soul. It is true that the physique of the Turk has been perfected over six centuries, thanks to the Circassians, Greeks, Bulgarians, Serbs, Armenians, Vlachs, Kurds, Arabs and Jews. But despite this, the Turk has not managed to rid himself

[19] Bedir Khān (1928 a), p. 9.
[20] Bedir Khān (1928 a), p. 30, quoting from *Vaḳit.*

> of the soul of Attila, Cengiz Khan and Helaqu.[21] His soul has remained and will always remain the same. How to force the Kurds to avow inferiority to a nomadic nation which had come in rags and in a nomadic state to territories where the Kurds had been living for more than 6000 years.[22]

2. *The Turkish Press and Conflicting Images of the Sheykh Saʿīd Revolt: Fanatics or Rebels?*

One of the most insurmountable obstacles to the Kurds' presentation of themselves was the Turkish control of the press coverage of resistance in the Kurdish provinces of Turkey: "The Turks have succeeded to a certain degree in painting for world public opinion these battles for liberation as acts of brigandage, and all these heroes fallen on the fields of honour as brigands" just as they had earlier charged the Kurds with perpetrating the Armenian massacres.[23] It is thus crucial to Bedir Khān's argument to discredit the veracity of the Turkish press as well as official statements. He is at least partially correct in charging that the recent Sheykh Saʿīd Revolt had been distorted by the Turkish press and official agencies to fit their own image needs. For fear that the revolt might mobilize smoldering religious resentment, it was portrayed within Turkey as a nationalist and separatist phenomenon which is, of course, the viewpoint that *Khoybūn* takes. On the other hand, in order to prevent the evocation of sympathy from a liberal European public for an ethnic minority striving for self-actualization, the Turkish government depicted the revolt to the Western public as religious reactionism. In this, the dual nature of the "nationalist revolt in religious garb" served Turkish purposes,[24] but as the author is able to demonstrate, their own press told a different story.

Almost half the pages of *Les Massacres* are devoted to translations from the newspaper *Vaḳit*, which covered the trials of the perpetrators of the Saʿīd Rebellion. It was a tremendous boon to T̲üreyyā's argument to quote from a source whose credibility could not be

---

[21] The Īlkhānid Hulagu (ruled 1256–65).

[22] Bedir Khān (1928 a), pp. 36–37.

[23] Bedir Khān (1928 a), p. 17.

[24] As Olson's (1989), p. 129, study of British archival material demonstrates, the British Foreign Office was well aware of this subterfuge.

refuted by the Turkish authorities.[25] There are excerpts from the interrogations of the accused, and quotes from the sentences explaining the reasons for handing down the death penalty. All of the passages document T̲üreyyā Bedir Khān's claim that the Turkish government never regarded the Saʿīd Rebellion as essentially a religious revolt and were aware that the leaders had used religion as a screen. Major Ḳāsim Bey, a Kurd who had been approached by a Kurdish ex-deputy to participate in the revolt, reported at the trial on the organization of the revolt.

> They wanted to use religion as a means. The goal was independence. I heard Sheykh Saʿīd say: to kill a Turk is better than killing 60 infidels . . . The aim of the revolution was to take the religious track, profiting from the ignorance of the Kurd, to arrive at independence.[26]

At the trial of Sheykh Saʿīd, the prosecutor charged that the perpetrators of the revolution had wanted to use religion "as a screen", while intending "to partition the fatherland. The revolution aimed at separating a part of the Turkish fatherland, which is an indivisible whole, from the rest of its body, thus leading to the dissolution of national unity and solidarity . . .".[27]

If, in the Turkish view, Kurdish rebels were religious fanatics (the view projected abroad) or traitors (the official view in Turkey) then T̲üreyyā presents the Kurds as heroes fighting for their political rights, for "national administration".[28] The Turks, on the other hand, he accuses of mass murder and other crimes against women and children, atrocities that he describes in detail. Once considered primitive in relation to the cultivated Europeans, the Kurds are now contrasted favorably with the tyrannical Turks. The very traits which once had been attributed to the Kurds: barbarism, wildness and

[25] Although I was unable to examine the Turkish articles in the original, I am inclined to believe that the articles were not falsified. After all, they contain elements which do not present the Kurds in a positive light and others which contradict nationalist doctrine, for example a certain Kurdish officer approached by nationalists to participate in the revolt had answered, "The idea of liberation made me laugh" (Bedir Khān 1928 a, p. 29, citing from *Vaḳit* May 31, 1925). On another occasion, a prominent Kurd who had participated in the revolts was asked which language he spoke best and he had to admit that he wrote and spoke Turkish better than Kurdish (Bedir Khān 1928 a, p. 22: *Vaḳit* May 7, 1925).

[26] Bedir Khān (1928 a), p. 29 (*Vaḳit* May 31, 1925).

[27] Bedir Khān (1928 a), p. 31 (*Vaḳit* June 7, 1925).

[28] Bedir Khān (1928 a), p. 41.

nomadism are transferred to the Turks, while Kurdish consanguinity with the Armenians is stressed.

The Turkish government's policy of assimilation is equated with the repression of revolt; both are seen as manifestations of a culturally inferior, bloodthirsty will, which the Western nations are morally obliged to oppose "at least out of respect and fidelity to the blood so generously shed".[29]

One of the articles selected from *Vaḳit* relates to the trial of Sheykh ʿAbdülḳādir, where a certain Seyyid Meḥmed, a member of a Kurdish club, testified. He linked this group with the Saʿīd Revolt, maintaining that his father, also a member of the group, had favoured autonomy while other members, including Emīn ʿĀlī and Kāmurān Bedir Khān, had been for independence. Emīn ʿĀlī Bedir Khān had "incited openly for the revolt and said that they were going to constitute a state with the Armenians".[30] It is, however, unlikely that the *Kürdistān Teʿālī Cemʿīyeti* had any links with the *Azadī* group, although it is conceivable that the former was involved in the Koçgiri revolts of 1921–1922.[31] Therefore, either Ṯüreyyā altered this section in order to stress his family's continuous preeminence in the struggle and early allegiance to the Armenians,[32] or the misleading statement may be attributed to trial officials or the official press, who wished to demonstrate the perfidy of Kurdish traitors.

Only in the last pages of the long pamphlet does Ṯüreyyā mention *Khoybūn* as a "national pact" to liberate "Kurdish national soil"[33] and demand that an investigative commission be sent to Kurdistan to view the situation and tell the world what it has seen. Such a commission would have to be established by charitable organizations since the League of Nations had not responded to similar pleas.[34]

---

[29] Bedir Khān (1928 a), p. 40.

[30] Bedir Khān (1928 a), p. 25 (*Vaḳit* May 19, 1925). The "Chakir Meḣmed" mentioned here must have been Şükrü Meḥmed Sekban.

[31] Olson (1989), pp. 28–34.

[32] Behrendt (1993, pp. 9–10) demonstrated a similar subterfuge to the same end in *La Question Kurde*.

[33] Bedir Khān (1928 a), pp. 40–41.

[34] Bedir Khān (1928 a), p. 39.

3. *The Same Turk*

The Case of Kurdistan against Turkey, published at the end of 1928, also articulates a demand for such an investigation and denounces the indifference of the Western nations toward Kurdish suffering, especially since it had been the callous and uninformed self-interest of the Allies which had allowed the Kemalists to perpetrate their crimes against the Armenians and Kurds. Several pages of the booklet describe in detail the interests—mainly regarding Mosul oil—which resulted in the complicity of the respective nations in Kemalist "crimes".[35] This section is preceded by a quote from the Gospel according to Mark. "And they crucify Him, and part His garments among them, casting lots upon them, what each should take".[36] The Allies are likened to the crucifiers of Christ and, by analogy, the losers of the Lausanne Conference (Kurds, Armenians and Greeks) to Christ. This particular analogy is characteristic of the ahistoric manichaeism of *The Case*. Kurdish-Turkish strife is presented as a struggle between Good and Evil or, more precisely, between a good nation (desiring only self-determination) and a bad nation (striving to enslave or destroy the other).

The expressed aim of *Khoybūn* to discredit Turkey is pursued here in a more comprehensive and systematic fashion than in *Les Massacres*. Including in its catalogue of accusations the massacres, deportations, duplicity, and the historical continuity of the evil Turkish character, *The Case* goes on to challenge every aspect of the supposed accomplishments and strengths of the Turkish Republic. Whereas *Les Massacres* was probably intended more for a European audience, *The Case* was written for an American public and in conjunction with Ṯüreyyā's visit to the U.S. *Les Massacres* was probably the earlier of the two publications, although the dates more or less coincide. The basic arguments are the same, but *The Case* is infinitely more sophisticated in terms of argument, language and structure, indicative of the assistance of a supportive editor, whose work was doubtless not

---

[35] Bedir Khān (1928 b), p. 43: "The Lausanne Conference was an unprecedented gathering of concession seekers, honest brokers and humanists, for the allotment among themselves of the bodies and properties of flocks of timid and trusting sheep, denominated as Armenians, Greeks and Kurds . . . and each nation pocketed the precise loot it coveted".

[36] Bedir Khān (1928 b), p. 43.

confined to the introduction and the copious footnotes accompanying Ṯüreyyā's text.[37] While certainly no less propagandistic in its simplistic, misleading and distorted interpretations of Kurdish and Turkish history and the conflict, and by no means more acceptable in terms of veracity, the authors of *The Case* attempt to convey the impression of a scholarly and sincere effort to clarify Kurdish grievances.

The Case consists of four parts: the editor's introduction, Ṯüreyyā's text (heavily annotated, apparently by both author and editor), lists of statistics delineating burnings, destructive acts and deaths perpetrated by the Turks in Kurdistan, and a selection of European and American writers and journalists who report on recent impressions gained traveling in Turkey. The text is illustrated with photographs of Kurdish patriots, urban notables, and tribal and religious leaders. The preponderance of Bedir Khāns (Ṯüreyyā, his two brothers, his father and uncle are pictured) suggests that this publication also aimed to establish firmly Bedir Khān leadership in the public eye.

The title of the editor's introduction, "The Same Turk", epitomizes the tenor of the entire booklet. Turkey has not, as its press would have the world believe, changed, because the Turk cannot change his nature. The editor[38] feels the world needs to know what is really happening—at Turkish hands—to the "traditions of a proud race which stretches back for a thousand years before the Turks came to Asia Minor".[39] Suggesting stability and authority, he refers to *Khoybūn* as the Kurdish National Council[40] and to "Prince" Ṯüreyyā as the grandson of "the last semi-independent Kurdish ruler", a competent scholar, and official representative of *Khoybūn* "with a mandate . . . to state the case of Kurdistan to the American people and

[37] The biblical quote is only one of many likely editorial interventions.

[38] Herbert Adams Gibbons, the author of the controversial *The foundation of the Ottoman Empire. A history of the Osmanlis up to the death of Bayezid I. 1300–1403*. London 1916. Gibbons worked as correspondent for the *New York Herald* in Europe and the Near East. Here, he elaborately demonstrates his knowledge of contemporary and historical affairs in Turkey. Along with the other authors and journalists selected for inclusion in the fourth part of the book, Gibbons appears rabidly anti-Turkish rather than enthusiastically pro-Kurdish. In any case, he is opposed to American policies in Turkey and especially those of contemporary American missionaries, who had become "Turkified" and "secularized". He likens them to Dutch traders in Japan who had not disdained "trampling upon the cross in order to gain admission to the country", Bedir Khān (1928 b), p. 8.

[39] Bedir Khān (1928 b), p. 5.

[40] On the title page of the booklet, *Khoybūn* is identified as the "Supreme Council of the Kurdish Government".

government".[41] Foreshadowing many of the charges made in T̲üreyyā's text, the editor asserts that the Allies and, in particular, President Wilson, were responsible for the present predicament of the Kurds and reminds readers that American soldiers had died in World War I for the right of self-determination.

At the centre of T̲üreyyā's text is the notion of an immutable Turkish character. Whereas oppositions, in particular Mongolian/Aryan, had been emphasized in *Les Massacres, The Case* focuses even less on developing an image of the contemporary Kurds.[42] A ten-page outline of their history depicts Kurds as Aryans who had lived in Kurdistan "from time immemorial" practicing their Zoroastrian religion and speaking their own language, which they eventually imposed on the Medes. No one was capable of long subjecting the Kurds until they entered a treaty with the Ottomans, the terms of which had not been honoured by the latter.[43] They are simply the victims of Turkish ill treatment, exactly as had been the Armenians and Greeks. Revolution was "the only honourable course open to them".[44] Turkish history, from the earliest times, is one of violence towards and exploitation of those who came under their rule.

---

[41] Bedir Khān (1928 b), p. 5.

[42] Two staples of Kurdish identity-building in the 1930's, the free and unveiled Kurdish women and Kurdish folklore as the "best interpreter of Kurdish sentiments", are mentioned only briefly, Bedir Khān (1928 b), p. 30, n.1 and p. 55. The accompanying photographs, however, provide the image lacking in the text. The photographs include six tribal chiefs, of whom two are said to be Yezidi. The pictures, which include a drawing of Sheykh Saʿīd, seem to aim at striking a balance between traditional (religious and tribal) and modern Kurds. Next to the photo of Midḥat Bedir Khān (founder of the newspaper *Kürdistān*), in Western attire, is an exotic looking man in traditional headdress, elaborate moustache and beard with the name of Dervish Bey. These and other juxtapositions suggest a harmony of interest despite disparate backgrounds. This statement is most clearly made in a large photograph of five Kurdish leaders: Three men in Western attire, Kāmurān and Celādet Bedir Khān and Memdūḥ Selīm are seated. Behind them standing, with their hands on the shoulders on the three leaders, are two unnamed "Kurdish volunteer leaders now in the field". They are dressed in festive "uniforms" and tall hats with tassels which are reminiscent of Janissary headgear. This photograph demonstrates the two worlds that the Bedir Khān brothers sought to unite: Modern Kurdish intellectuals and traditional Kurdish people, Bedir Khān (1928 b), pp. 51, 57.

[43] Bedir Khān (1928 b), pp. 21–31. Of these pages, easily half are devoted to the editor's notes on the various peoples living in the area since ancient times. This lends the appearance of a scholarly treatise to the section on Kurdish history.

[44] Bedir Khān (1928 b), p. 46 a.

The tenor is the same in both *Les Massacres* and *The Case*. The Kurdish struggle is eternal because the enemy has never changed. Although the paradigm of Mongolian-Aryan opposition was crucial in *Les Massacres*, in *The Case* it is mentioned only once by Bedir Khān, but with a particularly forceful footnote by the editor, who brings genetic theory to play in explaining Turkish inferiority. "The Turks of Turkey are basically of the most primitive and backward branch of the Mongolian race". Although they had mixed with all the races in the area, the Turks had retained their "primordial traits". To fortify his argument, the editor quotes a certain Madison Grant, who had applied Mendelian Law to anthropology. "... The result of the mixture of two races, in the long run, gives us a race reverting to the more ancient, generalized and lower type".[45] Similarly, Ṯüreyyā attributed the Turks' savagery to their "physical (numerical, MS) inadequacy, ... economic sterility and inability to survive. In consequence, due to the natural drive for self-preservation, they have sought to make up for and supplement their native defects in these respects by the *pacific or forced assimilation* of other races and by *loot*".[46] Thus, the overpowering image of the Turk is that of a parasite, able to live only by consuming others.

In a further distortion for simplicity's sake, the present revolt is asserted to be in its fourth year, implying that the revolt at Ararat was merely a continuation of the revolt led by Sheykh Saʿīd, which the Turks had not been able to put down. Similarly, the precursor to the present revolt is seen in the 19th-century Bedir Khān resistance[47] with no mention of other leaders of revolts such as ʿUbaydullāh. In addition to moral and pseudo-scientific arguments, the authors of *The Case* focus on pragmatic reasons why the Americans should not support the Turks. Whereas the Turks had made no progress and the country was in a shambles, the Kurds had produced many victories, including the successful repulsion of the Turks from Ararat, where they had attacked the "headquarters of the Kurdish National Army" in 1926. Needless to say, there was no Kurdish national army in 1926, and *Khoybūn* had not even been formed. But the point is

[45] Bedir Khān (1928 b), p. 15 n. 1.
[46] Bedir Khān (1928 b), p. 11.
[47] Which would have been successful had the Emir not been betrayed by his own cousin (Bedir Khān 1928 b, p. 29). The theme of betrayal is taken up by Celādet and Kāmurān in their works, discussed in the following sections.

to show that the Kurds are capable of victory if aided, and that the Turks will never be able to overcome Kurdish resistance.

All of the texts stress the catastrophic situation in present-day Turkey: poverty, an economy approaching collapse,[48] high public debt, an inept administration, corruption. The conclusion must be that the Kemalists lack not only character but actual or even potential resources for the maintenance of an independent existence.[49] Thus it makes no sense, either morally or economically, to support the Turks who not only threaten the lives of their own people, but also constitute a menace to the world with their Panturanian aims and close connection to the Bolsheviks.[50]

Ṯüreyyā's publications had a tremendous influence on later writing on the Kurds, but while clearly agitprop elements, such as the preposterous portrayal of the fundamentally evil Turk, were disregarded by subsequent nationalist writers, the statistics on deportations and losses contained in his booklets as well as his equally propagandist versions of historical events were integrated into many subsequent accounts of the Kurdish national struggle. If we assume that Ṯüreyyā is also the man writing behind the pseudonym Bletch Chirguh, then *La Question Kurde* demonstrates that he had made headway in a subsidiary concern, family-history writing. One aspect of Kurdish nationalism which was particularly painful to its proponents was the impression that the Kurds had missed a historic opportunity after World War I to establish a Kurdish state. Behrendt has examined an account in *La Question Kurde*[51] of a nationalist meeting in 1919 to take precautions against Turkish nationalism. Ṯüreyyā reported that three delegates of *Kürdistān Teʿālī Cemʿīyeti*, including the two younger Bedir Khāns, had met in Malatya "to prepare actions against the Kemalists". After they had been attacked by the military they assembled some 3.000 Kurdish fighters. But Major Noel was sent by Colonel Bell to demand that they withdraw their men.[52] Interestingly, the same incident was mentioned in *The Case*. However,

[48] Bedir Khān (1928 b), p. 9.

[49] Bedir Khān (1928 b), p. 59.

[50] Bedir Khān (1928 b), pp. 10, 18.

[51] I was not able to examine this Bedir Khān text, so I must rely on Behrendt, who was interested in showing how subsequent writers, from Nikitine (1975) to Küchler (1978), drew on Ṯüreyyā as a historical source. Behrendt (1993, pp. 8–13) convincingly demonstrates the fanciful inaccuracy of Ṯüreyyā's version.

[52] *La Question Kurde*, p. 29, quoted in Behrendt (1993), pp. 9–10.

instead of specifying the Bedir Khāns, the protagonists are referred to simply as Kurdish leaders. Neither is Major Noel, the loyal friend of the Kurds, mentioned. It is rather, in this account, Colonel Bell who encouraged the Kurds to let the Allies "solve the Kurdish case in accordance with their war pledges".[53] Ṯüreyyā concludes that, had it not been for the Allied betrayal, the Kurds would have been able to nip Kemalism in the bud.[54] *La Question Kurde*, as Behrendt showed, distorted both the significance and intentions of the Bedir Khāns. After his exile to France, Ṯüreyyā did not completely lose contact with the Kurdish movement, but in his contributions he followed the example set by his two younger brothers who began to chart a new course for Kurdish nationalism.

[53] Colonel Bell later commented on his travels through Kurdistan during the peace conference in Paris. He had been sent to discourage Kurdish hopes of a separate nation. "I had to go and say: 'Do nothing about it, it will all be settled for you at the Peace Conference'", Bedr Khan (1949), p. 246.

[54] Following the *The Case* strategy of coupling Armenian and Kurdish concerns, Ṯüreyyā goes on to argue: "There can be no doubt but that the Kurds were then more than able to crush Kemal, as the Armenian Republic of Erivan could easily have occupied Turkish Armenia. But both the Kurds and Armenians committed the unpardonable folly of giving full value to the words of the Allied and Associated Nations", Bedir Khān (1928 b), pp. 37–38.

CHAPTER SIX

SEKBAN, THE "TRAITOR": DENYING LEGITIMACY, ARGUING VIABILITY

If the point of Sekban's open letter of 1923 had been to formulate an argument against the assimilation policies of Turkish nationalists on the one hand, and to probe the possibilities of fighting the Kurdish cause on the other, *La Question Kurde*, published in 1933 in Paris, represented a complete about-face on all issues and goals regarding the national problem, and a dramatic departure from political activity.

Sekban had been involved in the Kurdish movement for at least three decades. After leaving Istanbul along with other nationalist leaders, he went to Iraq where he had a powerful protector in the person of Nūrī al-Saʿīd.[1] Sekban later claimed to have been minister of health in al-Saʿīd's cabinet, but the veracity of this statement must be doubted.[2] In 1927, he was one of the founders of *Khoybūn*,[3] so he must have avidly supported the uprising of Ararat, which was more or less the raison d'être of *Khoybūn*. Although involved in the

[1] Anter (1990), pp. 72 sqq., (1992), pp. 24–25.

[2] His name is not to be found in the pertinent handbooks, such as ʿAbd al-Razzāḳ al-Ḥasanī (1988). *The Iraq directory 1936* contains information on all ministers from 1921 onwards and a Who's Who of Iraq (pp. 566–607). Other than that of 1930, there was no longer a minister of health in Iraq, but rather a Directorate of Health, which was part of the Ministry of the Interior. However, it is quite possible that Sekban had some sort of ministerial job. As a policy of appeasement, Kurds were given positions, although of little political significance. Mīr Baṣrī (1987) does not mention Sekban. In any event, it is safe to say that Sekban maintained friendly relations with al-Saʿīd. After Sekban's return to Turkey, al-Saʿīd came to Istanbul on several occasions where he met with Sekban and recommended him to Adnan Menderes: cf. Anter (1990), p. 73.—I do not have any exact information about Sekban's whereabouts between 1923 and 1938.

[3] The sources differ as to whether Sekban was elected as chairman or one of the Bedir Khāns. Most sources name Celādet Bedir Khān. Contemporary press reports refer to either Aleppo or Beirut as the seat of *Khoybūn, Oriente Moderno* X (1930), pp. 295, 366. Sekban is mentioned as a Kurdish political figure in a Foreign Office report (FO 371/13032) from August 1928 ("Dr. Shukri Mehmed—Member of the former Kurd Teali Jemieti, Constantinople"): Alakom (1998), p. 146. In a French document (Sureté Générale du Vilayet d'Alep) from 1931, Sekban figures as president of the Baghdad branch of *Khoybūn*, Alakom (1998), p. 156.

Ararat uprising, at least from a distance, he and other Kurdish intellectuals did not participate in or actively support the uprisings in Southern Kurdistan under Maḥmūd (1930–1931) or the Barzanis (1931–1932).[4]

It has been maintained that Sekban was not even in favor of the cultural and educational efforts towards developing the Kurdish language and script, which had been supported in Iraq under the British Mandate. As nearly as I can determine, however, such assessments are made on the basis of statements in *La Question Kurde*, and do not necessarily indicate his attitudes throughout the preceding decade.[5]

The Anglo-Iraq treaty provided for an independent state of Iraq, but contained no express guarantees for the Kurdish minority.[6] Sekban and other Kurdish politicians who protested against the treaty in a petition to the League of Nations[7] were arrested in 1931 and imprisoned.[8] Hopes for Kurdish self-determination in any form had been quashed, and the isolation of the Kurds laid bare. The failures of the various uprisings and the tremendous suffering of the Kurdish population drove Sekban into a crisis: he spent a period in a German sanatorium to treat tuberculosis of the lung. His stay in Germany must have been some time in 1932–1933.[9] The theoretical underpinnings—if they may so be called—of *La Question Kurde* reflect an absorption of Turkish nationalist theories, which undergo a kind of idiosyncratic and hasty synthesis with the ideas of a German publicist, Max Hildebert Boehm, and also a sprinkling of national-socialist ideas.[10]

---

[4] There would have been many reasons for this. Most Kurdish intellectuals were skeptical of Sheykh Maḥmūd, Ibrahim (1983), p. 321. Perhaps more important, Kurdish nationalists had realized that the English were definitively not supportive of Kurdish separatist aims.

[5] Ibrahim (1983), p. 319.—Some Kurdish nationalists, the majority of whom spoke Kurmanjī, may well have been critical of the selection of Sorani Kurdish.

[6] Sluglett/Farouk-Sluglett (1991), pp. 24, 34 sqq.

[7] Küchler (1978), p. 401. Ibrahim (1983), pp. 319–321. Text of the petition in *Oriente Moderno* X (1930), p. 478.

[8] Ibrahim (1983), p. 321, note 1.

[9] Anter (1990), p. 75. Anter (1992), p. 25. There is no record of his stay in the files of the *Politisches Archiv* of the *Auswärtiges Amt* in Bonn as one would expect if he were really a minister. Sekban must have returned to Iraq by April 1934 at the latest, Gerede (1952), p. 279.

[10] Sekban mentions Boehm's book *Das eigenständige Volk*, published 1932. This also suggests that Sekban knew some German as the book had almost certainly not yet been translated. In his earlier publication (1923) Sekban uses the German word

Sekban had never been a theoretician of the Kurdish national movement—he had left the writing to the Bedir Khāns and others. His name is not found among the authors of the Kurdish newspapers. He was, by his own account, an orator and mediator. And, we might add, an idealist, but only as long as he had reason to expect positive results.

In his publication Sekban vehemently disputes the tenets of Kurdish nationalism which he himself had helped to propagate, and the goals which he had tried to realize. So intense, thoroughgoing and emotional is his refutation that one suspects he has come to see Kurdish nationalism as an illness. One might even speculate that his perceptions are coloured by his own attempts to regain his health. Contemporary and later nationalists saw the work as opportunistic.[11] However, I would argue that the text deserves more attention than it has previously received as it comprises an unusual documentation of the impingement of reality and failure on the nationalist consciousness and of disillusionment. Furthermore, I do not think it is an opportunistic document in the sense that it is motivated by some individual egotism. On the contrary, the writer seems sincerely concerned about the future of the Kurds, and acutely aware of his own share of responsibility for the injuries and losses sustained by the Kurds who had rallied to the calls of Kurdish nationalist leaders. Despite the contradictions, inconsistencies and misrepresentations, let us examine his "reckoning" with his old comrades and his confession.

In his efforts to explain his renunciation he destructs the system of Kurdish national ideas. According to Sekban, there was no reason to avoid assimilation because Kurds and Turks were members of the same race. Kurds were by no means Aryans but, rather, Turanian. This argument is redolent of Gökalp but Sekban does not mention him here, and purports to have it from unnamed German scholars.[12] While not denying that the Kurdish language was non-

Landtag. But Sekban's first foreign language was French mastered by most of the intellectuals in the Ottoman Empire from the middle of the 19th century on. In his years at the Military Medical School (*Ṭıbbīye*) his interest in learning French had attracted attention: Hatemi-Kazancıgil (1991), p. 57.

[11] Anter (1990), pp. 74–75. It was thought that Sekban had written the text in order to be included in the amnesty of 1933.

[12] "... Turc, Kurde, ce ne sont là que des prénoms, Touranien est notre nom de famille" (Sekban 1933, p. 36); p. 16: "... ces deux peuples du même sang ..."; p. 11: "Donc ... les Kurdes ne sont nullement aryens. Ils ne sont pas non plus des sémites. Ils seraient, d'après les prétentions de certains savants allemands d'origine touranienne".

Turkish and related to Persian, he disputes that Kurdish was the original language of the Kurds and, thus, that their language indicates they descended from the Medes.[13] Sekban develops the argument that the migration of the Kurds from their original homeland in Central Asia to the West had been prompted by climatic changes. The existence of Turks in Central Asia since early times makes the assumption of the Turanian origins of the Kurds probable.[14] These arguments resemble Turkish historical theories[15] which viewed not the Turks but the Medes as the colonialists who had conquered Kurdistan and imposed their language on the inhabitants.

Sekban is intent on destroying the dichotomy Kurd-Turk and refuting the argument that the Ottomans had thwarted Kurdish development. In his view, the Kurds had achieved greatness only in conjunction with other nations.[16] Describing Kurdistan prior to any association with the Ottomans he paints a desolate picture of disunity and the squabblings among Kurdish princes. Only during the Ottoman period had the Kurds been capable of greatness. Thus the true Kurdish heroes were not those who sought separation from the Turks but those who recognized "true Kurdish interests" as did, for example, İdrīs Bidlīsī, the architect of Turkish-Kurdish association. Even Saladin was, according to Sekban, Kurdish but not a Kurdish leader. Saladin had been the leader of a Turkish-Islamic realm. In his integrative function he was thus a great Kurdish model but not the symbol of a Kurdish state. Sekban likewise dismisses other Kurdish figures who had been raised to heroic heights by Kurdish nationalists because they were protagonists of Kurdish statehood. Asserting that an independent Kurdish state would be "a catastrophe for the true interests of the Kurdish people"[17] he goes on to characterize

[13] Western orientalists, officers and travelers had developed the theory of Median origin on the basis of linguistic evidence. Soane in Ibrahim (1983), pp. 107–108; Wilson and Sayce in Zeki (1977), p. 50. Minorsky in his theory of the affinity of Kurds and Medes relied on linguistic evidence, "Kurden, Kurdistān", *EI* (1) vol. II, pp. 1212 sqq. Cf. also Minorsky (1940). The Median origin of Kurdish has been contested by MacKenzie (1961) and (1986 = *EI* [2], vol. V, pp. 479–80).

[14] Sekban (1933), pp. 11–14.

[15] The history books in which the *Türk Tarih Tezi* was developed were published from 1930 onwards. It is quite possible that Sekban had read them.

[16] "Mais les Kurdes associés aux autres peuples et dirigés par ceux-ci ont fait toujours des merveilles" (p. 20).

[17] "Les événements ultérieurs ont montré que la constitution d' un Etat indépendant kurde eut été une calamité, un désastre pour les véritables intérets du peuple kurde" (p. 24).

the Kurds as being occupied only with themselves, blind to what goes on in the world: "Le Kurde ne connaissait que son district. Hors de son district, le monde lui était étranger. Il n'avait pas la curiosité de le connaitre".[18]

Sekban concedes that this isolation generates a kind of natural desire for freedom. But this freedom, Sekban argues, is not independence but, rather, a feeling of pride: "Il n'a presque jamais manifesté un sentiment national d' indépendance. Si certain chefs ont eu l'ambition d' étendre leur autorité sur plus vastes contrées, ils n' étaient point soutenus par un sentiment populaire de nationalisme".[19]

Having thus denied the boundaries separating Kurds and Turks as well as the ability or even the inclination of the Kurds to conduct their own affairs, while debunking the heroic figures who were to serve as models, Sekban moves to deal with Kurdish nationalists. In his open letter of 1923 Sekban had tried to minimize his own political involvement, dating it to after the end of World War I. Now he claims that he had already been interested in politics in 1896 and had possessed, even then, a "national consciousness".[20] He portrays himself as an influential member of Kurdish societies who had possessed the confidence of other members. For this reason he had always been well-informed. Drawing from his intimate knowledge of the societies, he disputes that they had ever had the intention of demanding privileges or independence for the Kurds. The aspirations of the Kurds had been limited to reforms of the six eastern provinces: construction of roads, reform of the judicial system. He claims to believe that the members of *Hēvī* had not demanded the separation of Kurdistan from the Ottoman Empire.[21] This of course is patently untrue since we do know that at least the radical wing of the Kurdish movement to which Sekban's *Kürd Teşkīlāt-i İçtimāʿīye Cemʿīyeti* belonged had envisioned independence. Not only is Kurdish separateness undesirable—he even discards the goal of

[18] Sekban (1933), p. 18. This judgment bears a certain similarity to Moltke's statement. "If ever a nation was bound to the soil it is the Kurds", von Moltke (1892), p. 290.

[19] Sekban (1933), p. 19.

[20] Sekban (1933), p. 20.

[21] Sekban (1933), p. 21: "Je ne crois pas que les membres de l'association des étudiants Kurdes Espérance (Hi-vi) constituée avant la guerre balkanique pensaient réellement à la séparation du Kurdistan. Car je jouissais pleinement de leur confiance; aucun d'eux ne m'en avait fait une allusion".

instruction in Kurdish language, asserting that after almost a decade the results of efforts in Iraq to develop the language and use it for schools were devastating. He contrasts this with the progress made in Turkey by reforming the script and conducting a literacy campaign. He calls on his compatriots to participate in this progress—but this participation is only possible on the basis of assimilation.[22]

Language, Sekban points out, is not a sufficient factor for nation-building. During his stay in Germany he read Boehm's *Das eigenständige Volk*[23] which, shortly after its publication, had provoked a lively discussion in the German media. Boehm's book is a "standard work"[24] of the so-called "Volkstheorie" or "Volkssoziologie", which dealt with ethnic groups ("Völker") not organized in the form of states. From the perspective of "Volkssoziologie", nations were organized according to criteria such as descent ("Abstammung") and language, that is according to the principle of objective nationality. Boehm emphasizes the independence ("Eigenständigkeit") of the people ("Volk") vis-à-vis other factors engendering mutuality such as state and society. In 1923, he had dealt with the irredentism of the national states established in Middle and Eastern Europe after World War I. Boehm concentrated especially on German ethnic groups not living within the boundaries of the German Empire of 1871. For him, language was an important, if not the most important, factor—others being race, customs, history, religion and region—in preserving the national characteristics of ethnic groups.[25] Language is an expression of the national character and the medium of literature and science: "Language reflects the intellectual development of a people . . .".[26]

---

[22] Sekban (1933), pp. 29 sqq.

[23] Published in 1932; reprinted in 1965. From the date of the publication (the foreword was written in April 1932) we may conclude that, first, Sekban's stay in Germany took place in 1932/1933, and second, that he had at least a reading knowledge of German, since so shortly after the publication a translation, for instance into French, is rather improbable. It is possible, too, that Sekban read articles of Boehm in his periodical *Deutschtum*. Boehm himself was a Baltic German.

[24] Lemberg (1967), vol. II, p. 12. Compare the statement of Mommsen/Martiny (1971), p. 640: "Sie (the "Volksgruppenforschung", MS) leugnete den staatlichen Charakter der modernen Nation und fand in M.H. Boehm (1932) ihren prononciertesten Vertreter".

[25] Boehm (1965), pp. 135 sqq.

[26] Boehm (1965), p. 227.

Undoubtedly, Sekban realized the importance of these ideas for the Kurdish question. He quotes Boehm: "Thus, language may be the first and the last—but in its huge possibilities lie great dangers".[27] These dangers, according to Boehm, are manifest ". . . if the language loses contact with "creed" ("Glauben", does Boehm mean religion?, MS) and delivers itself up to science . . .".[28] Although it cannot be ruled out that Sekban simply may not have understood Boehm's specific irredentism (especially since Boehm wrote in a very eccentric and obscure style) it is significant that Sekban refers to the dangers and not to the possibilities. He seemed to feel that if one took seriously the romantic concept of language as mirroring the spiritual and intellectual development of a people, then the Kurdish language, in its poverty (as he saw it), mirrored the deplorable state of the Kurdish people.

Sekban does not take a position regarding the official denial of the Kurds as a minority. He refers to the statement of the government to the effect that ". . . the Kurdish people will rule Turkey together with the Turkish people . . .".[29] He is convinced that Kurds and Turks are members of one race, and underscores the significance of the racial factor with the quote: "The basis of nations can be nothing but the unity of race".[30]

It is the roots of national identity, namely language und history, which Sekban wants to extract. He crowns his argument for assimilation and the rejection of the entire concept of a separate Kurdish identity with an allegory of three trees. The trunk of the first tree has been almost but not completely severed from its roots and lies uselessly on the ground. By virtue of the weak connection to its roots, this tree is still alive but not productive. Such a tree should be separated from its roots and removed. The roots of this tree are of interest and appeal only to a woodcarver. By contrast, the sec-

[27] Sekban (1933), p. 29: "So mag die Sprache zwar das erste und letzte sein—in ihren ungeheuren Möglichkeiten liegen aber auch ungeheure Gefahren". I could not determine the source of this quote; perhaps it is the periodical *Deutschtum*. In Boehm (1965, p. 228) there is a nearly identical passage: "Die Sprache hat ungeheure Möglichkeiten. Aber in ihnen ruhen auch ungeheure Gefahren".

[28] Boehm (1965), p. 228.

[29] Sekban (1933), pp. 34 sqq.

[30] Sekban (1933), p. 35. He ascribes this quote to one he calls ". . . one of the greatest statesmen . . .". Since he was a witness to the national-socialist seizure of power, it is not unlikely that Sekban was referring to Hitler.

ond tree is full of branches which produce, according to the season, foliage, lovely blossoms and delicious fruit. Such a tree is worthy of the care of its owner. Even strangers will protect this tree and, if extreme cold or other causes make the tree dry out, then all who are interested in the tree will be sad and shed tears. The third tree operates in opposition to the laws of biology, inhaling oxygen, producing carbondioxide and bearing poisonous fruit. This tree should be cut down without scruple.[31]

Considered in the light of Sekban's statements on the superiority of Turkish culture over Kurdish, it seems he has chosen a metaphor to express what is most painful.[32] The first tree represents Kurdish culture as barren, weak and of no use to anyone. It should be removed, i.e. there is no chance of resurrecting Kurdish culture as the nationalists had hoped. The Kurds should no longer devote their efforts towards keeping their culture or nation alive but, rather, turn to the healthy culture which is producing a viable society. Turkey, still in the process of Westernization, seems to be heading towards progress. The third tree, with its poisonous fruit, must then represent the product of the efforts of the Kurdish national movement: rebellions and exclusion from progress but, also, the Turkish reaction to such realities: deportations, repression and destruction. It is Kurdish nationalism, the poisonous tree, which he wishes felled.

But Sekban's metamorphosis from protagonist of self-assertiveness to advocate of Kurdish self-abnegation was perhaps not based solely on his experience of the failed rebellions and unsuccessful efforts regarding the language. His critics mention another motive for his change of mind: his wish to return to Turkey.[33] The precondition for his return was an amnesty granted by the Turkish authorities. Sekban, as mentioned earlier, had been a member of groups banned by the Kemalists due to their separatist activities or collaboration with the Allies during the War of Independence. As a matter of fact,

---

[31] Sekban (1933), pp. 31 sqq.

[32] Sekban's elaborately vented disillusionment with the Kurdish national struggle is reminiscent of another disappointed nationalist's more succinct statement: "I thought I was awakening the soul of Italy, and I see only the corpse before me" (*Encyclopaedia Britannica*, vol. 11, p. 728, 15th ed. 1978). Giuseppe Mazzini was appalled that his endeavours for the unification of Italy had ended in monarchy rather than a republic.

[33] In particular, his wife was said to be eager to return to Turkey: Anter (1990), pp. 74–75.

the date of the publication of *La Question Kurde* coincides with plans for an amnesty on the occasion of the 10th anniversary of the Republic. The reasons Sekban gave in the 1950s for the publication of *La Question Kurde* do not absolve him of the charges of opportunism levelled by former comrades. At that time he maintained in a conversation with the Kurdish writer Musa Anter that he had hoped to alleviate the repressions to which the Kurds were exposed.[34]

In 1938, Sekban returned to Turkey and settled in İstanbul, where he worked as a physician for the *Tünel* company.[35] He died in 1960. It was only after his death that *La Question Kurde* became an instrument of Turkish policy vis-à-vis the Kurds. For the government, it was most welcome that a Kurd had defended the notion of the Turkish origins of the Kurds. Sekban's booklet was translated and printed in several editions by a semi-official publishing house. It became a *vademecum* for Turkish officers and administrators in Eastern Anatolia.

The reactions to Sekban's withdrawal from the national movement varied. Dining with Celādet Bedir Khān in Damascus, Sekban asked him about the name of the dish which had been served. Celādet responded ironically: "This is eggplant, but you can call it zucchini".[36] Sekban realized this was an allusion to his ignoring the differences between Kurds and Turks. But other members of the Kurdish movement did not react as mildly as Celādet. Memdūḥ Selīm, a Kurdish activist since *Hēvī* days and one of the founders of *Khoybūn*, in a letter to Celādet in 1934 expressed his disappointment and anger that Sekban had betrayed his comrades.[37] A Kurd

[34] Anter was, in a way, the memory of the Kurdish movement in Turkey. He had participated in the revival of the Kurdish movement in the 1950s. In September 1992 he was killed by an unknown assassin in Diyarbakır. Shortly before his death, in an interview with Göldaş (1993, pp. 45–46), he claimed to possess the papers of the *Kürdistān Teʿālī Cemʿīyeti.*

[35] According to the *İstanbul Telefon Rehberi*, 1947 edition, Sekban lived at İṣtiklâl Caddesi 99. In the 1950's he lived at Samanyolu no. 52 in the Şişli district of İstanbul, cf. Sunguroğlu (1959), p. 453.

[36] Anter (1990), p. 75.

[37] "The doctor says, 'I am withdrawing from politics'. But this is not a withdrawal; this is a suicide. If only he had committed suicide because he was not able to reach the goal he had pursued . . . Is it not a kind of naiveté to desert from war and hand over one's comrades after surrendering to the enemy? In short, it is disgusting. We must think about a remedy for these treasons and betrayals", Alakom (1998), pp. 104–105. Uzun (1989, pp. 180–182; 1995, pp. 156–157; 1998, pp. 179–181) adapted this letter for his literary biography of Memdūḥ Selīm.

from Iraq, Rafīḳ Ḥilmī, published a vehement response.[38] If we can trust Ḥilmī, Sekban was not anxious for his book to be read by the Kurds. Only after submitting a written request did Ḥilmī receive a copy of *La Question Kurde*. Ḥilmī contrasts it with Sekban's open letter ten years earlier in order to expose his "distortion of history".[39] Ḥilmī's "true history" of the Kurds conforms to the nationalist version: the common origins of Medes and Kurds, the rejection of the theory of Turanian origin, and emphasis on the high educational level of the Kurds before the incorporation of Kurdistan into the Ottoman Empire. The Ottomans had been able to extend their rule over Kurdistan ("enslavement") only through "diabolic intrigues" and the discord sown by them amongst Kurdish rulers.[40] Not surprisingly, Ḥilmī differs from Sekban's verdict on great Kurds such as Saladin and Karīm Khān Zand. However, he does not characterize them as having been possessed of national awareness because such feelings were unknown at the time both leaders lived. Nevertheless, Saladin's Kurdishness was underscored by his emphasis on the existence of a Kurdish military aristocracy. That Karīm Khān had not pursued "Kurdish" policies was due to conditions in 18th-century Iran, where tribal solidarity preceded any notion of nationalism and patriotism.[41] Indignant at Sekban's claims that there had been no national feeling amongst the Kurds, Ḥilmī refers to the Kurdish societies, especially *Hēvī*. He asks why Sekban had boasted about his involvement with the KTC if he did not consider a union of the Kurds necessary. In view of the present "dangers" to the Kurds, Ḥilmī

---

[38] Curiously, Ḥilmī's booklet (1935) appeared in Baṣra in Turkish in the old script under the title: *Kürd mesʾelesi ṣafaḥātından . . .* Since the original was not available to me, I have used the latinized version in Bayrak (1994), pp. 144–176. An Arabic translation was published in 1956 (not available to me). Whether Ḥilmī wanted to address the Turkish audience, as Küchler (1978) writes, must remain undecided. Rafīḳ Ḥilmī was born in Kirkuk in 1898 and died in 1960 in Suleymānīya. He studied engineering in İstanbul. At the time of the publication of his booklet, he was working as a teacher of French and mathematics at a high school in Baṣra. Ḥilmī also published on the history of literature; for his extensive memoirs see Fuad (1970), p. XLVII; the memoirs (Hilmi 1995) were translated from Sorani into Turkish; they are mainly concerned with the revolts of Sheykh Maḥmūd Barzanjī whose close collaborator Ḥilmī was. Ḥilmī was the founder of the important *Hīva*-organization, which was not a party but rather a "coalition movement" ("Sammlungsbewegung") of Kurdish nationalists: Küchler (1978), pp. 194 sqq.; Ibrahim (1983), pp. 384–390.

[39] Bayrak (1994), pp. 145–147.

[40] Bayrak (1994), pp. 151–154.

[41] Bayrak (1994), pp. 157–159.

exhorts them to form such a union.[42] Assessing Kurdish nationalist activities more positively than Sekban, Ḥilmī attributes failures, such as that of Sheykh Maḥmūd, somewhat vaguely, to "circumstances".[43]

In support of his argument for Kurdish national aspirations, Ḥilmī quotes a passage from Gökalp which states that it is not necessary for one nation to be bound to another, even if the nation has lost its "personality" (*şakhṣiyet*) and language through long association. To find its way back to its own identity, a national awakening, such as the Irish and the Czechs achieved, was required.[44] One of the few points where Ḥilmī agrees with Sekban concerns the ineffectiveness of language schooling in Iraq during the Mandate.[45]

There are some parallels to Sekban's booklet in Mesut Fani's doctoral thesis *La nation Kurde et son évolution sociale*[46] which also appeared in 1933. Fani makes abundant use of secondary literature on the history, language and social organization of the Kurds, maintaining, as did Sekban, that there were no differences between Turks and Kurds.[47] Fani suggests, with somewhat more restraint than Sekban had exercised, that the Kurds were of Turkish extraction.[48] He concurs with Sekban in seeing the future of the Kurds in a strong Turkey

---

[42] Bayrak (1994), pp. 159–160.

[43] Bayrak (1994), pp. 165–166.

[44] Bayrak (1994), pp. 168–169. Gökalp explained the term *istimlāl* which is usually translated as 'assimilation', using the French word *dénationalisation*, see Beysanoğlu (1992), p. 125.

[45] Bayrak (1994), p. 173.

[46] He later took the family name Bilgili. He was born in Adana, but his family originally came from Suleymānīya. Mesut Fani served as *müteṣarrıf* of the district of Cebel-i Bereket (today Osmaniye) in the province of Adana. Along with his brothers ʿAlī ʿİlmī Fānīzāde (editor of the newspaper *Ferdā* in Adana), and Zeyn al-ʿĀbidīn Fānīzāde, general secretary of the *Ḥürriyet ve İʾtilāf*-party (cf. Tunaya, 1986, pp. 18–19), he had been on the list of the so called *Yüzellilikler*, e.g. the 150 persons who had been exiled because they had collaborated with the İstanbul government and the Allies during the War of Independence. Fani and his brothers returned to Turkey with the amnesty of 1938. In that year he also published a self-critique of his anti-Kemalist attitudes during the War of Independence. Mesut Fani settled as a lawyer in Antakya, where he died in 1980: cf. Soysal, p. 149. Goloğlu (1971), pp. 281–287, 327–329.—Fani's book was a doctoral thesis presented at the Sorbonne.

[47] Another Kurdish author who tried to demonstrate that Kurds are Turks, was Şerif Fırat (1894–1949). He belonged to the Alevi Khormek tribe, which had joined government troops in fighting the Saʿīd Rebellion. Fırat calls the Kurds "mountain Turks" (*dağlı Türkler*). Fırat's book first appeared in 1945 and was reprinted several times. President Cemal Gürsel wrote the foreword for the second edition (1961).

[48] Süslü (1993), p. 101.

where the Kurds can continue to live "under her/its protection". For Fani, the idea of an independent Kurdistan is a chimera, as without protection the Kurds would become slaves.[49] The rebellions since the 1920s he considers to be partly inspired from abroad, the result of an "artificial unrest" but not a "separatist movement". He writes: "If the Kurds would be separated from the Turks, this would be for the former a true catastrophe and suicide".[50] Apart from these parallels Fani, unlike Sekban, had not stood out as a Kurdish nationalist. Although Fani's views corresponded to the Turkish position, there were objections to some aspects of his thesis. In a critique of the book for the Turkish Historical Society (*Türk Tarih Kurumu*), Hasan Reşit Tankut[51] pointed out that Fani dated the settlement of Anatolia by the Turks to the 11th century, which was "useless for Turkey and the Turks".[52]

---

[49] Süslü (1993), p. 99.
[50] Süslü (1993), pp. 99–100.
[51] 1891–1980, a graduate of the *Mülkīye*. He took part in the formulation of the *Güneş Dil Teorisi*. Extracts of his writings can be found in Bayrak (1994), pp. 197–232.
[52] Bayrak (1994), pp. 125–128.

CHAPTER SEVEN

CELĀDET'S LETTER TO ATATÜRK: A LESSON IN KURDISHNESS

Turkish victories at Ararat and İḥsān Nūrī's flight into Iran spelled the end of *Khoybūn*'s leadership in Turkish Kurdistan in the summer of 1930. Although the Ararat region was not completely subdued until 1932 and Kurdish resistance in Dersim was only quashed in 1938,[1] the legacy of revolt was devastation and deportation. The Turkish Republic was clearly on the rise, and by the mid-1930s it had achieved rapprochement with its neighbors. The Saʿādabād Pact of 1937 guaranteed what had long been evident: assistance to the Kurds would not be forthcoming from Iran or Iraq.[2] In the face of such isolation and destruction Sekban had come to the conclusion that enough time had been wasted pursuing useless goals and that the only road to progress for the Kurds of Turkey was assimilation. Sekban advocated renouncing Kurdish identity and all the arguments which underpinned Kurdish political goals. The lesson Sekban had gleaned from the recent history of the Kurdish revolts was that there was too little substance in what the Kurds were trying to redeem and, because of this, there was little sympathy abroad with the Kurdish cause. Although Sekban explicitly refused to condemn his comrades, and resorted to the tree metaphor to challenge the legitimacy of continuing the struggle, the reasons for his defection and the implied accusations were clear enough to the remaining founders of *Khoybūn*.[3]

The Kurdish community of Syria, centered mainly in Damascus, however, seems not to have wavered in the aftermath of Ararat and

---

[1] Kendal (1988), p. 119. Bruinessen (1992 a), p. 291.

[2] Ibrahim (1983), p. 673: "Each act of the Kurds would have had all pact countries against them".

[3] A later generation of nationalists considered *Khoybūn* members responsible for the exorbitant losses and bloodshed of the Ararat revolt because they had begun it without first ensuring adequate preparation and weaponry, but this was partly a leftist-oriented criticism of what was considered the "aristocratic-bourgeois"stage of Kurdish nationalism, Kendal (1988), p. 116.

the demise of *Khoybūn* in their commitment to carry on the torch of Kurdish nationalism. The French administration tolerated cultural endeavours and the aim to develop Kurdish as a vehicle for education and written culture. But the main impulses came from the Kurdish community itself. It was a good environment for staying tuned to developments in Turkey, and a likely breeding ground for nationalist supporters, as refugees continued to arrive in Syria to request political asylum. However, there were perhaps a few too many spokesmen and men of letters. Intellectuals such as Memdūḥ Selīm, Ḥamzā, the editor of *Mem ū Zīn*, and the three sons of Emīn ʿĀlī Bedir Khān were among the most prominent advocates of the Kurdish cause. A lifetime associated with Kurdish nationalism had left an indelible mark on Ṯüreyyā, Celādet and Kāmurān. What they construed to be the legacy of their father, uncles and grandfather became their personal mission and determined their prominent status.[4] Celādet and Kāmurān remained wedded to the Kurdish cause for the rest of their lives.[5] In Damascus, however, the Bedir Khān brothers, along with other *Khoybūn* members, pashas, aghas and princes, lacked income and perspectives.[6] The displaced Kurdish patriots assisted other refugees and stoked the fires of their resentment. A new generation of Kurdish youth, many of whom were being educated in foreign schools but taught Kurdish,[7] became dedicated to awakening the Kurds and formed the organization *Hēvī* in

[4] Kāmurān and Celādet could no longer hope to return to Turkey. In his diary, Celādet quotes several lines from his sister's letter informing him that he and Kāmurān were not to be granted amnesty. Bekir Sami had argued that the brothers had activated troops to fight the nationalists in Malatya, Bedirhan (1995), pp. 49–50. Their collaboration with the British and later the Greeks would also have precluded amnesty. On the Greek-Kurdish connection involving Emīn ʿĀlī and Celādet Bedir Khān see Olson (1989), pp. 63–64.

[5] Ṯüreyyā lived for most of his life in Cairo. Exiled from Syria in 1930, he moved to Cairo and later to Paris, where he continued to make contributions to his brother's journal. He was killed in an automobile accident in 1938, Elphinston (1952), pp. 91–94.

[6] According to Elphinston (1952, p. 92) Celādet had told him that from the time he and his brother left Turkey they had to work for a living. Celādet had worked "as a gardener, writer, house-painter and type-setter". His printing skills later helped him to publish *Hawar*.

[7] Kurdish language education was a private endeavour which the French authorities tolerated but did not support financially, Vanly (1992), p. 149. Language instruction was not always permitted, however. A Kurdish writer, Mustafa Boti, was granted permission by the local authorities to teach Kurdish on the Turkish-Syrian border. Shortly thereafter, the French authorities withdrew their permission, Zaza (1982), p. 81.

1938. Availing themselves of assistance from Syrian Kurds and Armenians, they exploited the oscillating tolerance of the French administration in order to foster Kurdish culture.[8]

The border between French Syria and Turkey[9] gave rise to problems on both sides. First, the border arbitrarily cut through areas inhabited by Kurdish tribes whose socio-economic networks were impaired. France had a great deal of difficulty controlling this area, so that commerce between the tribal groups continued.[10] Rondot's "Les Kurdes de Syrie" affords us insight regarding the parameters of France's benevolence towards the minorities under its mandate and the dilemmas faced by the French. This carefully worded article reflects an official French attitude which was distinctly sympathetic to the Kurds, taking their wishes, aspirations and also criticism seriously, while at the same time trying to accomodate Syria's neighbours and the Allied interests. Rondot is firmly defensive about the correctness of French policies in view of the various interests and obligations within Syria and regarding its neighbours. The defense is addressed to both those who accused the French of not doing enough for the Kurds and those (in particular, the Ankara government and Syrian nationalists) who accused them of doing too much. Rondot was a general in the French army and an orientalist whose studies of the Kurds of Syria reflected his conviction that they had a strong sense of "communauté kurde"[11] and a cultural heritage worthy of preservation. The French had felt that the best way to assist the Kurds was to provide them with the security and stability needed to become worthy and supportive elements in Syria. On the political level, Rondot felt that the Kurds' "mission naturelle" was to use

[8] Zaza (1982), pp. 56 sqq. Noureddine Zaza, younger brother of a Kurdish physician from Diyarbakır who was forced to emigrate to Syria, describes his encounters with the large Kurdish community of Damascus, their social networks and economic straits. His brother devoted his life to providing medical services on the Turkish-Syrian border. Zaza recounts his "awakening" to nationalism. He later founded the Association of Kurdish Students in Europe and, subsequently, returned to Syria to become the leader of the Democratic Kurdish Party of Syria. Another Kurd from Damascus who played an important role in Kurdish nationalism was Ismet Chérif Vanly. He did his Ph.D. in Switzerland.

[9] Vanly (1992 a), p. 145.

[10] Rondot (1939), p. 88, states that the French government did not know until 1933 exactly which Kurdish groups fell under their mandate.

[11] Rondot (1939), p. 83. This sympathy for the Kurds corresponded to the French policy of counterbalancing Arab nationalism with strong minority communities, Fuccaro (1997), p. 302.

their energy to the profit of Arab, Iranian and Turkish states.[12] The French policy towards the Kurds was to grant them economic assistance if they "abandonnent le fusil pour la charrue". To a large extent, the refugees were grateful for the opportunity and turned the *Jazīra* into an important agricultural area, transforming rocky prairies into olive groves and vineyards.[13] However, many refugees had not given up the hope of winning back their homeland; some of them used the amnesty of 1928 to return to Turkey and participate in insurrections.[14] The activities of these provisional refugees who had contacts not only with the Kurds of Syria, including intellectuals and notables involved in Kurdish nationalism, but also with Turkish and Armenian refugees, prompted heated protests from Ankara. Having concluded agreements with Turkey, the French mandate government tried to restrain cross border movement and overt political agitation in Syria.

The Treaty of Lausanne had awarded part of the autonomous Kurdistan envisioned in the Treaty of Sèvres to Syria. It was no secret to the Kurds that the mandate's charter recommended supporting autonomy where the conditions were favourable. In 1928, some Syrian Kurds submitted a petition to the mandate government in Damascus demanding self-administration and the use of Kurdish both as an official language and as a language of instruction. The document also proposed that a Kurdish regiment be established to patrol the Turco-Syrian border. Such demands raised the ire of Syrian nationalists, who suggested that the Kurds establish independence in Kurdistan but not in Arab *Jazīra*, a "berceau arabe preislamique".[15] The French had no intention of awarding autonomy to the Kurds. That they encouraged Kurdish cultural development was motivated at least in part by a policy of weakening Sunni Muslim unity. The French even tolerated *Khoybūn* as long as their aspirations

---

[12] Rondot (1939), p. 103. He cites Sekban's *La Question Kurde* as support for this view.

[13] Rondot (1939), pp. 116–120. This assessment of the agricultural prowess of the Kurds quickly became part of the new Kurdish mythology being developed in this era, as a means of underscoring the viability of the Kurds as a nation. It crops up again in contemporary nationalists' portrayals such as Zaza (1982), p. 255, and Vanly (1992 a), p. 147, both of whom were Kurds from Damascus. In the next section it will be demonstrated how Kāmurān Bedir Khān injected this newly-found pride into his portrayal of Kurds in *Der Adler von Kurdistan.*

[14] Rondot (1939), pp. 112–113.

[15] Rondot (1939), p. 109.

did not extend to Syria and their activities had no serious political repercussions.[16] In 1930, several Kurdish nationalists were arrested on the occasion of the Ararat Revolt. Ṯüreyyā was evicted from Syria while Celādet was held under house arrest because he had supported Hajo, a tribal leader who had left Syria with his forces, intending to assist the rebels of Ararat.[17]

From 1932 on, Celādet published *Hawar*, which pursued cultural goals such as standardizing the language, creating language materials for instruction, and overcoming tribal prejudices against education.[18] Trying to maintain the solidarity of the forces which had merged in *Khoybūn*, Kurdish nationalists began to focus on building a collective identity not founded exclusively on opposition to Turks. But it was important to sustain the communality of the wronged and the premise of justified resistance to unjustified repression. The militancy of *Khoybūn*, which had been based on accusations of Turkish and Allied wrongdoing, had to be tempered so as not to test the limits of French magnanimity or arouse the wrath of Syrian nationalists.

The printing of Sekban's *La Question Kurde* coincided with the publication of an open letter addressed to Atatürk and written by Celādet Bedir Khān.[19] Possibly he had heard of the publication plans of Sekban and Fani and wanted to create a kind of counterweight which would neutralize the effects of their writings. But the main spur to Celādet's letter was the amnesty planned for the 10th anniversary of the establishment of the Turkish Republic. Celādet calls the amnesty "propaganda" and claims that Kurdish nationalists would not be

[16] *Khoybūn* had affirmed that their struggle concerned Turkey and not Iraq and Syria where the Kurds were content with the rights afforded by the mandate charter, Kutschera (1979), p. 91.

[17] Rondot (1939), p. 114. According to *EI* (2), vol. I, "Badrkhānī", p. 871, Celādet actually entered Turkey with Hajo's troops.

[18] Rondot (1939), pp. 121–123.

[19] There are two editions available: Bedirxan (1978) and Bedirxan (1992); I have used the latter. Bayrak (1993, pp. 575–579) has extracts. The Ottoman original was printed in Damascus in 1933. Since the original was not available to me, I have used the 1992 edition which has been latinized by Dr. Nuri Dersimi. I prefer that edition because it retains the old words whereas the 1978 edition contains many translations from Ottoman into *Öztürkçe*: Bedirxan (1992), p. 9. The open letter was finished, as is stated at the end, "on the shores of Tiberias [Sea of Galilee], Januar 8, 1933" (p. 96). Dersimi has attached to his latinization a "foreword" which is omitted in both editions, but included in Dersimi (1992), pp. 270–282. He gives as a date for Celādet's letter "end of 1933" (p. 282), and as the reason for his latinization his wish that it be read by the Kurdish youth.

impressed by it, because they were "goal-oriented", "persistent" and "willing to sacrifice": "They (Kurdish nationalists, MS) are not just any shortsighted individuals who would profit from a revolution or a coup d'etat today to become president or minister tomorrow".[20] But the very fact that Celādet was writing the letter indicates he knew well that some of his co-nationalists were weary and ready to abandon the cause and return to Turkey if they qualified for the amnesty. He draws attention once more to the extent of the assimilation policies and their results, hoping this will have a mobilizing effect on tempted comrades. Thus the open letter should be seen more as promoting Kurdish solidarity than appealing to the Turks to change their policies.[21] Moreover, addressing the Turkish leader as (no more than) a fellow interlocutor in the discussion of Kurdish affairs enables Celādet both to project himself and the Kurds as reasonable and willing to settle differences in a sensible manner and to draw attention to the continued focus on Turkey (rather than Syria).

Celādet accuses Atatürk of being responsible for the deportations and violent repression.

> You had Kurdish nationalists and fighters for independence brought before the independence tribunals. I don't know if it was intentional or accidental that you had the trials in Diyarbakır take place in a cinema. And the bloody film that is the Kurdish question you had played by actors specifically chosen for the task. For this bloodthirsty film you sacrificed many innocent people only because they were Kurds.[22]

No longer vilifying the evil Turk *per se*, Celādet raises specific questions of wrongdoing towards the Kurds, alternately decrying and deriding Turkish policies. In Celādet's somewhat tragicomic version of the results of the assimilation policies, the ban on speaking Kurdish had caused peasants around Diyarbakır to avoid the city. This in turn had led to obstacles in provisioning the military. For this reason, internal directives ordered that Kurdish be tolerated in such cases. But when the governor-general of the martial-law provinces visited Kurdish villages, all those who spoke no Turkish had to stay home and only villagers speaking Turkish, however badly, were shown to him.[23]

---

[20] Bedirxan (1992), p. 93.
[21] Bedirxan (1992), pp. 11 sqq.
[22] Bedirxan (1992), pp. 30 sqq.
[23] Bedirxan (1992), p. 32.

Professing to be aware of Atatürk's great interest in language, Celādet offers a "private reading" dealing with the Kurdish language. More than one third of the letter is devoted to laying out the similarities between Kurdish and Indo-European languages and the differences to Turkish. Celādet cites the research results of a German scholar, a certain Dr. Fric,[24] who demonstrated that out of 8,428 Kurdish words only 300 were of Kurdish origin, whereas 3,080 derived from Turkish and 2,000 from Arabic. Celādet disputes these results and refers to Jaba and Justi (1879) who counted 575 words of Turkish origin in the Kurdish language.[25] He quotes Gökalp, calling him "the greatest prophet of Turkism": "Kurdish is the richest language of the Orient, including Arabic".[26]

Celādet criticizes the resettlement plans of the government from an economic point of view with a detailed estimate. Several million Turkish pounds would be the cost of settling Kurdish peasants in the western part of the country and the Turks in Kurdistan. Aside from the fact that the state did not have the money, such a program was doomed to failure.[27] As a deterrent example of the results of the "extermination" or "assimilation" of a people, he cites the situation of the Native Americans in the US, where scholars were sent to the last survivors of tribes to record their language and customs for posterity.[28]

In Celādets' view, a solution of the Kurdish problem was "simple and clear" and, as he emphasizes, ". . . not as difficult as you think . . . If you recognize in an official proclamation the existence

[24] This must be Dr. Fritz whose identity I could not establish. In 1914 the book *Kürdler, Tārikhī ve İçtimāʿī Tedḳiḳāt* by Dr. Fritz appeared in Ottoman. It is doubtful whether there had been a German version. The book has been latinized by Şanlıer (1992). Bayrak (1994, p. 33) thinks that Dr. Fritz was a pseudonym for the Albanian-born "Unionist" (*ittihatçı*) Habil Adem. According to Malmîsanij (2000, p. 248), the book was authored by Naci İsmail Pelister (of Albanian origin), but it was presented as having been written by a German.

[25] Bedirxan (1992), pp. 37 sqq. Celādet claims to have amassed a Kurdish vocabulary numbering 13,090 words, confiscated by the authorities in 1918 when his house was searched. The manuscript was then sent to the Independence Tribunal in Elazığ and since then had disappeared: Bedirxan (1992), p. 48.

[26] Bedirxan (1992), p. 70. He mentions the Kurdish grammar written by Gökalp cited above. Kadri Cemil Paşa (1991), p. 29, relates that Khalīl Khayyālī, together with Ziya Gökalp, had written a Kurdish grammar and dictionary.

[27] Bedirxan (1992), pp. 86–91.—The law or a draft of that law was prepared on April 24, 1932, by the Minister of the Interior, Refik Saydam, and passed by parliament on June 14, 1934.

[28] Bedirxan (1992), pp. 94–95.

of Kurdistan and the historical, racial and cultural rights of the Kurds, an important and genuine step would be made. In this way further revolts would be avoided".[29] But if a peaceful solution is not reached, Celādet prophesies, hostilities will continue. "My Dear Pasha, you may be sure that it is more difficult to assimilate and imprison the Kurds than to kill them. The freedom of the Kurds is a steel which grows naturally". He then offers three quotes to illustrate Kurdish demands and threats:

> He who fights against steel will have his hands and arms ripped off (the Persian poet Saʿdī).
> Why do you enslave men? Their mothers have given birth to them as free men (the Caliph ʿUmar).

Finally, he quotes—without giving his name—Ernst Moritz Arndt, poet of the German wars of liberation and advocate of "Volkshaß" (ethnic hatred):

> Der Gott, der Eisen wachsen ließ
> Er wollte keine Knechte
> Darum gab er Säbel, Speer und Spieß
> Dem Mann in seine Rechte
>
> The God who let iron grow
> Did not want servants
> Thus he gave broadsword, spear and lance
> To man in his right hand.[30]

At the end Celādet threatens Atatürk with armed struggle, referring somewhat paradoxically, given the anticlericalism of both writer and addressee, to religious co-identity. "If you—despite everything—spill the blood of Muslims and do not pity the miserable Anatolians who are dying from Muslim bullets, then you should know that in the veins of Kurds so much blood flows in order to shed it dying and killing".[31]

---

[29] Bedirxan (1992), p. 95.

[30] Bedirxan (1992), p. 96. These are the first four verses in *Vaterlandslied* (1812). A complete version may be found in: E.M. Arndt (no date, [1894]), pp. 325–327. Although Celādet quotes the German original correctly, in the Turkish rendering he translated the word "Rechte" (meaning right hand) in the sense of the German plural of "Recht" (law, Turkish: hukuk).

[31] Bedirxan (1992), p. 96.

CHAPTER EIGHT

CELĀDET'S *DE LA QUESTION KURDE*

1. *Trick or Treason*

The "open letter" was the last Kurdish nationalist publication penned in Turkish to come out of Syria. Turkish, the language in which both Celādet and Kāmurān had published extensively, was no longer the language of a power responsive to their demands. French was now not only the medium for reaching a European public, but also the language of the nation that appeared to be the arbiters of the Kurds' fate. Certainly, for Celādet and Kāmurān, French presented the only context in which they could offer their services and advance Kurdish needs. Under the British in Iraq, Sorani was being developed as a language of literature and instruction. It was up to the Kurds of Syria to push forward with Kurmanjī, but few of them had actually written in Kurdish before. Most educated Ottoman Kurds had mastered Turkish better than Kurdish and it was likely that this situation had not yet improved. Until it did, French, which was understood by most of the Kurdish intellectuals in the Ottoman Empire, was a temporary crutch. Using French to inform the outside world, he could also address the educated Kurds about the tenets on which Kurdish solidarity was based. Certainly this consolidating function is more in evidence in *De la question kurde*[1] than in Ṯüreyyā's texts, which were almost exclusively oriented to the Western public.

De la question kurde, while purporting to be a critique of deportation practices, is more interesting as evidence of how Celādet dealt with the central concerns of the Syrian Kurdish agenda discussed above: building and expanding cultural identity and legitimacy (via the continued delineation of the ethnic and moral boundaries between Kurds and Turks) in order to perpetuate the polarity on which Kurdish solidarity and its legitimacy as an international cause rested.

[1] Bedir Khān (1934). The brochure was published under the pseudonym Herekol Azîzan. Azîzan was another name for the Bedir Khān princes, cf. Nikitine (1975), p. 86.

It must also be kept in mind that an emphasis on Kurdish-Turkish enmity was an important element in reassuring Syrian nationalists that they, the Kurds, harboured no claims regarding Syria, although the petition of 1928 had demonstrated otherwise.[2] It was vital to play the role of victim vis-à-vis the international community as well. However, this stance ran counter to the equally important task of portraying the Kurds in a positive light. This latter objective now assumed central significance in the task of rebuilding confidence in a Kurdish identity after the Kurds' failure to achieve nationhood.

As the chapter above on the Kurdish journals illustrated, the Kurds were justly concerned about not having a (written account of their) history. As ʿAbdullāh Cevdet had argued, a nation which does not "possess the history of its past and its future is not its own master". History was perceived as an essential block in the nation-building process. Celādet's text sheds light on how the Kurds in the 1930's, relieved of the demands of military struggle and free to engage in imaginative nation-building, approached history. Celādet and Kāmurān were no strangers to the business of history writing, having published an account of the Balkan Wars.[3] However, they did not, as one might expect, engage in the primary scholarship necessary to extend their knowledge of Kurdish history. I will venture the thesis that the Bedir Khāns were not interested in contributing to the repository of discrete details and processes from which historical narration is derived but rather regarded already available knowledge of the past as a stockpile from which they could choose at random episodes, facts, figures and concepts which could be adapted to support their arguments for legitimacy, identity, and the shared experience of victimization.

The basic premises of this argument were put forward in Ṯüreyyā's texts: Kurdish civilization had reached its zenith at the time of the independent Kurdish emirates. It was only when the Ottomans, an alien force, took away their independence that they descended into an age of darkness which was aptly described by the metaphor of slumber. This line of reasoning was the same as that employed by other Ottoman minorities and has remained a component of their

---

[2] In this petition demands were made for recognition of Kurdish as an official language and appointment of Kurdish officials in regions inhabited by Kurds.

[3] Bedir Khān (1329/1913–14). In the preface the authors express the wish: "May Ottomanism remain, may Islam be eternal!" (p. 8).

historical attitudes today. One salient difference to the Balkan Christians, however, concerns the concept of ethnic survival. Christians were wont to attribute the survival of genuine ethnic traits to the heroic efforts of their national churches rather than to the Ottoman *millet* system, which assigned the tasks of socialization to the religious heads. But the Kurds, as part of the Muslim *millet*, had not been distinguished from the Turks. How then could they explain enduring distinctiveness? I believe it is in this context of establishing a matrix for survival that we must view the insistence on the longevity of the Kurdish question or the age-old resistance of the Kurds to Turkish assimilation efforts.

Celādet begins his account of the Kurdish question, which he asserts to be so necessary for understanding the framework of the laws governing deportation, with a topographical clarification of the origins of the question. First of all, he reminds readers that the Kurds of Syria and Iraq had been created only after the Great War when these areas were detached from the Ottoman Empire. Historically, the Kurds had been divided between Turkey and Persia. As for the Kurdish question in Persia, he relates the following episode from the golden age of the great Kurdish emirates, of Ardalan, which eventually lost its Kurdish character as it assimilated to Persian court culture. I will quote his account at length as it illustrates a resourceful appropriation of history to enhance his own portrayal.

> Comme on sait d'ailleurs la Perse qui, jusq'à ces dernières années, sommeillait dans la léthargie et l'incapacité n'avait ni forces ni moyens pour imposer son autorité aux kurdes et résister aux révoltes de leurs princes. La dernière principauté du Kurdistan de la Perse, l'Ardelan, qui plusieurs fois avait menacé le trône des chahs de Téheran, ne put être détruite que par ruse, par les empereurs de la Perse. Pour y parvenir, les chahs ont été jusqu'à contracter des parentés d'alliance avec les émirs kurdes d'Ardelan. Les princesses de la cour de Téheran, mères des émirs d'Ardelan, accomplissaient fidèlement et avec beaucoup de succès les instructions de leur père impérial, à la cour de Sinandiz.[4] Jusqu'à l'entrée de ces princesses à la cour des émirs d'Ardelan, l'opium, très répandu en Perse, et tout autre boisson alcoolique étaient inconnus des émirs kurdes.

In Celādet's account, another negative consequence of these marriage alliances was that the Kurdish emirs embraced Shiʿism, thus

[4] Sanandaj, also known as Senneh.

losing the respect of their subjects. As for contemporary Persia's policies towards the Kurds, it merely imitated the Republic of Turkey, including the banning of the Kurdish language and calling the Kurds "les persans montagnards", just as Turkey had begun calling the Kurds "mountain Turks".[5]

What aim is Celādet pursuing in the way he relates the Ardalan episode? It seems to me that as a purveyor of nationalist history he has two main interests in the past: as it provides evidence of the eternal struggle of the Kurds against their oppressors (the Kurdish question), or as furnishing proof of greatness and thus the potential for nationhood. The Kurds of the İstanbul clubs and journals had promoted, along with Saladin, Karīm Khān Zand, who had been the Shāh of Persia, as an object of pride and a model for emulation. But the princes of Ardalan had achieved eminence and prosperity by virtue of their relationship with the Ḳājārs, whom they assisted in vanquishing the Zand dynasty. The Ḳājār rulers had adopted the strategy of cooperating with rather than trying vainly to exclude popular Kurdish tribal leaders. When possible they had pursued marital alliances, the practice of taking hostages to ensure good behaviour, and naming tribal leaders to governorship posts. The result was that the Ardalan princes were more partners than vassals to the Ḳājārs.[6] Celādet frames these pragmatic policies as invidious, part of a long-term Persian scheme to undo the Kurds. As far as the many princesses who were alleged to have successively contaminated the court of Ardalan in the interest of their father, the fact is that the last Ardalan prince to occupy the position of *vali* was Khosrow Khān, the son of Amānullāh Khān who had given "... une allure royale à sa petite capitelle",[7] Sanandaj. Khosrow Khān, whose mother had been a Persian court slave, was brought up at the Persian court, corresponding to the hostage practice. He was married to the daughter of Fatḥ ʿAlī Shāh, who later succeeded her husband and ruled in their sons' name. Valiye Khānum's rule paved the way for further Persians to occupy the position of *vali*.[8]

---

[5] Bedir Khān (1934), pp. 4–5.

[6] A similar strategy was followed by the Safavids vis-à-vis the Ardalan, see Strohmeier and Yalçın-Heckmann (2000), pp. 72–73.

[7] Nikitine (1975), p. 169.

[8] Nikitine (1975), p. 169.

Why does Celādet choose to speak of the Ardalans rather than the Zands? I would propose that here he is less concerned with introducing heroic figures, a useful practice in rallying hope and instilling admiration, but not particularly effective in banishing the trauma of defeat and unachieved statehood. I believe that the crucial, if unstated concerns of much of the literature after the Ararat defeat are explaining why the Kurds failed in their aspirations, and overcoming the internalized aspects of defeat such as feelings of weakness and inadequacy. In a narrower sense, this involves the question of why the Kurdish leaders had encouraged their people in an endeavour which had ended so calamitously for many. In Celādet's account of the fall of the Ardalan dynasty, we find two main elements which have become *topoi* in Kurdish nationalist literature: 1) decline due to stealthy and/or systematic infiltration and contamination by an alien nation, i.e. involuntary assimilation, and 2) an enemy's success in defeating the Kurds by trickery and treason. The fate of the last Kurdish principality in Iran is seen from the perspective of the Turkish experience. The author superimposes the framework elaborated in Ṯüreyyā's writing where healthy, good Kurds faced evil, unhealthy and racially inferior foes. Celādet, unable to make the racial argument in regard to the Persian foe, charges instead that the Persians had introduced debilitating factors such as opium and "other alcoholic drinks". Even the conversion of the *vali*s to the religion of the rulers, a familiar pattern in creating and strengthening alliances, is seen within the framework of moral contamination. The "last Kurdish emirate" in Persia evokes the parallel of the much-cited Botan, where the last remaining Kurdish ruler had revolted against Ottoman centralization efforts. In most accounts of the revolt, the elder Bedir Khān, an emblem of Kurdish leadership pretensions, was defeated "only by a ruse", betrayed by his cousin.[9] It was central to face-saving endeavours to attribute defeat to a tricky, dishonourable enemy or traitor. This left the Kurds strong and honest to a fault, dependable; keeping their word, adhering to treaties, they are the victims of those who are less constant. This argument is employed not only in regard to endemic foes but also to the Western powers, who had likewise deceived and betrayed the Kurds.

[9] Bedir Khān (1928 b), p. 29: ". . . succumbed only to a ruse by Bedir Khān's nephew". Nikitine (1975), p. 186: ". . . après une série de défaites infligées aux Turcs, succomba trahi par son cousin".

2. *The History of the Kurdish Question in Turkey*

Celādet locates the beginning of the Kurdish question in the 16th century when the Kurds, caught between the warring Ottomans and Persians, had to choose sides. Despite their common roots in "la grande famille aryenne", the Kurds and Persians had religious differences. For this reason, the Kurds had supported Selīm as the head of the Sunnis. Celādet explains that the manifestation of the Kurdish question in this era was different from that of the 20th century because of the supremacy of the religious factor at that time. Due to the Turks' belonging to the Ḥanafite rite, and the Kurds to the Shāfiʿite rite, there had been some conflicts.[10] But following these religious conflicts the Kurdish tribes began to revolt and recover ". . . leur liberté et la divine indépendance qui leur est aussi que la vie".[11] Celādet suggests that all Kurds are Sunnis.[12] As a member of several Kurdish societies, he would have been aware of the large number of Kurdish Alevis. He should also have known that many of the Kurds of Persia, in particular those close to Kirmanshāh and Lūristān, were Shiʿites. His two brothers had been fascinated with the Yezidis and other non-Muslim Kurdish groups, who they felt had retained original Kurdish traits. Celādet himself had had close connections to Hajo, head of one of the most prominent Yezidi tribes. However, these religious differences are passed over in *De la question*, where Sunni identity is affirmed. There are several more, similar references in the text, which may be seen as evidence of consolidation efforts. While ostensibly explaining religious homogeneity to the outsider, he tacitly reminds the likewise-targeted indigenous reader of one of the main bonds among Kurds. He remarks in a footnote on the differences between Sunnites and Shiʿites, that the latter consider the former to be more foreign than non-Muslims: ". . . si un sunnite boit dans le verre d'un chiite, le chiite considère

[10] The only evidence of such "conflict" as far as I can determine was a petition of Kurdish sheykhs which called for filling the positions of *ḳāḍī* and *muftī* by adherents of the Shāfiʿite rite. As Jwaideh ironically remarked, this would have amounted to "the establishment of a Kurdish national church", quoted by Olson (1991), p. 17.

[11] Bedir Khān (1934), p. 7.

[12] Ever since Sharaf ad-Dīn in his Sharafnāme stated that the Kurds are Sunni, Kurdish authors stressed the Sunni affiliation of the Kurds, probably wishing to argue Kurdish loyalty to the Sunni Ottomans.

le verre comme tellement souillé qu'il ne peut plus être rendu propre par le lavage et il le casse, pour que ses lèvres ou celles de ses coréligionnaires ne le touchent pas".[13] In fact, such sentiments were characteristic of the Yezidis towards all other groups: Christians, Muslims and Jews alike.[14] I am not entirely sure why Celādet emphasizes this particular boundary. Sunni-Shiʿī distinctions were central to the Iraqi Kurds' aspirations. They argued that the Kurds should not be forced to integrate into an Arab state, as the Arabs of Iraq, divided as they were among Shiʿites and Sunnites, could not even be said to constitute a nation.[15] One must assume that Celādet, a fairly astute observer of French policies, was aware of their efforts to divide the Sunni Muslims of Syria.[16] On the other hand, why should he risk excluding the very sizeable and influential group of Yezidis from the Kurds and Kurdishness? One possible answer might lie in French-British controversies over the Yezidi Kurds in the *Jazīra*, many of whom had come to Syria from Iraq in order to escape conscription.[17]

Leaving the earlier manifestations of Kurdish striving for freedom, he turns to the "purement national" concerns of the Kurdish question today. This national orientation was not recent, but could be observed as early as the 17th century in the writing of Aḥmad-i Khānī. He reiterates his assertions in his open letter to Atatürk.[18] After this brief reference to Khānī, Celādet quotes extensively from Nikitine on the three phases of the Kurdish question.[19] According

---

[13] Bedir Khān (1934), p. 5.

[14] According to a petition to the Ottoman government in 1872 explaining matters of the Yezidi faith, a Yezidi was not allowed to ". . . drink from the cup of a Muslim or of one who belongs to one of the other religions", cited by Kreyenbroek (1995), p. 7.

[15] [National Central Committee] (1930), p. 348.

[16] Later in his pamphlet, Celādet quotes at length from an article from an Arab journal in Damascus. This would point to the possible existence of a dialogue between the Kurds and Arabs of Syria, or at least the attempt to initiate one.

[17] Fuccaro (1997), pp. 570–574.

[18] "Le grand poête kurde Ahmedê Khani, né en 1061 de l'hegire, peut être considéré à juste titre comme le véritable apôtre du nationalisme kurde. Khani qui a puisé le sujet de son oeuvre (Memozîn) dans une légende nationale ne parle que du kurdisme et du Kurdistan. Ses personnages sont des symboles. Il figure en prison la personne qui symbolise le Kurdistan et il montre à ses hommes et ses amis les moyens et les efforts à déployer pour le sauver", Bedir Khān (1934), p. 7. Cf. Bedirxan (1992), p. 21.

[19] Conforming precisely to the three-page quote of Nikitine's rendering of Kurdish history is a long footnote on Khānī, which constitutes a significant subtext, Bedir

to Nikitine, the first is the feudal period, when Kurds were vassals of the Ottoman Empire. In the second stage, the last Kurdish feudal principality, Botan, was dissolved, destroying the political equilibrium; this had prompted a series of revolts against the regime. The third stage was characterized by the legal and territorial transformation after the war which lead to the building of a modern, Kurdish elite inspired by the same aspirations "... que nous apprend l'histoire d'émancipation des peuples depuis la grande révolution française".[20]

Celādet elaborately lays out the solemnly propagated aims of the states which had formed the League of Nations. It had been instituted for "... la défense des droits des petits peuples qui n'étaient pas maîtres de leurs destinées et qui, sous la domination d'autres nations, étaient victimes de persecutions et de vexations. En effet, aussitôt la guerre finie, les puissances victorieuses avaient proclamé par des déclarations solenelles, qu'elles ne laisseraient aucun peuple sous la domination d'autres nations et que tous les peuples, maîtres désormais de leurs destinées, auraient le droit d'auto-détermination".[21] It was in this context that Kurdish leaders during the armistice had attempted to attain their rights at the peace conferences with the result that the Turkish government accused them of high treason and executed those who could not seek refuge abroad. But these leaders, as Celādet sees it, were themselves the victims of European treason. "La trahison de l'Europe consiste en ceci que les grands états européens, comme à tant d'autres petites nations, après avoir promis aux kurdes de faire valoir leur droit, plus tard sans scrupule les ont livré aux mains de leur bourreau".[22] Without naming the nations thus accused, he points out that they had not even assumed

Khān (1934), pp. 7–10. Here was a Kurdish intellectual, long before nationalism had become established in Europe, who espoused nationalism despite the "religious fanaticism" of the era and the fact that he had been educated only at *medreses*. He quotes at length—possibly for the first time in a European language—the verses of the prologue to *Mem ū Zīn*, which as we have seen earlier, were most preferred by nationalist authors. It is interesting that, even in 1934, Celādet was still referring almost exclusively to the prologue and only summarily to the epic poem itself, although the poem had been published in İstanbul by the same Ḥamzā who was now one of Celādet's cohabitants in Damascus.

[20] Bedir Khān (1934), pp. 7–11, quoting Minorsky, *Le Dictionnaire Diplomatique*, vol. I, pp. 1201–1204.

[21] Bedir Khān (1934), p. 12.

[22] Bedir Khān (1934), p. 15.

a neutral stance, but had actively assisted the Turkish military in their combat against Kurdish rebels, by letting Turks use the railway in Syria to transport their troops.[23]

3. *The Deportation Law*

Having "established" the pattern of betrayal and deceit to which the Kurds had been subjected, Celādet now comes to his actual subject, an analysis of the law governing deportation. He had already made clear on the title page what the results of the law would be. "Les kurdes déportés de leur sol natal et dispersés parmi les turcs, à travers les siècle oublieront leur langue maternelle, perderont leurs moeurs et coutumes, s'assimileront au turquisme et deviendront des turcs". The text of the law, reproduced in its entirety, does not contain the word "Kurd", but Celādet explains that the law aimed at destroying the living conditions, social networks and culture of the Kurds. The law stipulated several zones from which sectors of the population would be removed and into which they would be moved, and specified the ratio of Turks to non-Turks. Turks from abroad would be encouraged to settle in previously Kurdish areas. Tribal chiefs, beys, aghas and sheykhs would be removed from their land and separated from their followers. Celādet's analysis consists mainly of explaining why the law will not work. First of all, the Kurds would never accept the measures. Second, the Turks would not want to live in Kurdistan; even if they did, the costs would be exorbitant. The intention of the government to invite ethnic Turks from Azerbaijan and elsewhere to inhabit Kurdistan is also dismissed as Celādet claims they would not want to come without financial incentives and those who came would not manage to survive the inhospitable climate.

His aim—part of a larger strategy to deconstruct the powerful Turks—is to deride Turkish policies and show that they cannot be effective. On the contrary, the only possible results were failure and revolt. To support his argument, he turns to historical precedent, viewing the present measures as part of the age-old Ottoman ". . . système de déportation et de déracination des kurdes de leurs montagne . . .".[24] In a page-long footnote he cites a text by Helmuth von

[23] Bedir Khān (1934), pp. 15–16.
[24] Bedir Khān (1934), p. 22.

Moltke who had been an eyewitness to Ḥāfiẓ Pasha's attempt in 1838 to transform the Kurds of Kharzan Dağı into loyal subjects of the Sultan by removing them from their inaccessible mountains where, he promised them, they would receive large plots, be freed for three years from all taxes and tributes, and become rich by cultivating silk and horses ". . . au lieu de faire le pasteur dans les montagnes".[25] But he might as well ". . . proposer à un poisson de se construire un filet".[26] Both Moltke and Celādet relate the episode to illustrate the depth of the Kurds' attachment to their homeland. Although Ḥāfiẓ Pasha's troops were able to overcome the rebels, they had to abandon the project of the colonization of the plains.[27] Up to this point, Moltke's text suits Celādet's purposes, but Moltke goes on to lament the lack of unity among the Kurds. "None of these lesser princes exercises a stable rule over a large area of the country and only in times of great need and distress were men such as Rewanduß-Bey [Rāwanduz], Bedehan-Bey [Bedir Khān] and Sayd-Bey [Saʿīd] able to rally a considerable number of their compatriots behind their banners. They deserted them (their leaders, MS) just as quickly and each one defended exclusively his own hearth. Therein lies the weakness of the nation. They would be invincible if they were united, but the one side has never stood by the other and whenever Reşīd and Ḥāfiẓ Pasha invaded a district, the others rejoiced for the time being in their freedom until their turn came".[28]

Moltke's description of the lack of unity and solidarity among the Kurds recalls Khānī's lines, which Kurdish nationalist writers had invoked so often before as an exhortation to unite.[29] But Celādet

---

[25] This is Celādet's translation (Bedir Khān, 1934, p. 22). In fact, Moltke's exact words were: ". . . instead of picking mulberries and tending sheep" (Moltke, 1892, p. 294). Celādet obviously felt that this phrase was derogatory and thus deleted it. It should be remembered that Celādet spent the years 1922–1925 studying in Germany, so we can assume he had a good command of German.

[26] Moltke's exact words were: "Aber man könnte ebenso gut einem Fisch vorschlagen, künftig ein Nest zu bauen" (One might as well suggest that a fish build a nest). Celādet confuses the German word "Nest" with "Netz" (net). Moltke's remark emphasized the uselessness of the government's endeavour, while Celādet's "filet" (net) makes it seem insidious.

[27] Whereas Moltke speaks of the "complete defeat" ("gänzliche Besiegung") of the insurgents, Celādet translates this as "écrasement complet" ("complete destruction"), Bedir Khān (1934), p. 23; Moltke (1892), p. 295.

[28] Moltke (1892), p. 295.

[29] Celādet, too, had quoted the same verses in his long footnote which preceded the note on Moltke by 13 pages. "Les kurdes, autant ils sont zélés dans la bravoure,

omits Moltke's comments on the inability of the Kurdish leaders to control their areas, as this remark contradicts the version of the long-lived rule of the Azīzan over Botan. The author likewise leaves out the remarks about the lack of solidarity. He changes the last two lines to: "Et si Hafiz pacha dans cette expédition avait réussi à atteindre, dans un court laps de temps, son but, le principal motif consiste en ceci, que dans cette guerre on avait utilisé des kurdes contre les kurdes".[30] Thus the burden of blame for the lack of unity is shifted to the Ottoman authorities who had used the Kurds.

But it was not only a natural love of their land that explained why the Kurds would resist all efforts to remove them from their native soil. Ill-conceived Turkish educational policies had done their part as well. Thinking they could assimilate the Kurds by training them to love Turkey, the Turkish government had tried to spread Turkish culture via the schools. "Mais les jeunes gens kurdes qui étudiaient en langue turque et recevaient une éducation turque au lieu de suivre le grand chemin du 'Grand Touran' avec le flambeau du savoir qui vint en leurs mains avaient commencé d'examiner les profondeurs de leur conscience nationale et de voir là des vérités qui jusqu'ici étaient inconnus pour les kurdes illetrés".[31] Again, the Turks are shown to have bungled it.

The portrayals of the Kurds as weak and lacking in solidarity are no longer desirable. As we have emphasized, Celādet and, before him, Ṯüreyyā were concerned with projecting a positive image of the Kurds and demonstrating both the legitimacy of their struggle and their viability as a nation. Aḥmad-i Khānī's 17th-century remarks on the Kurds—long before Europeans had formed nation-states—were less threatening than Moltke's more recent statement that even

---

autant ils détestent de supporter le fardeau de la dépendance. C'est pour cela qu'ils sont toujours désunis, et qu'ils sont en discorde et n'obéissent pas l'un à autre. Si nous nous unissions et obéissions l'un à l'autre, ce turc, cet arabe, et ce persan, tous, ils nous auraient servi de serviteur", Bedir Khān (1934), pp. 8–9.

[30] Bedir Khān (1934), p. 23.

[31] Bedir Khān (1934), p. 24.—A strikingly similar assessment was given of Syrian educational policies by a Syrian Baʿathist in a secret study of the Kurds in Syria written in 1963. "The Kurdish tribes of Jazira . . . have this one desire which gives them their strength: the dream of a Kurdish homeland which is today deeply rooted in the mind of every Kurd, thanks largely to the education we have so generously lavished upon them, and which is being turned as a weapon against us. The idea of Arabizing them through education is misguided, for the results are the opposite of what we expected", quoted in Vanly (1992 a), p. 155.

the likes of Bedir Khān had not been able to sustain unity or support. This was a serious indictment of Kurdish unruliness and detracted from their argument that it was not their weakness but rather Turkish oppression and the League of Nations' neglect, betrayal and egotism which had prevented them from attaining nationhood.

But if the law was so impracticable, why did Ankara want it? Celādet asserts that the Turks were seeking reasons to justify atrocities. The law had generated resistance. This is a crucial aspect of the law for Celādet as he clearly wishes to deny any present association of Kurdish leaders in Syria with revolts in Turkey. The incidents, in his view, were unorganized cases of resistance, a "legitimate defense" according to natural and penal law.[32] No doubt Turkish authorities were claiming the revolts were results of outside intervention and that the responsibility for bloodshed lay in the Kurdish camp. But Celādet denies any such accusations, asserting that Kurdish leaders were not anxious to present Ankara with an excuse to ". . . faire couler le sang kurde".[33] But resistance would be inevitable as long as the Turkish government continued its policy of repression and deportation. Celādet professes to have received word that in different parts of Botan members of notable families had recently been arrested in order to be deported. The government, however, had been forced to do a volte-face as the people were so incensed that the authorities feared armed resistance. At the same time, a dozen singers had been arrested and accused of stirring up popular sentiment by singing about fallen Kurdish revolutionary heroes. Celādet remarks that Kurdish folklore is of "considerable richness", having recorded the "gloire des anciens émirautés" and, since the revolt of 1925, had preserved the events affecting the Kurdish people such as ". . . les élégies des martyrs kurdes, l'exode des chefs kurdes aux pays étrangers et leur effort pour le salut de leur patrie".[34] It was this recently discovered reverence for traditional culture that was to constitute a new orientation of Kurdish nationalist scholars.

[32] In support of this view, Celādet quotes an article in an Arab newspaper on Kurdish resistance to the law of deportation, Bedir Khān (1934), pp. 33–36.

[33] Bedir Khān (1934), p. 36.

[34] Bedir Khān (1934), p. 38.

PART THREE

A "NOVEL" APPROACH TO PRESENTING THE KURDS

CHAPTER ONE

THE BEDIR KHĀNS AND FRENCH ORIENTALISTS

Among the French officers and administrators of Syria, there were a number with scholarly interests in Kurdish affairs. The orientalists Roger Lescot and Pierre Rondot, both of whom had been military officers in Syria, and Father Thomas Bois published extensively on Kurdish history, culture and literature until well into the 1960's and 1970's.[1] Like the British Kurdish experts Noel and Soane, they intervened in administrative and political affairs.[2] Their collaboration with Kurdish intellectuals—both Lescot and Bois had wide-ranging contacts with Celādet and Kāmurān[3]—was integral to a new phase of imaginative nation-building. One of *Khoybūn*'s aims was to build cohesion amongst the different strata of Kurdish rural and urban society, by stressing a common Kurdish culture. Endeavours to delineate a Kurdish identity underwent a change in focus as these scholars overhauled and replenished the arsenal of cultural markers, seeking to map the terrain of the Kurdish soul which was held to be manifested in their traditional culture.[4] They discovered the widespread appeal of songs and legends and the utility of the romantic code which provided, as it were, passwords in the ongoing struggle to be admitted to the world of nations.

We have seen in earlier chapters how the dual concerns of "awakening" the Kurds and representing their nation to potential allies in

---

[1] Cf. Edward Said's discussion (1978) of the relationship of orientalists as "agents" to their fields of study. Certainly, Said's assessment of the dichotomy of "us" (advanced, civilized) and "them" (primitive, incapable of self-rule) holds true for the paternalistic role of the French orientalists in Syria.

[2] Noel and Soane, in contrast to other orientalists dealing with the Kurds, were both passionate advocates of Kurdish self-determination although they differed regarding the methods for achieving it, McDowall (1996), pp. 156–8 on the conflict between Noel and Soane on the retribalization of Kurds in Iraq.

[3] Nazdar (1988), p. 410 n. 1.

[4] Thus the title of one of Father Bois' contributions was: *Kurdische Volksdichtung. Spiegel der kurdischen Seele.* Many of the other publications in this vein were printed in *Hawar*, a journal edited by Celādet in Damascus.

the Western world engendered borrowings and adaptations of various aspects of what was perceived as the universal model for acquiring nation-status. Whereas early Kurdish nationalists had viewed nations as those peoples who had achieved a high level of civilization, thereby demonstrating their qualifications for membership in an elite club which was not about to accept members unable to meet its standards, Kurds writing in the pre-World War I journals could find few redeeming qualities in contemporary Kurdish culture. Kurdish leaders after Sèvres began to focus on the assumptions underlying the clauses of the peace treaty which recognized their wish for self-determination as an unalienable right of all nations regardless of their economic or cultural development. The Romantic glorification of the "Volk" which had been the basis of German nationalism from its inception[5] offered the possibility of viewing Kurdish "primitiveness" differently, by seeing it as containing all the unadulterated, authentic and noble qualities which had been lost in cosmopolitan culture.[6]

The new focus on songs, legends, proverbs, religion and superstitions represented a departure from the attitudes about what constituted cultural achievement expressed in the first decades of Kurdish nationalism. For the first generation of awakeners, Khānī's *Mem ū Zīn* had been the main proof of a worthy and distinctive culture; Kurdish folk songs had been denigrated.[7] In the post-Saʿīd period, Kurdish intellectuals seem to have realized that their elite had spent too long bemoaning the shortcomings of the Kurds, and deriding their "own" culture rather than imaginatively translating it into something inherently valuable. Ṯüreyyā Bedir Khān was the first to project the Kurds as a heroic people viciously wronged by the Turks (as opposed to a lethargic "nation" needing to be awakened). It remained, on the level of cultural argumentation, to project positive existing traits instead of focussing on high culture—a perspective which could only lead to the assessment expressed in Sekban's tree analogy: Kurdish written culture was a wasteland. Written culture

[5] Among numerous studies on the subject, I found Greenfeld (1994) and several articles in Giesen (1991) to be particularly informative. Parallels between German and Kurdish nationalism can only be briefly suggested in the course of this study.

[6] The affinity to the national socialist ideal of the pure Aryan peasant is apparent and will be discussed in the following.

[7] See note on ʿAbdurraḥmān Bedir Khān, p. 34.

was less important in a *Volk*-oriented definition of cultural distinction. Orientalists, moreover, who were interested in folk songs, religion and fairy tales had contributed to the nationalists' realization that their people's songs were a kind of cultural capital. Kurdish scholars and supporters, such as Safrastian[8] and Nikitine, almost invariably stressed the musical nature of the Kurds.[9] By absorbing the findings and attitudes of European scholars, Kurdish nationalists, and in particular Kāmurān, were adopting a strategy which compensated for the lack of high culture with an equally respectable "low" culture[10] as well as a code for favorably presenting the Kurds to the world, ever the concern of the image correctors.

The Bedir Khāns developed an interest in the subject of Kurdish women. Stories of Kurdish women who assumed political and military functions among their people were put forward. The most prominent of these was ʿĀdila (Khān) of Halabja who, even before the death of her husband ʿO<u>t</u>mān Pasha, the chief of the Jaf, had taken over leadership of the tribe.[11] Such women could capture the attention of Western audiences as they contradicted the stereotype of the sequestered, powerless Muslim woman. Kāmurān and Ṯüreyyā, in particular, elaborated on the freedom of Kurdish women which became a *topos* in accounts of Kurdish society.[12] The West was taking

[8] In a chapter titled "The evolution of the Kurd and his prospects" Safrastian cites their ancient customs, development, high morals, physical and moral health—"totally devoid of any sign of neurosis"—as justification for their right to better treatment. The highlight of his personality portrait is an episode illustrating Kurdish men's and women's sensitivity to music. He himself had experienced a scene in which an entire group of men and women broke into sobs as a Kurdish bard sang a tragic love ballad, Safrastian (1948), pp. 94–95.

[9] Soane (1913, p. 160) characteristically wrote in his Kurdish Grammar: "The Kurds being generally a people who love legends, bravery, freedom and withal are naturally gifted with the linguistic sense, have evolved, or we may say, perhaps always possessed songs, some of which are worthy of high rank as dignified verse, the finer that it is purely spontaneous. The folk-songs are untrammelled by the intricate conventions of the 'ilm i 'arud which makes Persian, Turkish and Arabic verse so unconvincing, and often so floridly pointless".

[10] The merits of this "low culture" were enhanced when it was found to articulate a sense of injustice at enemy hands, as in songs which recounted the events of the Saʿīd Revolt, Bedir Khān (1934), p. 38 n. 9.

[11] The "uncrowned queen of Sharizar", as Edmonds called her, was a staunch supporter of the British administration, Edmonds (1957), p. 50.

[12] Nikitine (1975), pp. 99–102, summarizes Soane's and Minorsky's first-hand accounts of ʿĀdila Khānum as a ruler. Soane had lived in disguise at her court. Nikitine quotes other known cases of influential Kurdish women recorded by other Western travelers and scholars such as Hartmann and Millingen. Nikitine recounts

an avid interest in Turkish advances in educating and liberating women from their traditional roles. It is not surprizing that Kurdish modernists would wish to demonstrate that their women, too, were advanced, and did not even require a cultural revolution imposed from above to make them so. Kurdish women's strength, superiority and independence illustrated in tales printed on the pages of *Hawar*, became one of the planks of Kurdish self-representation.[13]

the views expressed in Kāmurān's article on Kurdish women which had appeared in *L'Orient* (Beyrouth) in 1933. This article, stressing the freedom of Kurdish women, related again the story of 'Ādila, going on to assert that women were the main creators of Kurdish poetry and mainstays of Kurdish nationalism as it was they who taught their children the Kurdish national songs. This latter view is taken up and elaborated on in Bois' chapter on Kurdish women (1985, pp. 73–93). Kāmurān also relates the practice of giving children the names of their mothers instead of their fathers in cases where the wives had been superior to their husbands, a fact he reiterated again in a speech before the Royal Central Asian Society (Bedr Khan 1949, p. 241). Bois (1985, p. 119) mentions an article of Kāmurān's in *Hawar* (no. 19, pp. 294–296) titled "La femme kurde". Ṯüreyyā attended an international congress in Brussels in 1935 and presented a paper entitled "The Kurdish Woman and her social role" (Bois 1985, p. 119 n. 28). The theme of courageous Kurdish women is central in *Der Adler von Kurdistan* (Bedir Khan/Oertel 1937, p. 141) to be discussed in the following.

[13] Cf. Bedir Khan (1963, p. 23): "The Kurdish woman not only has the same rights as the man, but is also able to assume the same responsibilities as he does . . . This is probably the greatest and most striking difference between the Kurds and their neighbours". Nationalists today still like to point to the freedom of Kurdish women. Bruinessen (2000, pp. 9–21) demonstrates that historically there has been a greater readiness among Kurds to accept the wives of fallen or absent tribal leaders in their positions. Women, however, have been able to arrive at such positions only by virtue of their relationships to powerful men.

CHAPTER TWO

KĀMURĀN'S LITERARY CAREER

Both Celādet and Kāmurān Bedir Khān's studies and life in Germany[1] had brought them into contact with romantic nationalism and related ideological currents in the Weimar Republic. It is hard to see how they, frustrated nationalists, would not have felt some affinity for the bitter German nationalists who were congregated in rather large numbers in Munich. A certain sympathy for German nationalist writers, as seen in Celādet's use of Ernst-Moritz Arndt's verses in his open letter to Atatürk in 1933, may have obscured for the brothers the anti-Semitic tendencies expressed in the putsch of November 1923. When they returned to the Middle East, they reported back for duty in the Kurdish struggle, participating in the establishment of *Khoybūn* and its activities until its disbanding. Rather than relinquish the role of national protagonist when the military option was eliminated, they turned to cultural matters. Celādet remained for the most part in the Near East, publishing in Damascus and developing first a Latin alphabet, which was used in teaching the refugees to read and write in their mother tongue, and later a grammar. Kāmurān also pursued a career as a Kurdish man of letters and spokesman, an endeavour which eventually led to a teaching position at the *Institut National des Langues et Civilisations Orientales* in Paris, where he later became the editor of the *Bulletin de Centre d'Etudes Kurdes*. In the 1960's he was spokesman for Mustafa Barzani. In 1935 a slender volume of poems appeared in a German translation titled "The Snow of Light. Kurdish poems".[2] Kāmurān, who was said to

[1] Celādet's diaries of the years 1922–1925 spent in Munich unfortunately do not yield many impressions of current events and ideologies. To the putsch of Munich in November 1923 (pp. 52 sqq.) he allots a few lines, devoting more attention to everyday concerns such as procuring food and accommodation which were difficult given his and his brother's lack of funds and the serious inflation. There are also accounts of frequent visits to museums, concerts and excursions in the vicinity of Munich and trips elsewhere in Germany.—There is now an excellent study of the center of national socialism: David Clay Large: *Hitlers München. Aufstieg und Fall der Hauptstadt der Bewegung*. München 2001.

[2] Bedir Khan (1935/1968).

speak very little Kurdish in 1921,[3] had contributed to Ottoman Turkish and Kurdish newspapers[4] and written a history of the Balkan Wars in Ottoman Turkish.[5] He spoke and wrote Kurdish in this period, as demonstrated by his articles in *Hawar*,[6] but could he, in one decade, have acquired not only the linguistic but also the lyrical skills to compose Kurdish poems? Or did "Kurdish poems" refer merely to the "nationality" of their author? My scepticism is reinforced by the fact that neither Joyce Blau in her various articles nor Bois (1985) ever mention these "Kurdish poems" in their reviews of Kurdish literature, nor are they cited in Celādet's grammar, which avails itself of all of the meagre material available in Kurdish. Vanly, listing well-known Kurdish poets who published in the pages of *Hawar*, calls Kāmurān "a fine poet in his own right", but does not specify any lyrical publications.[7] And while Father Bois, who was certainly no disinterested judge when it came to Kāmurān,[8] praised the lyrical qualities of his writing, the one "lyrical" passage he actually quoted at length, was originally written in French.[9]

Naturally, we can attribute the choice of language to his intention to extend the discourse on Kurdishness to a European public; but it is also possible, in the case of the poems, that his high level of Kurdish was exaggerated in an attempt to round out his cultural leadership profile. In any case, at the beginning of the 1940's, Kāmurān had a position as Kurdish speaker at the *Radio du Levant* in Beirut, where he also organized Kurdish courses to teach the Kurdish community to read and write Kurdish and edited *Roja Nū*.[10]

---

[3] E.W. Noel, known as the "Kurdish Lawrence", who spoke Kurdish very well himself, recounted that Kāmurān, his traveling companion to Kurdistan in 1921, spoke no Kurdish (Behrendt 1993, p. 372 n. 36). On the other hand, Kāmurān proposed that Kurdish be the "official language" of the meetings of the Bedir Khān in 1920. Although the proposal was unanimously accepted the minutes continued to be written in Turkish, cf. Malmîsanij (2000), p. 28. Furthermore, according to Celādet's diary he or Kāmurān or both gave Kurdish lessons in Munich (Bedirhan 1995, p. 19).

[4] E.g. in the newspaper *Serbestī*, cf. Olson (1989), p. 18.

[5] Bedir Khān (1329/1913–14).

[6] Kāmurān also translated parts of the Kuran from Arabic into Kurdish, Bois (1985), p. 104.

[7] Vanly (1992 a), p. 150.

[8] Pater Bois and Kāmurān's close collaboration included several bible translations in Kurdish overseen by Kāmurān. Their views and the material cited to support these views corresponded closely to one another. See Bois (1985) and Bedir Khān (1949, 1963).

[9] Bois (1985), pp. 31–2.

[10] Vanly (1992 a), p. 150. Zaza (1982), p. 246 n. 49.

The majority of Kāmurān's poems deal with themes of love; several, however, are concerned with the patriotic struggle and allude to the suffering and loss suffered at enemy hands. In "Site of Memory" ("Stätte des Erinnerns") and "Native Country" ("Heimat") the poet laments the loss of family, dreams, places and the "blissful happiness, without hatred, without envy" of his youth when the "great song of freedom" was sung.[11] In 1937, he co-authored a novel in German with Herbert Oertel, a bookshop owner in Potsdam, who had already published several juvenile novels.[12]

We can only speculate about what led to this partnership of prince and hack writer, or the precise modus of cooperation, but it is not surprising that Kurdish nationalists should turn to the novel as a vehicle for promoting nationalist issues.[13] It must be remembered that Armenian nationalists had actively supported *Khoybūn*,[14] and thus Kurdish intellectuals would have been aware of the sympathy Armenians had reaped with Franz Werfel's novel, *The Forty Days of Musa Dagh*,[15] in which the heroic resistance of Armenian villagers against Turkish efforts to deport them was led by an emigré Armenian who had been virtually assimilated in France. The novel was set at Musa Dağı which was very close to the Syrian border through which many of the Kurds had escaped. Perhaps Kāmurān hoped, in launching a publishing career in Germany, that his book might have a similar impact. However, he would also have been aware of the fact that Werfel's novel had been among those banned and burned by the Nazi authorities, and that Werfel himself, a Jew, had gone into exile. Seeking access to the German book market from which so many serious writers had been excluded—whether by force or due

[11] "Heimat", Bedir Khan (1968), (without pagination). Some of these motifs appear again in Bedir Khan/Oertel (1937).

[12] E.g.: *Schirokko—und der Heiner weg. Eine dalmatinische Geschichte*, published by the same publisher as *Der Adler von Kurdistan*. Anon. (1939), anon. (1988). Interestingly, after this novel about Kurdish heroes (see below), he went on to write a book entitled *Ein türkischer Freiheitskämpfer: Geschichte eines Lebens* (n.p.) which was not available in German libraries.—Oertel was born in Leipzig, and may have met Kāmurān while the latter was studying there.

[13] In Soviet Armenia, the most prominent Kurdish writer, Ereb Shemo (1898–1978), had published what must have been the first Kurdish novel in Kurmanjī: *Shivanē kurd* ("The Kurdish Shepherd") in 1935, Vanly (1992 b), p. 209. Passages from this novel are reprinted in German by Reso (1978), pp. 87–88.

[14] According to Fuccaro (1997, pp. 308–09), one of the Syrian Dashnak leaders was a member of the Aleppo branch of *Khoybūn*.

[15] *Die vierzig Tage des Musa Dagh*. Wien 1933. The English translation appeared in 1934.

to emigration—was best assured in the form of war-glorification literature. Aside from providing a possible source of income and introducing himself as a Kurdish spokesman, Kāmurān, the image corrector, would have been intrigued by a reading public whose primary or sole impressions of the Kurds had derived from the popular *Durchs wilde Kurdistan* ("Through Wild Kurdistan") by Germany's favourite author of boys' books.[16] The Kurds in this novel are portrayed as a humourously ignorant group possessing, however, many endearing qualities such as honour, bravery, loyalty and hospitality. The Turks, on the other hand, are portrayed as arbitrary and brutal oppressors. Quite possibly, Bedir Khān and Oertel speculated that the interest generated by Karl May's novel would ensure a substantial reading public. In any case, the co-authorship by a writer of adventure books for boys would have facilitated clearance by the censorship authorities.

Kāmurān might have hoped at the outset that he would be able to achieve a novel of the stature of Werfel's with similar benefits in terms of public sympathy generated for the Kurds. But the constrictions of publishing in fascist Germany, the limitations of war glorification, Kāmurān's own lack of experience with the genre of novel, as well as the uninspired writing of his co-author all conspired to produce a propagandistic novel with little, if any, artistic merit. The book is of interest to this study, however, as it represents the attempt to create a new context for the discourse on Kurdish issues using a new instrument, the novel. Moreover, it is a response to many of the issues left unresolved in the aftermath of the premature flight of *Khoybūn* leader İḥsān Nūrī and the failure of the Ararat campaign. It is likely that writing a heroic novel about the Kurdish struggle offered Kāmurān the opportunity to resolve symbolically the anguish of defeat by framing the events in the more positive light which fiction afforded. At the same time, as long as Turkish Kurdistan had not been completely subdued, the Kurds needed—as Ṯüreyyā's analysis of the Turkish press treatment of Kurdish affairs had made clear—a spokesman to present their case to the West. This was ever more true at a time when Turkish leaders were disclaiming the ethnic rights of Kurds, and carrying out policies of assimilation.[17] The

---

[16] Karl May: *Durchs wilde Kurdistan*, 1892.

[17] It is relevant to mention that the situation of Kurds in Syria had deteriorated after the French-Syrian agreement in 1936, with the growing anti-Kurdish propaganda of Syrian nationalists, Fuccaro (1997), p. 318.

role of spokesman was a position to which Kāmurān felt "called". *Der Adler von Kurdistan* ("The Eagle of Kurdistan")[18] was intended, I would argue, to establish his reputation abroad and to continue the tradition of Kurdish propaganda (so ably initiated by Kāmurān's older brother Ṯüreyyā) by transposing it to the level of fiction. Borrowing the genre of the militant nationalist novel, Kāmurān was able to create a textual representation of the Kurds which emphasized their cohesive identity, and legitimated their struggle. The image of Kurds which grew out of the scholarly research and *Khoybūn*'s mobilization activities bore certain similarities to idealized versions of the German nation currently en vogue in Nazi Germany. Portraying the Kurds by means of a code familiar to German readers encouraged the latter to substitute German for Kurd. This was a useful tactic not only in bypassing censorship hurdles but in eliciting sympathy via identification. To this end, he did not disdain to borrow a number of elements from contemporary fascist ideology. It must, however, be clearly stated that Kāmurān cannot be suspected of sympathizing with national socialism. The implications inherent in Kāmurān's "borrowings" are easier for today's reader to recognize.[19]

The "Eagle" is peopled by self-confident paragons of moral excellence, superior to their oppressors in every way except in numbers, financial resources and weaponry. They are patriotic youths whose identity and sense of duty are consonant with the heroic fighting men portrayed in national socialist literature. Individual concerns are insignificant for these heroes, who march with discipline and even desire towards their deaths,[20] which are seen as necessary in the struggle for freedom and nationhood. Their blood will fertilize the soil of their beloved fatherland.[21] Kāmurān's makeover of the Kurds,

---

[18] Hereafter referred to as "Eagle".

[19] One year after the appearance of *Der Adler von Kurdistan*, a book was published in French: *Le Roi du Kurdistan*, subtitled *roman epique kurde* (not available to the author). Emir Kamuran Aali (sic) Bedir-Khan and Adolphe de Falgairolle are listed as translators, which leads me to believe that *Le Roi du Kurdistan* is a translation of the German. Moreover, in the German version, the hero is referred both as an eagle and the king of Kurdistan. Adolphe de Falgairolle wrote novels, nonfiction books and literary criticisms, especially dealing with Spanish literature. He appears to have had sympathies for the anti-Franco forces during the Spanish Civil War. He obviously did not consider Kāmurān's German nationalist borrowings to be offensive.

[20] See Loewy (1969), whose classic analysis of national socialist ideology in the poetry, novels and other writing of the Third Reich, is relevant to an understanding of the "Eagle".

[21] This was one of the main themes of the notorious *Blut und Boden-Dichtung*

which emphasizes their integrity, their will to action and their almost obsessive willingness to make any sacrifice for their fatherland, not only brings the Kurds closer to Germans but also, by inference, sets them apart from two groups reviled in Nazi racist ideology: the "indolent" Orientals as well as the "morally depraved" "Asiatic" Jews; thus the reader might see a parallel between the invading Turks and the Jews.[22]

To do Kāmurān and his co-author credit, the novel is not racist. Whereas T̲üreyyā had striven to draw the racial distinctions between the "Aryan" Kurds and the "Asiatic" Turks, there is scant reference to race ideology in the "Eagle". But the writers fully availed themselves of another, equally opprobrious cornerstone of national socialism: the cult of the leader who embodies the will and historic mission of the nation and thus legitimately demands of individuals voluntary submission to and submersion in the collective. The Kurdish heroes and patriots are thus characterized by their unrelenting struggle to implement their leader's will and their absolute intolerance of nonconformity on the part of their compatriots.[23] Their leader's aims no longer derive solely from opposition to specific oppressors, but rather represent the attempt to purify the fatherland, a Kurdistan which is not only a geographical-topographical entity but also a sacrosanct, mythic-metaphysical force inspiring a love and reverence which exceed even that reserved for the leader.

T̲üreyyā's portrayal of the Kurdish situation had been anchored in the opposition of the evil Turk and the victimized Kurd. The more important opposition in the dramatic framework of the "Eagle" is that of patriot-traitor. The Turks, not once called by name, are referred to only as the enemy.[24] They figure much less prominently in the plot than those Kurds who have not supported their heroic

("Blood and Soil Literature"), where such ideas as "The nation is born in blood" abound, Loewy (1969), p. 154; however, Celādet (Bedir Khān 1934, p. 36) also found favor with such imagery.

[22] Herder had called the Jews an "Asiatic folk foreign to our continent", Greenfeld (1992), p. 383.

[23] Turkish political culture in the 1930's exhibited features associated with Nazi ideology, among them, a similar leader cult, Berkes (1997), pp. 161–162. The leader cult of the "Eagle" is a borrowing from German militaristic novels, but may also reflect Kurdish wishes for a charismatic reader capable of consolidating the Kurds as Atatürk had done for the Turks.

[24] Nor are the words Turkish or Turkey mentioned, a practice initiated by T̲üreyyā (Bedir Khān, 1928 a).

leaders—whether due to ignorance, opportunism or coercion. Blaming Kurdish traitors for the continued oppression of the Kurds is a way to rationalize the weaknesses and failures of heroes and patriots by attributing their failings to the machinations of the inner enemy, a practice indebted to the Nazi demonization of traitors. In post-World War I political discourse, special blame for Germany's defeat in the war and present malaise was placed on politicians who had betrayed their nation[25] and on writers such as Erich Maria Remarque, author of *Im Westen Nichts Neues* (1929), who published anti-war literature which was seen as demeaning the military.[26] In the "Eagle" the imperative to strike the traitors in their midst generates much of the plot.[27]

The existence of the "Eagle" is not acknowledged by scholars of Kurdish history and culture or by nationalist writers[28] despite the prominence and near reverence enjoyed by Kāmurān. The pro-Kurdish German journalist Günter Deschner does mention the title, but falsely characterizes it as a book of poetry and fairy tales[29] confusing it on the one hand with the volume of poetry mentioned above, and having heard perhaps of the Siyabendo tale framed by the preponderantly militaristic novel. The later Kurdish spokesman[30] certainly would not have been anxious to publicize his exploitation of a number of fascist concepts as it could have challenged his democratic credentials.

---

[25] Cf. Loewy (1969), pp. 154–155, on the theme of betrayal and the "Dolchstoßlegende" ("myth of the stab in the back") according to which the German nation would have been victorious in World War I had it not been betrayed by its own politicians.

[26] All such writers landed on the book pyres of 1933, Loewy (1969), p. 11.

[27] Interestingly, traitors also play a large role in Nūrī's account of the Ararat revolt. Although he could hardly remember the details of battle, he remembered very well and related with satisfaction the ill-fated stories of prominent traitors. He devoted an entire chapter to "Kur Hussein Pasha" who though he had been forgiven by *Khoybūn* would surely in Nūrī's estimation meet harsh "divine punishment" for the sin of treason. While Kur Hussein Pasha was merely opportunistic, another traitor, "Tamor Kiskoyi", had not recognized that one did not choose one's nationality—it was decided by birth. The Turks, moreover, no matter how faithfully one served them, would always finally consider a Kurd an enemy, Nouri (1986), pp. 117–126.

[28] This author's attention was attracted by an entry in the bibliography of Nikitine's volume. Aside from the title, Nikitine does not further refer to the novel.

[29] Deschner in his preface to Bois (1985), p. 10.

[30] He acted as a foreign speaker for Barzani and was involved in talks between Iraqi Kurds and Israelis, Ibrahim (1983), pp. 711, 804. He came to Eastern Germany in 1960 on behalf of Kurdish scholars and students, Bedir Khan (1960).

Clearly, behind the rather crude product there was an ambitious project to assemble a new image of the Kurds, by relating the nationalist struggle to the aspects of culture and personality which had emerged from the scholarly pursuits of the Syrian years. The following pages will deal with the writers'[31] efforts to pool their resources of language and information and superimpose aspects of the German model of militant nationalism on the Kurdish quest. There is no way of knowing how positively Kāmurān viewed this temporary juncture of Kurdish nationalism with elements of national socialism. One can only assume that the German model could have had some attraction for kindred Kurds who had also been humiliated by the Great Powers and who would be encouraged by one nation's apparent ability to recover and fight back. Whatever appeal this model had was short-lived and stayed in the realm of fiction.[32] Since the volume is rare, I have gone into greater detail and quoted more widely than would otherwise have been the case. I have largely followed the order of the plot.

[31] It is difficult to assess how authorial responsiblity was shared. For simplicity's sake, I will generally refer to the authors in the plural.

[32] In fact, there was a brief and inconsequential collaboration between Iraqi Kurds (Sheykh Maḥmūd Barzanjī and a member of *Hīva*, Ramzī Nāfiʿ Rashīd) and German military intelligence in the early 1940's. In return for access to the oilfields in Kurdistan the Germans would drive out the British from Iraq and allow the Kurds to establish their own state, Dağlı (1996), pp. 101–118.

CHAPTER THREE

"THE EAGLE OF KURDISTAN": HEROES, PATRIOTS, TRAITORS, FOES[1]

The story is narrated in the first person singular by a young man returning from Constantinople to his native town in Kurdistan.[2] Superficially, the character bears some resemblance to the hero of Werfel's novel who, nearly assimilated after decades of living in France, returns to his fatherland for family reasons, only to be engulfed in the events which are taking place.[3] The town to which the narrator returns has an infectious air of mystery and excitement connected with rumors that a certain Jado and his riders have attacked a garrison and made off with ammunition.[4] Having been absent from

[1] The first chapter is preceded by two lines in Kurdish: "Ne botî me, ne gerzi me, xulamê axa Kurdistan; ne mîrim ez, ne axa me, peyayê dewleta kurdan. B-K." The quote is somewhat unclear; Ludwig Paul suggested the following translation: "I am not from Botan . . . (unclear) I am a slave of the agha Kurdistan; I am not a prince, I am not an agha, but rather a soldier of the state of the Kurds". The German co-author contributed a dedication preceding the text. It reads as follows: "Erich Finger, dem treuen Kameraden zugeeignet: Wer andere recht machen will, muß selbst recht sein, und wer das nicht in seinem Herzen erfahren hat, dem öffnen sich nicht die Tore des Himmels".—I have kept the names as they appear in the German text.

[2] The name "Constantinople" is the only reference to a Turkish city and it is mentioned only this once. Thereafter his previous life in the city is refered to as "in the foreign country" or "among strangers".

[3] Gabriel Bagradian, too, is transformed by the encounter with the smells and sounds of his childhood although he initially resists the pull. But Werfel projects ethnic identity as a powerful if at times latent force which has only to be awakened to exert a decisive, positive influence on character. Bagradian in France had been a somewhat weak character. Returning to his fatherland he becomes an important man. Whereas Bagradian, however, becomes a leader, the Kurdish prodigal son becomes a follower.

[4] The name and the first action associated with the heroic leader of Kurdish revolt, Jado, warrant closer attention. Although the "Eagle" is anything but a faithful presentation of the events at Ararat, Kāmurān does make some allusions to actual occurrences and persons associated with the revolt. It will be remembered that leadership in the Ararat Revolt was shared by İḥsān Nūrī, the *Khoybūn*-sent military leader, and Bro Haski Tello. Jado, in contrast, is neither an educated military man nor a tribal leader. He makes his appearance here as a bandit, attacking government forces and stealing enemy weapons. In fact, the Ararat Revolt had begun under Tello's leadership as a traditional revolt against state authority, and

his native land for many years, the youth is ignorant regarding the identity of Jado and the significance of his actions until his cousin visits him on his first evening home in the fold of the family. His cousin is described as a brave man who hates the inactive life and the narrowness of cities, in contrast to the narrator.[5]

The cousin mediates between the world of Kurdish patriotism and the young Kurd who has forgotten his true identity. This first encounter sets off a process of self-criticism which quickly results in the prodigal's conversion to the Kurdish cause. The opposition of city-country, whereby the land, and in particular the mountains, are projected as the proper life centers and as constituting the essence of Kurdishness, and the cities are referred to as places where life is artificial and inimical to the Kurdish character.[6] The young Kurd's reimmersion in his native culture is as much a revelation as his cousin's clarifications.

"The entire family was collected around the fire. We sang our old songs,[7] which I had not heard for such a long time in the foreign country, and my cousin recounted the deeds of the Kurds. I felt at once frightened and happy. Never before had the love of my country risen so hotly in me. . . .".[8] His cousin, noticing the fervor he has aroused, begins to proselytize: "In this night he spoke enthu-

---

the guerilla bands followed in the footsteps of social bandits. One of the prominent leaders in the Saʿīd Revolt had been a certain Yado, with a reputation for having been a social bandit. After the failure of the revolt, he took up his former lifestyle in the mountains. In the "Eagle", Jado (which would be pronounced Yado in German) several times scoffs at the fact that the government righteously considers him a "bandit".

[5] The heroes and patriots of the "Eagle" are all portrayed as men of action—see Greenfeld's discussion of this ideal in German romanticism, pp. 342–343.

[6] Although the realization that the Kurds must return to their native homeland to truly effect change had been expressed in the early Kurdish journals, this was a pragmatic assessment and not a denunciation of city life *per se*, which is instead a motif of German romanticism.

[7] Songs play an important role in characterizing Kurdish culture and in inspiring and reflecting patriotism in the "Eagle".

[8] The excitement and enthusiasm for the Kurdish cause are associated throughout the novel with images and attributes of fire: glowing, hot, to catch fire, fever, suggesting physical arousal and its satisfaction in action and battle. One of the most influential writers of pro-military bent in the late Weimar period, Ernst Jünger (1895–1998), used similar language to describe the height of emotions involved in battle: "blood boiling in the veins", Loewy (1969), p. 162. Kurdish patriots, however, display such sensations even when listening to talks about the fatherland or battle plans. Loewy interprets the frequent use of fire imagery as follows: "It is no wonder that the metaphors flame, fire and blaze recur again and again. In them undisguised violence is revealed; everything must be destroyed so that the new sun can rise in the German sky", Loewy (1969), p. 239.

siastically of the life of our people who had once been great and brave and now lived under foreign rule. These foreign rulers were our misfortune, having destroyed us by wiping out our entire culture and imposing their will, their customs and language upon us. For this reason it was imperative to gain freedom in any way. He spoke again and again of Jado, who would lead our people to freedom, of his tireless work and persistent struggle".[9]

The first scene is characteristic of the abstract-reductionist tendencies of the novel. Aside from Jado, other characters are rarely called by name. Even the narrator, who is the protagonist, is only once referred to by name. The characters are flat, lacking any individuality; they represent only idealizations or types. Although the language describing the scene in the bosom of the family suggests a number of members, only the mother and the cousin are actually mentioned, and neither by name. His own mother is marginal to the story, present only at the beginning. While significant mother, wife and daughter characters do emerge later in the story, they are not members of the narrator's family, but rather figures in the struggle against the enemy. Only one father (Jado's) is mentioned, but he appears only as a prop on the novel's stage. In the "Eagle", the true family is made up of comrades, and the only authority commanding loyalty and obedience is the leader.[10]

The young man responds to his cousin's appeal to join the battle with the feeling that "the great goal to save our nation was my goal too".[11] He is given the task of bringing help to Jado's wounded brother who has found shelter in a mountain hut. Thus the narrator embarks on a journey which will lead him ultimately to the great Jado in the true heart of his fatherland, the mountains of Kurdistan.

The mountain-hut scene is the first in a sequence of episodes which serve as stages to portray types relevant to the Kurdish struggle and platforms from which to deliver the Kurdish "J'accuse" in speeches on behalf of the Kurdish nation. Here the narrator meets the two pillars of Kurdish society: the warrior and the traditional Kurd. Before he is allowed to meet the model of heroic behaviour, Jado's brother, he first comes face-to-face with the true custodian of

[9] "Eagle", pp. 8–9.

[10] See below for Theweleit's interpretation of why fathers were missing in "volunteer corps" (*Freikorps*) literature.

[11] "Eagle", p. 9.

Kurdish tradition. Arriving at the mountain hut, the narrator makes the acquaintance of the Kurdish shepherd who found and rescued Jado's brother and was now guarding him. This individual embodies the ideal of the distinctly and purely Kurdish man. His physique and clothing are described in loving detail as attesting to the unbroken line of Kurdish tradition. Neither his language (emphatically poetic) nor his religion (decidedly non-Muslim) has been sullied by the foreign occupiers. He represents the virtuous, honourable wild man in his natural habitat, strong by dint of perseverence, loyalty, attachment to his cultural roots and the continuous battle with wild animals and the elements.[12]

> For the first time in a long time there appeared before me a young man of my people, who lived and worked as had his fathers and grandfathers. Out of the gaunt face shone black eyes; he was tall and slender. He wore the wide trousers and tight vest of the Kurds, and over this a coat of fur. On his head he wore the high white *Kolos*, a felt hat.[13] A color-print silk scarf was wrapped around (the hat, MS) with the tip of it hanging down onto his shoulder.[14] His dagger was stuck in his belt and a rifle hung over his shoulder.[15] In his simplicity a proud man of our nation—I thought and immmediately formed a comrade's trust in him.[16]

[12] Actually, as a shepherd and thus at least a semi-nomad, this figure embodies the most representative Kurd qua livelihood and social structure in the novel, but the writers are nowhere interested in realistic portrayal and the stylized shepherd is here the eternal, never-changing Kurd. He is a revised version of Karl May's valiant Kurd.

[13] In Nikitine's summary of various accounts of Kurdish men's dress, which amply demonstrate that there was not a unified Kurdish national costume, there is frequent mention of a white felt hat (1975, pp. 90–92). Karl May's *Durchs wilde Kurdistan* depicts on the front cover a Kurd in traditional clothing, wearing a large white hat. Sykes (1908, p. 477) described the headdress of the Jibranlī men as follows: "An enormous white felt tarbush about a foot high bulging out like a busby; around this is wound a very small turban of silk".

[14] Compare Soane's admiring account of the Mukrī Kurds' rich headdress which consisted of a red hat around which a large, colourful, striped silk scarf was wrapped and held in place by an abundance of sashes (Nikitine, 1975, p. 91).

[15] This is one of several descriptions of dress in "Eagle" which allude to Kurdish dress as having distinctive characteristics. Bruinessen (1989 a, pp. 614–615), traveling through various parts of Kurdistan could not ascertain any traces of a national costume, but rather, great variety in all symbols of separateness, including dress, folklore and cooking. He remarks on attempts in the 1970's by Kurdish nationalists in Turkey to invent a unified Kurdish dress. Behrendt (1993), pp. 30–31 reports on other attempts to determine secondary symbols such as common articles of clothing as support for the case for a common cultural identity of the Kurds.

[16] "Eagle", p. 10.

When the shepherd's first words "Greetings in the name of the god of light"[17] are uttered, the narrator realizes furthermore that "this was a man who did not give a damn about the commands coming from the capital, who spoke exactly as his father had taught him". However, up close the shepherd's face appears to be "fearful, bold and reserved. In his eyes however, the unshakeable wish to be free was reflected clearly".[18] Jado's brother, referred to only as "the wounded" and the "warrior", demonstrates enthusiastic self-sacrifice for his nation and unquestioning admiration for the leader. Despite his terrrible condition, he is humming a Kurdish lullaby, a theme which reverberates throughout the novel. His words are awaited anxiously as if he is about to divulge a "secret", "important news", or perhaps a "legacy".[19] In a monologue[20] reminiscent of battle-rousing speeches, he delivers a justification of the Kurdish struggle and a rather eloquent account of all the little things which arouse proprietary feelings in the true nationalist patriot. This monologue also

---

[17] In a characteristic attempt to depict the Kurds as unified, not only in terms of aspirations, but in history and culture, attempts were made to further distinguish Kurds from their Muslim neighbors by asserting their true religion was Zoroastrianism. The Bedir Khāns did not invent just any claim, but based it on the findings of European scholars, many of whom who had been fascinated by the Yezidis, commonly known as "Devil Worshippers". Layard's detailed account of Yezidi rites had found its way into Karl May's account of the Kurds. Other studies, such as that of Empson (1928), concluded that there were striking similarities between the cults of the Yezidis and the Zoroastrians. The Yezidis were a numerically weak group among the Kurds; the predominant Sunni Muslims often refused to accept them or the considerable Alevi minority as Kurds. However, the manifest dissimilarities between Yezidis and Muslims (although scholars such as Empson had also pointed out many similarities, and Roger Lescot had argued an Islamic origin for the Yezidi religion [Nikitine (1975), p. 226]) made them—in the nationalists' selective perception—a possible link to their true past prior to their being conquered by Islam. To this effect, a piece of leather on which verses had been inscribed relating an eyewitness account of the destruction of the Zoroastrian religion in Kurdistan in the seventh century was fabricated. Ṯüreyyā made the "document" available to Nikitine and thus an additional myth was substantiated, see Behrendt's detailed account of the forgery (1993, p. 59, n. 7). Kāmurān published a study dealing at least in part with the Yezidis entitled "Le soleil noir, Coutumes du pays des Kurdes" in *Hawar* no. 26 (Bois [1985], p. 117, n. 7), and another entitled "Le culte du soleil chez les Kurdes" (Nikitine [1975], p. 231).

[18] "Eagle", pp. 10–11.

[19] "Eagle", p. 13.

[20] Most of the messages of the novel are delivered in speeches which belie the authors' lack of narrative skills, their inability to embed the important messages in dialogue or at least to schedule the speeches where they would make sense—in front of a large crowd, for example, as opposed to an audience of three, as in this scene.

contains two of the main themes of the "Eagle": outrage at being treated like a foreigner in one's own country, and the determination to punish harshly all traitors to the Kurdish cause.

> Not the foreigners who own our lands and have control over us are at fault in our misfortune . . . We Kurds alone bear this responsibility. Many of us have forgotten our grand aspirations in order to gain small advantages. They were rich but they wanted to become richer . . . They entered the service of foreigners instead of remaining with us and fighting at our side, and they accepted pay in foreign currency. They betrayed their nation and the foreigners were glad that there were such men without backbone who sinned against their own blood out of egotism. Only a few remained free and derided all offers. We paid for their guilt with our blood, but our blood, and I know this for certain, will nourish the young tree of freedom. It will grow and one day be strong and its branches will spread out and provide comfort and refreshment for those who have lost their way.[21]

Coughing and choking on his blood, the warrior turns to the programmatic part of his speech, which brings him not only to a description of the battle in which he was so brutally wounded, but also to the second great theme of the novel: dealing with traitors.

"Our unit[22] has set as its goal to fight even more fiercely against the traitors in our midst than against the external enemy. We have decided to proceed against them without mercy for there is no excuse for their actions, and the slowest death is too quick for those whose actions render even the Kurdish infant in his cradle a slave in the hands of the foreigners".[23] He goes on to describe the execution of the first traitor, a Kurdish member of parliament, who, blinded by "foreign money", had forgotten the welfare of his people. With a characteristic concern for image, and consistent with the tradition of honour killings, the executioners had chosen a public place in broad daylight so as not to appear cowardly and "so that everyone could see how the Kurds punished a Kurdish traitor".

---

[21] "Eagle", pp. 13–14.—One cannot help but hear echoes of Sekban's tree imagery in this passage. In this sense the passage is not only a refutation of Sekban's thesis that Kurdish nationalists had produced only destruction but also a threat to traitors of Sekban's ilk.

[22] This is the first mention of the military organization of the Revolt at Ararat and one of the novel's few realistic details, a fact attested in Nūrī's memoirs (1986, p. 44).

[23] The reference to the Kurdish infant hearkens back to the lullaby sung by the warrior.

Appropriately, the café where the parliamentarian meets his friends, other high officials, is a place which denies its Kurdishness. Jado spends the night before the execution with his bride, who lives in this town.[24] Jado's brother, accompanied by his father as well as two other warriors who will later likewise die in patriotic self-sacrifice, enter the café to await Jado, who is to appear disguised as a beggar in order to be able to approach the traitor's table without arousing suspicion.

> Each of us chose a different table, close to the exits. Lost and alone I sat, a foreigner in the middle of the life taking place around me, alone with my thoughts about what we had to do. But this solitude, the many people around me and the danger which grew every second only made me stronger, and more certain about what was necessary. Better to die than lead a life such as this, I thought, and observed the sunny room with revulsion . . . A gramophone played songs, but they were not our songs; people were speaking loudly in confusion, but it was not our language; no one wore our costume. I looked at the many foreign faces which eyed me coldly. 'What do you want here!' I wanted to cry. 'This is our home. Go back where you came from. Can't you see that out there the sky is blue for us? That it is our sun which is shining, that our mountains are greeting us through the open windows and that the mild breeze blowing this afternoon wants to feel us and not you?'[25]

When Representative Emin finally arrives, accompanied by the military commander of the city, Jado's brother notices how familiarly he speaks to the military officer. "He no longer felt that he belonged to us".[26] This insight confirms the narrator's determination. "How right we had judged in the name of all Kurds according to an unwritten law." When Jado approaches the table to ask for alms, Emin

[24] This is one of several loose ends in the novel. The existence of a bride is not mentioned again. Perhaps the reference was a concession to the need to demonstrate Jado's manliness. In Theweleit's study of "volunteer corps" literature (1977, p. 85), which was both an important precursor and mainstay of national socialist literature, he concluded that there were a number of things fighting men were allowed to love: their nation, the fatherland, the soil, the uniform, their comrades, the leader, weapons, battle and animals, but not women. There was no room for erotic relationships. As Loewy (1969, p. 104) phrased it, "The erotic had no place in expedient love relationships which . . . served only to provide the state with children and cannon fodder".

[25] "Eagle", pp. 14–16.

[26] It is tempting to speculate that Representative Emin was modeled after Fevzī Pirinççīzāde, one of the most prominent and perhaps most deeply-resented Kurds who had cooperated first with the Young Turks and later with the Kemalists, see pp. 44, 82–83.

recognizes the "judge of his actions", but before he can defend himself Jado shoots him twice, risking his own life to make sure the traitor is dead before fleeing through the window into the mountains. Covering Jado's flight, his brother is wounded. Then he too, as a true Kurdish warrior, flees to the mountains where the ultimate tests of manhood, battle and death, must take place.

Now, in the mountain hut, he eulogizes his brother. "What were any of us compared to him, the body and spirit of our unit! And what would we be without him! Like a herd without a shepherd and dog would we live without him, abandoned to every sort of force".[27] Even in dying he thinks of the sacred duty of protecting his brother and rises to grab a rifle lying on the table and attack Jado's pursuers.[28]

As the dead hero's eyes are closed by the shepherd, the narrator's eyes are opened. It is the much apostrophized awakening. Appropriately, the next chapter is titled "The Conversion" (*Die Bekehrung*), and describes the epiphany brought on by what the narrator has heard of Jado, the execution of the traitor and the bravery of the dead hero. "It seemed to me that my heart was like a piece of raw iron laid on an anvil, and the last sentences of the young dead man the hammers which beat it to steel". He looks back on the falseness of his life in the foreign city, where everything he had seen, learned and spoken in his fatherland was looked down on, and which had seemed old-fashioned to him too, in his desire to become like the city people.

Although the story contains other episodes concerning the theme of betrayal/treason, the narrator's betrayal is of particular (and historical) significance as it reflects the danger faced by the first generation of cosmopolitan, Istanbul-educated Kurdish youth, to which Kāmurān and his brothers had belonged. They were prone to seduction by the more sophisticated, but "foreign" culture of the capital and thus to being waylaid in their true mission to liberate their nation. In a sense this is also the theme of Gabriel Bagradian, who

---

[27] Loewy (1969), pp. 72–73, describes how, under the Nazis, the element of individual decision was eliminated from manly action. Only those actions were recognized "which had been predetermined in the commands of the charismatic leader".

[28] "Eagle", pp. 18–19.—That a warrior's emotions could range from a kind of ecstasy to frenzy was attested to by many writers who glorified war both as an inner experience which led to manhood and as a means of experiencing an absolute lack of restraint. See Loewy (1969), pp. 153–174.

had been so taken in by the charms of Parisian society, that he had slowly forgotten where he came from.

> Now I saw it clearly: the foreign city had bewitched me with its brilliance and charm. My work had been to write pretty poems for delicate ladies; my task to believe in a religious community which was remote from the actualities of life. My ambition strove to speak the foreign language better than my own, and to forget the language my mother had taught me. I betrayed my country, my friends, the traditions of the fathers; I betrayed my ancestors, and demeaned my race.[29]

Feeling shame that his vanity and need for approval had allowed him to be deceived as to his true identity and to betray his fatherland, he realizes that he must begin a new life. "My Kurdish heart did not belong to me; it belonged to my people". And just as he has made this decision, he is addressed for the first time as Remo, and feels he has "awakened, as though from a dream".[30] With this awakening, Remo acquires an authentic identity and, with it, clear obligations. It is telling that he goes on to announce to his companion that it is their duty to stay and bury Jado's brother and father. Although the shepherd had described finding a dead older man and the dreadfully wounded brother, not once was any reference made to the father. Nor did the dying warrior express feelings of regret or sorrow towards his father—simply that he had been a member of the ring and thus involved in the action. All his feelings, attachments and loyalty are for Jado, and this is his legacy to Remo. The only father to appear in the novel is introduced only to be immediately buried.[31]

The Kurds of the "Eagle" are most musical, with hardly a scene in which some traditional or newly composed patriotic song is not sung, hummed or recited. Most of these songs are presented in their entirety in the text. In the realm of this novel, song is the main evidence of a Kurdish cultural tradition. Although written proclamations and letters make appearances, no reference is made to a literary

---

[29] "Eagle", pp. 20–21.

[30] "Eagle", p. 21.

[31] Theweleit (1977, p. 140) explains the absence of father figures, and the preponderance of mother-figures in volunteer corps literature as a reflection of the ignominious abdication of "Father" Wilhelm II. Although Celādet and Kāmurān's generation might have felt the leadership of the previous generation had missed opportunities and made mistakes, there is no clear indication that the lack of father-figures in "Eagle" had any direct bearing on their self-conception.

tradition.[32] Not all of the songs in the "Eagle" may be attributed to the reevaluation of folk culture discussed above. With the exception of the long Siyabendo tale, the songs and lullabies are, for the most part, of the militaristic sort, glorifying soldierly and nationalistic values, or the leader Jado.

In the night they spend together in the hut the remaining three men hum the lullaby which Jado's brother had been singing earlier, a lullaby in which the mother urges the child to sing so that he "will quickly become a warrior" and then protect her.[33] The functions of bearing and rearing children as well as duties of adulthood are subsumed into the all-encompassing realm of patriotic duty.[34]

> Your mother is here to guard you
> Sleep, so that you may quickly become a warrior
> Sleep, you whom I protect today
> Who will protect me tomorrow.[35]

Now that the awakening of the narrator has been completed, the authors turn to softer means of enhancing the image of the Kurds and substantiating their viability as a nation. The cousin's estate, to which the hero now proceeds, is located not in the rough mountains but rather in a gentle valley full of vineyards, fruit orchards and a small river. The mountain is an important locale and symbol in the novel, but it cannot stand alone. A petition submitted to the League of Nations by the National Central Committee of Iraqi Kurds in August 1930 illustrates that the mode of establishing legitimacy has changed. Practical concerns replace moralistic-legalistic arguments. Five reasons were listed and elaborated on to support the Iraqi Kurds' belief that they had "the right and the ability to form an independent state": 1) the numerical strength of the Kurds 2) homogeneity (in terms of "wit, language, religion, culture, manners and traditions, and even climate") 3) their soil and natural resources 4) "large water-courses" and "other benefits which Nature has bestowed

[32] Khānī, for example, is mentioned only in the epilogue, i.e. not in the novel proper, "Eagle", p. 143.
[33] "Eagle", p. 22.
[34] There are many references in the story to mothers proudly sacrificing their sons in order to save the fatherland, a notion common to volunteer corps and Nazi literature, cf. Theweleit (1977), p. 131, on the strong mother who nevertheless must be protected from the enemy by her sons. As regards the mother as a symbol of Kurdistan, cf. Roosevelt (1988), p. 235.
[35] "Eagle", p. 22.

on our fatherland" 5) the people's awareness "of their strength and destiny".[36]

The chapter titled "After the test" (*Nach der Prüfung*)[37] must be seen in the context of demonstrating and celebrating aspects of Kurdishness that roughly correspond to the points made in the petition above. The cousin's estate is the venue of two quite different, though interrelated congregations. He is host to a large group of guests who are enjoying his hospitality, and also to another group, hidden from their view, who are planning the Kurdish revolt. The first evening, Remo meets only the first group and is happily submerged in the richness and vastness of Kurdish material culture, imagination and folk tradition. The following day, he encounters the superior world of the politically committed Kurdish youth.

[36] [National Central Committee] (1930), p. 348. The third point is worth quoting completely: "Our soil, by its natural resources, can sustain a Kurdish people and a Kurdish state, and even allow its inhabitants to export a by no means negligible surplus. These natural riches consist of grain—corn, barley, rice, maize, and so forth; of petrol in unmeasurable quantity; of wood and coal; of all kinds of fruit; of beasts and all their produce—wool, butter, skins, and so on. In short, our country is reckoned by the best qualified observers to be of the richest in the world".

[37] "Eagle", pp. 24–40. The title refers to the task of bringing help to Jado's brother as a test to be passed before being entrusted with a mission in the Kurdish struggle.

CHAPTER FOUR

CELEBRATING THE KURDS

In one part of the large home, a group of guests are being entertained in opulent style by a flock of servants. Everything about the cousin's home suggests wealth, tradition and high social standing. The renowned hospitality of the Orient, also much touted in Karl May's novel, was an indispensable element in portraying the Kurds to a European public. This scene, however, is obviously intended not just to highlight the hospitable nature of the Kurds but also to draw attention to their vast resources and capabilities. The cousin's house is a repository of the precious legacies of Kurdish culture: Kurdish carpets, weapons, old Kurdish silver, Kurdish linens and silks, and a virtually endless supply of Kurdish food. In fact, everything about the lavishness suggests the trappings of an *agha* or a noble, although this is not explicitly stated.[1]

The rituals and foods connected with the "genuine Kurdish meal" are described in elaborate detail as if to counter the view that Kurds are "wild" or "poor" and to provide local color. Cushions are rolled out on for the guests to sit, and the mutton is served with deference and temerity as it would be humiliating for the host if the meat did not fall, soft and tender from the bones.[2] Almost three pages are required to describe the abundance and richness of the food: various meats, wheat, bread, buttermilk, rice, many kinds of vegetables, a "genuine Kurdish salad" and, when the first round was finished, another started again with more meat, vegetables, followed finally by a description of the preparation of the traditional dessert, and an account of fruits which are so big and firm that they must be cut

[1] The only explicit *agha* figure in "Eagle" is a traitor figure. In the public view the cousin plays the role of traditional *agha* while in private he is a dedicated patriot. This reinforces his introductory function as a mediator between worlds, a sort of undercover agent. He is not portrayed with the pathos awarded to warriors, all of whom—in this novel—fall in battle. Both the cousin and Remo are educated men whose primary role it is to support the battle with mental muscle.

[2] "Eagle", pp. 27–28.

with a saw, and other fruits so delicate that they must be held between the fingers.[3]

The meal is crowned by a performance by two minstrels who sing in antiphony facing one another "as was the custom". The common ways of the Kurds from Persia and Turkey are suggested as one of the singers was from Van; the other from Senne.[4] They sang the "Legend of the Mountain of the Thousand Lakes where the Euphrates has its source". Curiously, the minstrels' tale is narrated, not directly, but by Remo, who describes and simultaneously interprets the reaction of the audience to the legend. "Oh, how gloriously they sang! All of us were glad of heart and with dreaming eyes we gazed at a remote, dimly perceived vista, there where the source of eternal happiness was located, of which the singers sang, and which we had lost". From Hessar Gol (Thousand Lakes, MS) the "glorious plateau", the "happy land", the listeners could see the "eternally ice-covered mountain tops of the fatherland", among them the mountain of Sipan, "which is the protective spirit of lovers".[5]

With this the narrator breaks off his account of the minstrels' song; the guests depart and he retires. In a state between sleep and waking he "hears" the words, "Siyabendo, awaken!" It is not clear whether the minstrels are continuing their tale or Remo is dreaming.

---

[3] In a speech in London where Kāmurān once again sang the praises of his country by focusing on all the aspects which might endear it to a Western country and promote sympathy for the injustice it has endured: the ancient history, the virtues and abilities of the people and its natural resources. The description of the abundance and strength of its fruits surpasses even that in "Eagle", with "40 different kinds of grapes" a bunch of which "weighs from six to ten lbs". The watermelons of Diyarbakır are so enormous that a camel can carry only two of them, and they must be cut with a saw, Bedir Khān (1949, p. 239). The fertility of the land and the strength of its agricultural products remained staples of the argument for the viability of a Kurdish nation. Nureddin Zaza, who had probably been influenced by Kāmurān during their time together at *Radio du Levant*, improved on the portrayal of the productivity of the land, claiming there were over 60 kinds of grapes produced in Kurdistan, Zaza (1982), p. 255.

[4] The singer from Van is described as having blond hair. The singer from Senne (Sanandaj) has brown hair. Many accounts of the Kurds stress that in some areas blonds predominate. See also "Eagle", p. 69, on the white-skinned, blond men of Motkan. Blondness is a feature mentioned by Bedir Khān (1963), p. 23. Distinguishing the Kurds from their Arab and Turkish neighbours he asserts: "The Kurds in general are blonder (or less brunette) than both . . .". Yaşar Kemal, in his preface to the German translation of *Siya Evînê* by Mehmed Uzun, claims that ". . . a considerable majority of the Kurds is blond, has blue and green eyes . . .", Uzun (1998), p. 7.

[5] "Eagle", pp. 30–31.

This is a rather sophisticated twist considering the otherwise striking paucity of narrative devices. Instead of simply recording the minstrels' words as in the monologues, delivering important political messages (such as Jado's brother's speech), the narrator splits the minstrel's narration—focusing at first on the images of the lost Kurdish Garden of Eden the bards have evoked in the minds of their audience, and then removing the legend from the traditional configuration of minstrel and listeners to the realm of imagination and dream. This has the effect of demonstrating how deeply rooted patriotic love and legend are in the imagination itself. In fact, there is another reason for splitting the tale. The legend of the Thousand Lakes is the Kurdish version of the biblical Garden of Eden, where eternal life was lost.[6] This "traditional" tale, however, shares only the venue with Kāmurān's Siyabendo tale, which begins on the mountain Hessar Gol.[7] Kāmurān drew from another traditional tale, Siyabend and Xece.[8] In adapting two tales from the oral tradition to create a version more in line with his nationalist aims, Kāmurān is following in the footsteps of Aḥmad-i Khānī. Like *Mem ū Zīn*, Kāmurān's tale

[6] Published by Herekol Azîzân (Celādet Bedir Khān) in *Hawar* (no. 11, pp. 166–167) as "La Legende de Bingol", cf. Bois (1985), pp. 33–34, 117. The tale relates how a shepherd who saw a wounded serpent emerging from a lake cured of its affliction, runs to tell the ailing agha about the miracle, in the hope that he too may be cured. By the time he returns, however, each drop of water off the snake's body has turned into a lake, making it impossible to find the original body of water.

[7] Bois erroneously translates Bingöl as meaning "rose fragrance" and derives the name from the fact that the place is transformed into a large garden of flowers in the spring. He describes Bingöl correctly as being south of Erzurum and north of Muş. He is referring not to the city but to the mountains of the same name. Bingöl is Turkish for "thousand lakes". Hessar Gol, the name used instead of Bingöl in the novel and in Bedir Khān (1949, p. 238), should not be confused with the lake of the same name south of Elaziğ. In "Eagle" (p. 30) from the "mountains of the thousand lakes" which he designates as the source of the Euphrates, one could see as far as Sipan, a mountain crowned by two stars which is the "patron saint of lovers". In Bedir Khān (1949, p. 238), Kāmurān attributes the two stars to Hessar Gol, which "is considered to be the stronghold of happiness, the refuge of pure and candid love". He then tells the story much as it appeared in *Hawar*, but the ailing *agha* becomes an ailing prince. While the Bedir Khāns obviously took seriously the task of collecting Kurdish folklore it is also clear that Kāmurān was not beyond adjusting the raw material of an orally transmitted tale to fit his conception and the exigencies of Kurdish self-presentation.

[8] Cf. Erdem (1990). Apparently, there are two fairy tales bearing the names Siyabend resp. Siyamend, *EI*, s.v. "Kurds", p. 481.

of Siyabendo incorporates elements from the traditional Kurdish tales but also displays marked differences.[9]

In the epilogue, which will be examined at the end of this chapter, Kāmurān directly appeals to the nostalgia of the reader for lost worlds that existed before the railway and airplane destroyed all mystery, claiming that "the blue flower of romanticism still blossomed . . . on the shores of Lake Van, in the shadows of Ararat, on the Kurdish plateau". Considering both the extent to which the Siyabendo tale and the entertainment scene correspond to the evocation in the epilogue of a romantic, paradisiacal world and the divergence of these scenes from the body of the novel which is firmly embedded in militaristic concepts, it may be safely assumed that these scenes, more than any other parts of the novel, most distinctly reflect Kāmurān's orientation and strategies for presenting Kurdishness: to demonstrate the richness of Kurdish life, portraying a world which not only inspires admiration but a yearning for qualities which lost to more sophisticated, technological societies. The Siyabendo tale, "documents" lyrical patriotism and the perseverence of a traditional Kurdish musical tradition. The tale is not a foreign body in the novel; it contains strong parallels to the characters and plot.

Born on the mountain of the thousand lakes, the orphan Siyabendo grew up in harmony with nature. When he is sixteen, a beautiful young girl traveling with a caravan crosses his path. Peri-Khan has turned to regard an eagle following the caravan as Siyabendo sees her face, more beautiful than nature itself. Without speaking, the two exchange rings and Siyabendo's existence is changed forever. Three years later he is finally driven by restlessness to leave his homeland and search for Peri-Khan.[10] He sets out on the "path his longing showed him, a path without fixed direction", accompanied only by his wild, but fiercely loyal horse, Djalag. He traverses wild and harsh mountain landscapes, facing constant danger from avalanches, wild animals and strong currents, but "a benevolent fate"

[9] The deer, their antlers, the hero's death resulting from the attempt to kill the deer to procure food, as well as the roses at the lovers' grave are elements contained in the orally-transmitted tale. In the traditional tale, Siyabend was a troublesome child who only later became heroic. More striking is the change in name of the beloved from Xece to Perikhan. The significance of the latter name will be discussed below.

[10] This is the way the name is given in "Eagle".

protects him, and the image of his loved one drives him on. For weeks upon weeks he rides in search of the sound of the language spoken by the people in the caravan, which he finally hears in Hewraman.[11] Although the word "Kurdish" does not occur in the tale, the references to language suggest that Siyabendo hears his language all along the way, but with different accents. In a series of steps involving typical fairy-tale motifs such as the recognition of the ring and submitting the youth to a test of manhood, he acquires the consent of the bride to carry her off just before she is to be married. The couple, at last united, flee homeward, pursued by her seven brothers. Once they reach the mountain Sipan, they are safe, but Siyabendo is attacked by a stag he attempts to kill so that Peri-Khan will have something to eat. The wounded animal knocks him off the cliff with its antlers. When Peri-Khan looks down into the gorge she sees her dead lover impaled on tree branches resembling the stag's antlers. Her dreams destroyed, she sings a lullaby "as if at the bed of her child" and plunges to her death, to be with him forever. "At that spot a rose tree grew, every year surrrounded by two butterflies".[12]

Siyabendo's tale both reinforces certain already-introduced themes and foreshadows others. In keeping with the marginalization not to say neutralization of mother and father figures, Siyabendo is an orphan. But growing up alone and educated by the example of nature, he embodies the virtues of the noble Kurdish peasant and, as such, foreshadows Jado. It is not educated men, such as Remo, who personify Kurdish virtues and ideals, but rather the uneducated child of nature, Siyabendo, and Jado, the son of peasants. Siyabendo's journey over unfamiliar, hazardous terrain to take possession of what he knows must be his, parallels the way to Jado and the struggle to take Kurdistan back from its occupiers. The eagle, symbol of the magnificent force of Kurdistan embodied in Jado, is linked with Peri-Khan (who is gazing up at the eagle at the moment Siyabendo first sees her). Thus she becomes associated with the lofty quest for patriotic fulfillment.

---

[11] This is roughly between Sulaymāniya and Sanandaj.

[12] Aside from the exchange of rings and the rose tree growing at their grave, the quest of the lovers for unity echoes themes in *Mem ū Zīn*. In some ways the quest for Peri-Khan is *Mem ū Zīn*'s spiritual journey taken to the mountains. The butterflies, which may be a touch of Sufism, are reminiscent of the moths surrounding the candle in *Mem ū Zīn*.

The name Peri-Khan had a special significance in Kurdish studies of the 1930's, when two tales of fighting women were published. One of these, certainly an invention, told of Perîxan, the young daughter of a murdered Kurdish nationalist, who avenges her father and her fatherland by presenting a bouquet of flowers in which a bomb is hidden to the Turkish governor during festivities marking the Turkish national holiday.[13] A second Perîxan was the widow of an agha, "as intelligent as she was pretty", who took over the "battle against the central government even more doggedly than her husband". Her fame was greater than her husband's and her children were called by her name rather than his.[14]

That Jado must mature before setting out on his mission reflects Remo's own somewhat belated initiation into Kurdish patriotism. Here, too, as in the story at large, the Kurdish landscape has mythical dimensions. It is a primeval force, at once protective and wild, offering shelter and taking its own back again. Death is a return to the beloved soil; death is renewal, new life. Both Siyabendo and Jado die on the mountains: Siyabendo, struggling to feed his bride; Jado, in battle against the occupiers. Both, in dying, spawn new life: in Siyabendo's case, the rose tree; in Jado's, the continuation of the struggle by the Kurdish youth. While the mountain represents a lofty, noble and inexorable force, the duality of the landscape is portrayed:

[13] Bois (1985, pp. 93–95, 121), recounts this tale which appeared in *Hawar* no. 27 entitled "Hevîna Perîxanê" by Nuredin Usif. Other details are even more dubious than the bomb-bouquet. Her father had founded a secret resistance committee in 1907. Perîxan had learned the verses of Khānī's *Mem ū Zīn* by heart as a child, studied the history of the Kurds and collected their heroic deeds. She even had a map of Kurdistan on her wall. The dating is particularly ludicrous, as there were very few Kurdish families with national sentiment at this time. According to this tale, when the bomb exploded, the Turkish soldiers scattered, enabling the "occupied" people to storm the seat of government and raise their flag. Later, Perîxan's corpse was found, her hands still around the throat of the governor.

[14] Cf. Bois (1985), p. 97, on an article by Diya Ferzo (Bruinessen 2000, p. 17, footnote 18, suggests that this may be a pseudonym for Celādet) titled "Perîxan" in *Hawar* no. 40. This practice of naming sons after warrior mothers is referred to in "Eagle", p. 57, and is cited again by Kāmurān (1949, p. 241) as evidence of the special status of Kurdish women. It also finds its way into Nikitine's account of Kurdish women (1975, pp. 99, 102), where he mentions Kāmurān's brief reference to the chief of a tribe who bore the name of his mother, Perîxan. Bruinessen (2000, p. 17) discusses the case of Perikhan Khatun who indeed ruled her Raman tribe after her husband's death until she was succeeded by her son Emin, who became a famous tribal leader and did in fact assume his mother's name. As Bruinessen points out, Perikhan and other powerful Kurdish women were able to achieve such status only through male relatives.

on the one hand rocky, barren and wild mountains; on the other gentle, fertile valleys. Siyabendo originates in the former; Hewraman,[15] where he finds Peri-Khan, is located in the latter. Thus, their union is a wedding of both elements—a theme of the cousin's speech which directly follows the tale—and reflects also the unity of Kurdistan. Similarly, the struggle at Ararat is joined by Kurdish leaders from areas and towns in Iran and Iraq, although the countries themselves are not mentioned. Thus, the boundaries of the homeland are subtly delineated, at least for the informed reader, and this leads into the next chapter.

[15] The beauty of Hewraman was the subject of a lyrical introduction to Kāmurān's study of the Yezidis ("Le soleil noir, Coutumes du pays des Kurdes" in *Hawar* no. 26, pp. 415–418), quoted in Bois (1985), pp. 31–32.

CHAPTER FIVE

THE BATTLE FOR KURDISTAN

The following morning, the narrator is granted brief admission to a group of Kurds whose Kurdish has a strange accent. The group is busy planning the "great revolt" for the following spring (it is now autumn). He is just in time to hear his cousin's long, impassioned speech in which he appeals to all Kurds—represented symbolically by the five present—to invest all their strength in the battle for freedom.

> Kurds must stick together; not even small groups can stand apart. The terms Upper and Lower Kurdistan no longer exist. Foreign flags, foreign passports cannot separate us. The land, the sky, blood and language unite us. The proud man who lives in the mountains and the modest man in the valley must shake hands. The call which comes from every corner of the land must reverberate in all hearts. . . .[1]

"Upper" and "lower" were not just euphemisms for Turkish, Iraqi, Persian and Syrian Kurdistan. Kāmurān may have been alluding to the lack of solidarity between the semi-nomadic tribes (the "proud man of the mountains") and the non-tribal Kurdish peasants. The latter were looked down upon by tribal Kurds who did not even consider them Kurds.[2] Remo's cousin goes on to articulate the imperative of liberation and rebellion, and to justify punishing those whose life plans diverge from the nationalist mold.

"Oaths forced on us by foreign powers are invalid in the face of our duty towards our own fatherland . . . We must come forward as a unified force. No one may be allowed to stand aside. No area, no tribe, and no leader of a tribe[3] may be allowed to act as they see

[1] "Eagle", pp. 41–42.

[2] Commenting on the centrality of mountains in the concept of Kurdish society, Behrendt (1993, p. 49, n. 37) quotes Nikitine (1925), p. 4: ". . . la notion de *kuestân* (montagne, pays montagneux) remplace pour le Kurde l'idée de la patrie, car pour lui tout ce qui est *decht* (plaine) ne peut être habité que par les étrangers . . ."

[3] This is the only mention of tribes in the novel, despite the fact that the majority of the Kurdish population and Kurdish rebels in particular were members of tribes. Fuccaro (1997, p. 310) remarks on the difficulties *Khoybūn* encountered in

fit".[4] After hearing the speech Remo is given a sign to leave—he is not to be told the secrets of the plan. But this does not diminish his enthusiasm for his new role. He realizes that the indulgence and merriment enjoyed nightly by the guests invited to his cousin's house are not "real life"; that was taking place in the study upstairs where plans were being made to liberate the Kurds. Remo is given the task of forming a unit of four warriors with the mission of making their way to join forces with Jado. His unit includes a medical student, a teacher and the son of a peasant. The narrator is both impressed and shamed by their expertise and enthusiasm; they had been active in intelligence service and weapons transports, while he had lived in ignorance and inactivity in the city.[5]

Taking leave of his mother, he tells her, as his cousin has requested, that he is leaving to attend a friend's wedding.[6] For both the narrator and the reader this pretext anticipates the eventual union of Kurdish rebels in the chapter "The wedding begins . . ." (*Die Hochzeit beginnt . . . .*).[7] The first step on their adventurous journey, fraught with dangers, is to acquire rifles, and there is little doubt as to their sublimating function when they are described "as lovely and pure as a spring day".[8] In their first contact with government troops, from whom they are able to seize ammunition, they fight "with the strength of a mountain" and with honour following the motto: "To defeat is heroic; to destroy cowardly".[9] In this and many other scenes the Kurds are shown to behave with clemency and honour towards their enemies, who respond with cowardly, deceitful and brutal treatment. They later pay for their forbearance when enemy troops launch a counterattack in which two Kurdish comrades are killed. Pursued by the enemy, they are aided by Kurds along the way, among them a heroic, fearless young woman, herself active in the Kurdish struggle.

In the Pura Neschat[10] scene, Kāmurān takes up a theme which was at the forefront of his contemporaries' concerns in portraying

mobilizing tribes, due to the military organization which would require tribal leaders to subordinate themselves to centralized command.

[4] "Eagle", p. 42.
[5] "Eagle", pp. 42–45.
[6] "Eagle", p. 46.
[7] "Eagle", pp. 70–87.
[8] "Eagle", p. 48.
[9] "Eagle", p. 54.
[10] The woman possesses the same name as the village which they were about to reach when enemy troops attacked the unit, "Eagle", pp. 54–56.

the Kurds: the heroic, fighting woman.[11] This was not, however, part of the militaristic repertoire, wherein the battlefield was an exclusively masculine domain and the camaraderie of men provided the decisive social and emotional framework. Women acquired significance in this world only as nurses or enemy accomplices.[12] The scene betrays the rather subtle influence of more antagonistic attitudes towards women—so subtle that Kāmurān might not have been entirely aware of it. Pura Neschat, a feminine counterpart of Jado, is a creature of beauty, virtue, power and somewhat ambivalent sexuality. Her desirability as a woman, the sole erotic element in the plot (aside from the Siyabendo tale), is not perceived by the chaste Kurdish warriors whose minds and desires are pure and directed only by heroic concerns, but is reflected, rather, in the dishonourable behaviour of the enemy.

> She must have been in her mid-30's, wearing her full blond hair like a crown. As she approached me the skirt which she wore under her shawl gleamed blood-red.[13] The golden bracelets and necklace told me that she really was a woman, but amidst the men she seemed to be a warrior. She stood fearless, surrounded by her loyal friends, and not one of them considered her less worthy than one of their best comrades. I thought silently: she is surely one of those women of our nation whose sons are given the names of their mothers and not their fathers because the deeds of the women outshine those of the men, like the sun the stars at night.[14]

For her Kurdish comrades, then, the woman commands respect devoid of lust. Although she is not past the child-bearing age she is not portrayed as a mother, but rather as a comrade. Pura Neschat relates to the narrator how, during her husband's absence, an enemy

[11] While Pura Neschat is not actually shown in battle, there are several patriotic women who die heroically in the last battle depicted in the "Eagle": the mother of a Kurdish fighter and four young girls who had disguised themselves as boys in order to be allowed to join Jado's troops, "Eagle", p. 87. The epilogue contains two more references to proud, heroic women who were not only good leaders of their people but also effective representatives of Kurdish concerns with the powers-that-be.

[12] See Theweleit's chapter on "Gunwomen" (*Flintenweiber*) (1977, pp. 96 sqq.); Loewy (1969), pp. 154–156.

[13] It is interesting to compare the description of women's dress in the epilogue where Kāmurān prefers "scarlet" to "blood red" in describing women's trousers (not skirts) worn under emerald-green sashes; Kāmurān later uses "blood-red" to describe the color of roses in Kurdistan, "Eagle", p. 142.

[14] "Eagle", p. 57.

commander had abused her hospitality. She had offered him accommodation for the evening according to the etiquette of hospitality. Exploiting the proximity of his room to hers, he had made sexual advances. When she realized his intentions she called for help, and her servants defended her and tied the evildoer to a tree. When her husband returned, he admonished the officer for showing a lack of respect for Kurdish hospitality and turned him loose. For this, her husband had been imprisoned, another example of how Kurds are punished in the end for their merciful treatment of the enemy.

The episode entails some ambivalence. If the woman was strong enough to fight in battle, why was she not able to defend herself? The prurient reader might ask what a beautiful young woman might have been thinking, to lodge the enemy at such close quarters. And the husband's reaction seems too mild considering that defending a woman's honour was a maxim of the Kurdish code of honour. The incident is one of several which betray a certain tension between the various interests of the authors. The woman-warrior was becoming a staple of Kurdish self-presentation, but did not easily fit the format of German popular literature of the period.[15]

After an arduous and perilous journey, during which they constantly fear being caught by government troops, Remo and his unit finally approach the area where they are to meet Jado. It is a dramatic moment in the plot and a pause is interjected. The narrator and his friend take time to mourn the comrades lost on the way, and to reflect on the significance of dying for the fatherland. Remo is sad that his friend Khurshid, killed when they had seized the enemy's munition, will not be there to meet the great Jado. On the other hand, he tells himself, his friend's deed had probably made it possible for them to get so far. "The sacrifice of his life meant the realization of our deed". In honour of their dead comrade they sing a funereal, dirge-like song which had been one of Khurshid's favourites, about orphan children weeping in front of burned village walls and about the hope that the evening wind bringing coolness from the lands of the East will also bring a happy message.[16]

They find Jado in a clearing under a mighty cliff. The place is like a "landscape of giants" and an "eagle's nest", and Jado is the

---

[15] However, such near-rape incidents were frequent in volunteer corps literature, cf. Theweleit (1977), pp. 132–133.

[16] "Eagle", pp. 64–65.

"Eagle of Kurdistan". His dignity is compared to that of a prince, his leadership to that of a shepherd. A "clever judge", "star of stars", "king of kings" and "hero of heroes", Jado is of peasant origin, but "his soul comprised the entire nobility of Kurdistan". This, the narrator marvels, was "the man for whom the mothers of Kurdistan bore children".[17]

Jado's comrades are warriors from all over Kurdistan, famed for deeds already commemorated in songs. "The people who were close to Jado had to be beyond reproach in every respect. He had to be able to ask the utmost of each. Valour alone was not sufficient". There follows a long list of regions and tribes represented in Jado's army. In these pages the mental map of Kurdistan is extended into Persia and Iraq, but not into Syria or the Caucasus.[18] There are fighters from Urmiya, Senne and Khoy in Persia, from Hewler (Arbil), Rewandis (Rawanduz) and Barzan in Iraq, Dersim and Botan in Turkey. Here, as elsewhere in the novel, local patriotism is characterized as something unifying rather than divisive. The only differences amongst the Kurds are attributed to the different landscapes, handicrafts, and natural products of their home regions. In their interests and goals, however, they are of one mind. Dersim[19] is characterized as the "holy land . . . as the western birthplace of the Kurdish religion. They venerate Zoroaster, who worships light. Sacred are the waters of the land of Dersim, sacred its fires, sacred its forests".[20] The author allows himself some local patriotism by characterizing Botan, the home of the Bedir Khān family, as the "land of the giants".[21]

Remo has arrived in time to be involved in crucial preparations for the spring revolt. However, the battle is first to be carried out in the realm of propaganda. As the enemy has already been informed of their plans, Jado has written a proclamation containing the rebels' demands. By seeming willing to negotiate, he hopes to deter the

[17] "Eagle", pp. 66–67.

[18] The map inserted in "Eagle" (pp. 136–137) seems somewhat arbitrary. The word Kurdistan does not appear, nor do many of the locales which figure in the novel such as Kulp, Mush or Hewraman. The map, which depicts a large section of Asia from the Mediterranean to the Caspian Sea, provides only a vague orientation.

[19] In this area, resistance to the Turkish government was still being conducted when the "Eagle" was written.

[20] "Eagle", p. 69. Kāmurān returns to this theme of an original, non-Islamic Kurdish religion in his epilogue to "Eagle". He later dropped this particular distinction between the Kurds and their Muslim neighbours.

[21] "Eagle", p. 69.

enemy from sending larger units to the area. Remo's first task is to distribute the proclamation throughout Kurdistan, making sure it reaches all governmental offices. The proclamation, consisting of a list of grievances and demands and a call to the Kurdish people is a conglomeration of all the arguments employed by recent Kurdish agitation. This is clearly one of the sections almost exclusively conceived by Kāmurān, in apparent disregard of Nazi categories and priorities, indicating that he was unwilling to abandon completely Kurdish self-representation to the constraints of analogy. Thus, specific Kurdish concerns such as their endangered language and culture and their recent history, otherwise almost totally absent from the novel, are articulated here.

> No foreign nation has the right to rule Kurdistan. The powers who live as occupiers in our country never conquered Kurdistan. Kurdistan concluded agreements with these nations. It is a historically undeniable fact that Kurdistan always faithfully adhered to these alliances, and fulfilled its obligations. But the foreign powers constantly intervened in internal disputes among the princes and tribes, exploiting them for their own purposes. In this way the power of the country was broken, and out of the agreements grew step by step an illegal occupation.[22]

After establishing the illegitimacy of Turkish[23] rule and renewing the argument for separation, which was at least as old as Khānī (that the Turks had taken advantage of disunity among the Kurds, and impeded their development), the proclamation goes on to describe contemporary oppression.

> In the last 15 years, the situation has deteriorated to the point that even the existence of the Kurdish nation as an entity ("Volkskörper") is denied. In all the cities of Kurdistan the Kurdish language is forbidden by the foreign powers. Kurdish records have been destroyed; magazines, newspapers and books forbidden. The possession of a book in Kurdish is considered a punishable offence. Singing Kurdish songs is viewed as a crime. Two thousand Kurdish schools have been closed, places in which the Kurdish language, literature and history were taught. One hundred and fifty thousand children wake up with no schools of their own. All Kurdish clubs are closed, their members

[22] "Eagle", pp. 71–72.

[23] Even though some of the historical argument applies to Persia as well, the authors are obviously referring here to the Turks, as the ensuing list of grievances demonstrates.

arrested or sent into exile. The possessions of those arrested have been confiscated. Local industry is completely destroyed. The smallest incident suffices to bombard settlements and kill defenseless women and children. This situation cannot continue. The Kurdish people demand recognition as an ethnic group. Nationality is a secondary question. The Kurds demand freedom of language, culture and the press; moreover, the reopening of schools or at least two hours' daily instruction in the Kurdish language. These are the minimal demands of the Kurdish people. The Kurds would rather die than tolerate a foreign language, a foreign culture and a foreign race as rulers. The Kurds have no further demands. They wish merely to act as they see fit regarding their own land, the hereditary, ancient possession of their princes. They hold no enmity towards the powers presently occupying it. As soon as the foreign governmental posts disappear, the Kurds will live in peace with the present rulers.[24]

These moderate demands, reminiscent of the remonstrances following the Turkish subdual of the Saʿīd Revolt, appear somewhat incongruous in the context of the militancy of Kurdish warriors in "Eagle", expressed in the speeches of Jado's brother and Remo's cousin, and suggests there may have been some discord between the authors on this point. The narrator, reading the petition, remarks that the demands "seemed to me still very mild".[25]

But the following paragraphs, which address "the Kurdish people themselves", are very much in keeping with the rhetoric of the "speeches". Weaving together the themes of the inextricable unity of landscape and people, and the strength and will of the "race", raised by its mothers to fight and die for the country, the authors formulate the essential case for Kurdish independence.

At the sources of the Euphrates and the Tigris, there where the Mountain Ararat, upon which the ark of the new men beached very long ago, soars into the sky, lives the nation of the Kurds. Uncontrollable in our striving for freedom, confined by foreigners, we have been fighting a heroic battle since time immemorial for our own way of life and independence—a battle for our freedom, for the simple right of every proud and decent nation: to belong to itself and to be allowed to govern itself. In the valleys and meadows of the Taurus Mountains lives an austere and strong race which has been made strong in the clear and dangerous mountain air in which the eagles, too, live. As long as just one Kurdish heart beats in longing for liberation, the flags

[24] "Eagle", pp. 71–73.
[25] "Eagle", p. 73.

> of freedom will flutter on the never-conquered mountains. Strict mothers raise a hard race here: With your shield or on it is the motto that they pass on to their manly sons as they go off to battle.[26]

In his speech before sending his warriors off to mobilize for the revolt, Jado reminds them that they will encounter Kurds who do not understand what they are fighting for. But Jado's warriors should not forget that "we embody the will of the Kurdish nation. Perhaps we will not reach our goal this time, but when the banner of freedom moves just a few steps forward, that too is a victory and the blood of all Kurdish heroes who died for their fatherland will not have been in vain". He reminds them that the "sacred blood" of all fallen Kurdish heroes will "fertilize the earth" and proclaims that "the wedding feast of the Kurdish nation has begun". The marriage metaphor implies that the individual achieves fulfillment only in battle for the fatherland, that the true objects of his affections are his land and comrades. All are obliged to merge in this "wedding", a union which supercedes all other bonds and relationships. Thus united as one will, one body, their blood sacrifice will conceive the precious child, freedom.[27]

As Remo rides off on his new mission, his gaze sweeps over "Kurdistan, my fatherland. These were our mountains, and I loved them no less because they were rocky. The valleys far below me were our valleys and the fruit harvested by Kurdish farmers was our fruit . . . I swore that I would do everything I could for this land which was more sacred[28] than my life".[29]

Rejoining forces with Jado, in a surprise attack the Kurds manage to assume control over a Kurdish city (Muş) occupied by government and military officials. Availing themselves of the telegraph, they are thus able to send the proclamation directly to the government. The town is rapidly transformed, with people expressing their newly-found freedom by singing Kurdish songs and performing tra-

---

[26] "Eagle", p. 73.

[27] "Eagle", pp. 74–75. See Loewy (1969), pp. 153, 158 on images of war and fertility. On the wedding of "Volk und Führer" see Loewy, pp. 264–265.

[28] References to religion are not common in "Eagle". However, in İḥsān Nūrī's account, Kurdish fighters were said to have begun to treasure their black cliffs as much as the black stone of Mecca. And in the "National Kurdish Song of the Agri Revolt", the mountain is said to have become "the Mecca of the Kurds" (1986, pp. 65, 98).

[29] "Eagle", p. 76.

ditional dances, donning Kurdish costume and raising the Kurdish flag which had been buried in old chests.[30] Members of Jado's group assume the administration of the city, and everyone comes to Jado, who listens to their petitions. Meanwhile, their show of strength convinces many Kurds from the surrounding area to join forces with them. Equipped with weapons seized in this garrison town, the recruits are a welcome addition to Jado's fighting forces. As the narrator views them, he begins to imagine the battle in which their efforts will culminate. "I had the feeling that we had become an army which would not be so easy to beat. I saw before me the mountains and the battle that we would fight there, man against man". Remo makes the rounds, talking to people, and reports back to Jado how satisfied everyone is with developments. Jado seems pleased, but the narrator realizes their leader would not have wavered even if this had not been the case.[31] Jado's near indifference to popular support indicates the firmness of his conviction that he has the prerogative to make decisions for his people. It must be remembered that, in Muş, Jado is no longer merely a military commander but has taken over the administration, thus providing a preview of what a liberated Kurdish city would look like. If Muş is any indication, citizens will not be governing themselves, but rather accepting orders from their charismatic leader, who will carry out his mission without consultation or accountability.

Several historical incidents are reflected in the course of events taking place in Muş.[32] In an attempt to create detente and initiate negotiations with the rebels at Ararat, the Turkish government in 1928 "stopped deportations and suspended executions". In a letter to Haski Tello, the tribal leader who was the "governor" of Ararat, the Turkish governor offered amnesty if the Kurds would give up their pointless battle,[33] arguing that "We are all Muslims and you live in the mountains like bandits".[34] According to Kutschera's account,

[30] Since flags were the most common of national symbols, it was desirable that they, too, be "traditional". Although the Kurdish flag is described as an antique object handed down through families, in fact it was allegedly created during the brief existence of *Kürd Teşkilāt-i İçtimāʿīye Cemʿiyeti*, of which Kāmurān was a member.

[31] "Eagle", pp. 77–83.

[32] In the following I rely on the only two sources I am aware of which relate these incidents: İḥsān Nūrī (1986) and Kutschera (1979). The latter probably based his account on Ṯüreyyā's books.

[33] Kutschera (1979), p. 95.

[34] Nouri (1986), p. 78.

Haski Tello refused the offer, admonishing the government for thinking the Kurds stupid. "We have had experience and know the world. The wild man exists no longer".[35] İḥsān Nūrī's account of the refusal is less motivated by image correction, and has a more truthful ring. He points out that it had been only the threat of deportation by the government which had forced him to leave the comfort of his home and flee to the mountains "to find security beneath the cliffs of Agri".[36] İḥsān Nūrī was also approached by Turkish government representatives and offered promotion in rank, a pension and a posting to a European capital. He also declined the government's offers.[37]

In a telegraph from the president of the government, Jado receives an offer of pardon provided that his troops depart from the city they have occupied. Jado is much chagrined at the use of the word "pardon". "Since when do the guilty pardon the innocent? We are fighting for our land, for what belongs to us . . . If we had touched as much as one stone of your possession, you would have the right to speak thus". The government responds to his indignant protests with an offer of high positions in the administration for Jado and his friends. This offer is icily refused. "This is not about personal ambition. We are talking about the survival of a nation". The government's next step is to send airplanes which distribute leaflets warning the population to refrain from involvement with "rebels" and "bandits", who will soon be defeated by the government. Jado's response to the government action is the Kurdish proverb: "Lion, put your faith in your paws".[38]

Despite their success, Jado's forces feel obliged to depart from the town in order to spare it reprisals. They withdraw to Ararat, where preparations continue for the great revolt, organized by men who would be the "nucleus of the coming government of our land if we are victorious". Jado assigns Remo to the communications department because "Words come easily to you and the feather in your

[35] Kutschera (1979), p. 95.

[36] Nouri (1986), p. 78.

[37] According to Kutschera (1979), p. 96, the Turkish *kaymakam* made this proposal. In his memoirs, İḥsān Nūrī (1986, pp. 91–92) describes a visit made to him by a Turkish delegation which included two members of the National Assembly and several officers who had been his friends in Istanbul.

[38] *Eagle*, p. 85. Part of the academic agenda of the Kurdologists was the study of proverbs. The most frequently quoted Kurdish proverb was this one. For Bois (1985), p. 102, who had argued that Kurdish adherence to the *sunna* was rather marginal to their everyday life, this proverb indicated that the Kurds relied on their own strength and did not wait for divine assistance.

hand does not quickly dry up". In his new function, which corresponds to the division of labor envisioned by *Khoybūn*[39] (with the difference being that *Khoybūn* carried out these activities outside Kurdistan), the narrrator comes into contact with foreign newspapers and is astounded "how little understanding for us there was out there in the world. Hardly anyone understood what we were fighting for. From the security of their own lives they wrote of 'robbers' and 'blood-thirsty savages'". The Kurds also publish their own newspaper on Ararat.[40]

Remo is pleased with his hard work, pleased to belong to the "great" Kurds who were the workers and peasants (plus a few members of the nobility) working on sacred Mount Ararat for the good of their nation. He belittles those scholars, scientists and teachers who aspire only to their own advantage. They have names in the big world but are small in the eyes of the patriots of Ararat.

Three dramatic episodes precede the last battle on Ararat, each dealing with a different prototype: a traitor, a hero and a heroic mother. The narrator is ordered to travel to the city of Beyazid[41] to extend the communications network. One of his contacts there is a Kurdish composer who has just completed a freedom song to celebrate the impending spring revolt. Although the texts of other songs have been presented to the reader, this song, surprisingly, is left to the imagination. Instead of the song, the reader hears the remarks of the composer, which are relevant to the subsequent betrayal scene. As the short monologue employs the image of a tree and roots as a simile for a man and his companions, one is tempted to interpret the passage as an allusion to Sekban's departure from the nationalist camp and the three-trees passage which illustrated his criticism of Kurdish nationalism. "Behold how strangely similar the things of the world are. A man puts his life behind him year by year as does a tree, which sprouts branch by branch; and the friends he loves are the earth on which he stands. In them are the roots of his strength. He cuts off his own support when he rashly jeopardizes genuine friendships, thus losing himself and his friends".[42]

---

[39] Nouri (1986), p. 44.

[40] "Eagle", pp. 98–99. İḥsān Nūrī (1986, p. 122) relates that a newspaper handwritten in Kurdish called *Agri* was distributed at Ararat but, due to the lack of paper, there were few copies.

[41] This corresponds to Doğubeyazıt.

[42] "Eagle", pp. 104–105.

Just as he has finished these words, the comrades learn that one of their friends, Tello, after being arrested and tortured, has given information about their weapons depot to the enemy. The group includes Tello's brother and ersatz father, whose first impulse is to liberate his brother. The comrades, however, make him appreciate the necessity of swift and radical punishment. Remo is to participate in the execution of the "blood-brother" who, although himself a martyr, must be punished. "Terrible was the law of necessity, indescribably terrible". The traitor himself, when he sees the group the following day, commands that they shoot him. True to the conventions of "Eagle", the enemy is spared but not the traitor in their midst. The boy is executed, but his persecutors are not attacked.[43]

In the tale of Atman and his mother the two authors' intentions and strategies merge effectively. First, Atman, who had been commanding troops bringing supplies to Ararat is ambushed by the enemy. After prolonged battle, only Atman and his servant (who lives to tell the tale) remain. They take refuge in a cave and, just as they have found a passage which would lead them to freedom, the hero is seized with a yearning to fight to the death rather than retreat and face Jado emptyhanded. "The cold corpses of the victimized comrades seemed warmer than his own life".[44]

Subsequently, the enemy captain calls Atman's mother to the village square and empties a bag at her feet which contains the bloody head of her son, asking her if she recognizes it. Instead of weeping, she answers stoically, with "the pride of all the mothers of our land": "I know the head. It is the head of a lamb but the rams up in the mountains will continue to live" on.[45] When Jado hears the story he

[43] "Eagle", pp. 106–112. There were many instances in Germany of members of the *Freikorps* (volunteer corps) or secret national organization taking it upon themselves to execute comrades whom they had accused of treason, usually for revealing the locations of weapon depots, Theweleit (1977, p. 35). What is emphasized in the Tello episode is the inexorable nature of the laws which transcend the dictates of personal survival and the ordinary loyalties of family and friendship. Tello is obviously a more sympathetic figure than Representative Emin, and thus is allowed to die proudly. But the unhesitating conviction of his executors recalls the words of Jado's brother at the outset of the story, that Jado and his men are determined to "pursue Kurdish traitors even more relentlessly than the enemy", "Eagle", p. 14.

[44] "Eagle", p. 116.

[45] "Eagle", pp. 119–120. Cf. Theweleit (1977), pp. 133–141, for tales of heroic mothers who do not cry in volunteer corps literature. Significantly, such mothers are never one's own. In volunteer corps literature the mother image is split: the narrator's own mothers were soft and loving while the hard side is represented in

decides to punish the offending Turkish officer who, he learns, is residing at the house of a Kurdish *agha*. Immediately winning over the magnificently garbed bodyguards of the *agha*, Jado gains access to the *agha*'s "castle" and is reproached by the *agha* who hears of his intention. "Punish? What do you mean punish? Who gives you the right to do this? You mean to violate a man who is my guest? You call yourself a Kurd and you do not honour the law of hospitality?" This is a remarkable scene in that it is the only one to juxtapose Kurdish freedom fighters with an *agha*, who represents a world which, in its organization and mentality, stands as squarely in the way of Kurdish national aspirations as does any foreign nation. In vain does the *agha* invoke the traditional, tribal code of honour to ward off Jado's vengeance. The *agha* is shot by his own freshly converted bodyguards, who announce that although their ancestors had served his ancestors, from this day on they wished to serve their people. Thus the conflict of the two value systems is resolved. The point is not that the law of hospitality had lost substance for loyal Kurds,[46] but that the patriotic code was absolute and supreme. While the Kurdish traitor is swiftly and harshly dealt with, the enemy is awarded a manly death. Jado scorns the captain who reaches for his pistol. "You, as a soldier and I as a bandit—for this is what you call me—yes, we can tolerate pain longer". They do battle with daggers rather than the cleaner, swifter pistols, and it sounds as if "two rams were locking horns". When the officer lies dying at his feet, Jado, himself seriously wounded, remarks thoughtfully, "You are lucky your mother cannot see you in this condition".[47]

Offending Atman's mother is the only crime apart from betrayal, for which retribution must be direct, swift and uncompromising. In

---

the "iron" mothers of fallen comrades. Theweleit discusses also the absence of fathers in this literature, either as heroes or important opponents, as a result of the disgraceful abdication of Kaiser Wilhelm II. "The father had failed: they (the sons, MS) now strove to be his successor with Mother Germany".

[46] The hospitality of the Kurds was a *topos* of Kurdish portrayal in the accounts of scholars, travelers and the Kurds themselves from the 19th century on. In several scenes, the authors of "Eagle" depict Kurdish patriots trying to harmonize traditional etiquette with the demands of their struggle. In one scene, Remo and his comrades learn from their host that there are enemy soldiers in the village who are transporting weapons. The youths decide immediately to attack the *agha*'s house where the soldiers are staying. Their host discovers their plans and accuses them of abusing his hospitality. He points out that he and the entire village will suffer from their actions. The Kurdish fighters postpone their plans, "Eagle", pp. 50–52.

[47] "Eagle", pp. 122–124.

comparison, the punishment of Pura Neschat's would-be molester is very mild. Mothers are sacred, not because of individual ties—as we have seen, aside from Atman's mother no other figure is portrayed with respect to a parent figure—but because of their lofty function of raising and then sacrificing sons for the fatherland. So Jado, who has not once spoken of any familial ties, after avenging the offender of his comrade's mother Nessrin, visits her. Embracing her brings forth a torrent of emotion which surprises the narrator. "Can a man like Jado cry? He cried like a child. A long while they held on to one another and tears rolled over their faces". Wordlessly, Nessrin removes her scarf (symbolizing her role as wife and mother) and cuts off all her hair (her womanhood). With directions to the remaining family members—a child and a man referred to as uncle—that her hair be buried with her son's head should the burial place become known, she leaves her family to join Jado.[48]

United with the mother figure, and accompanied by several young girls who have earlier joined the group, Jado's forces set out for Ararat. The mountains are full of enemy troops and the warriors realize Jado has decided that "on this mountain our fate would be decided". In the ensuing battle many comrades fall, including the girls. Nessrin kills herself rather than fall into enemy hands: Finally, Jado is mortally wounded. Before shooting himself in the head he commands that his comrades carry his head to another valley and bury it there so that he will remain the "terror of the Kurdish mountains which can never be conquered". He dies full of optimism, "The land will remain. Our people will live".[49]

The story ends fittingly with a burial, much as it began. Remo lays Jado's brother's ring in the grave. Finished with the burial, the comrades hear voices. "From West to East, the Kurdish youth came down from the mountains. The rising sun of the young day shone in their faces. From a thousand directions echoed in the mountains the song of the Kurdish freedom fighter from their fresh lips".[50]

---

[48] "Eagle", pp. 126–127.
[49] "Eagle", pp. 130–134.
[50] "Eagle", p. 135.

CHAPTER SIX

"EPILOGUE": THE GLORIES OF KURDISTAN

If *Der Adler von Kurdistan* focused on the heroic battle for freedom, the "epilogue" (*Nachwort*) to the book is a sweeping argument for the singularity and charm of the nation, its people and landscape. Ostensibly leaving the realm of fiction, the author offers the German reader a frame of reference for perceiving the Kurds: nostalgia for a world which existed before technical progress, the railway and airplane destroyed all mystery. But the "blue flower of romanticism"[1] continues to blossom "on the shores of Lake Van, in the shadows of Ararat, on the Kurdish plateau". But, notes the author sadly, "Who knows anything of Kurdistan? Was the name not mentioned at the peace negotiations? Didn't one hear of Kurdish revolts?".[2] As in the "Eagle", the words "Turkey" and "Turks" are not mentioned—only a fleeting reference is made to the government and soldiers. Kurdistan is spoken of as if it were *de facto* free and prosperous, in full possession of its resources, developing its potential. Kāmurān speaks of the Kurdistan which might have been as if it really existed.

Lest the reader ultimately be unable to identify with the image of single-minded if virtuous fighters lacking the charms and comforts of a familiar civilization, the author uses the "epilogue" to round out the image of Kurdish culture, reiterating some points not made in the novel proper, that would have been out of place in the austere here and now of revolutionary struggle. He locates Kurdish society between the poles of tradition and progress, embodied by two groups: peasants and educated young men. But at the heart of the distinction between Kurds and others is their authentic religion; while not explicitly denying they are Muslims, he insinuates they are not.

Reducing controversies as to the origins of the Kurds to a debate on whether Kurdistan had been the "cradle of humanity" or a "refuge

[1] "Die blaue Blume der Romantik" refers to the ideal society longed for by the Romantics, see Greenfeld (1994), p. 342.

[2] "Eagle", p. 138.

for dispersed Aryans" he turns to the living proof of the unchanging legacy of the past, the Kurdish peasant, who still "sowed and harvested in the manner of his ancestors and prayed with hands raised to the sun".[3] One of the Bedir Khāns' contributions to the delineation of Kurdish identity had been their contention that the true religion of the Kurds was Zoroastrianism, a religion which the Kurdish peasant supposedly still practiced. "The sun cult of Zoroaster is alive here, which affirms the great and wonderful life and wishes to know nothing of promises for the future and the reward of paradise for death". Though Zoroastrianism as a religion had the advantage of allowing a clear-cut distinction between Kurds and Muslims, Kāmurān had only a weak case for this claim: the small number of Yezidis whose religion was said to derive from Zoroastrianism, and various references made by European travelers and scholars who referred to other pagan or Persian survivals.[4] This was not an idea which had any lasting effect on the course of Kurdish nationalism,[5] proving that you cannot invent just any nationalism.

But the future of Kurdistan is not in the hands of the venerated peasants. Nor is the romantic land of Kurdistan only a place of nostalgia. On the contrary, Kāmurān does not hesitate to attach any attribute of modern Western society to his Kurdistan of the mind. The Kurdish reality he purports to describe is an exercise in wishful thinking.

> We are Aryans, stress the young Kurds who prevail in the cities of the land, who studied at European and American universities and work for freedom. Scholars confirm that they are descendents of the Medes, the oldest proven pure Aryan race. Appearances convince even the layman. The customs of the Kurds are pure . . . their movements have a rare vitality in the indolent Orient.[6]

Another aspect particularly dear to his heart is the subject of the importance of women in Kurdish society. In the novel, this aspect

---

[3] "Eagle", p. 139.

[4] E.g. Sykes (1908), p. 467, who found most of the Dersim tribes to be ". . . apparently Pagan, who call themselves Shias, their religion as far as I could ascertain, being a mixture of magic and nature worship, which again develops into Pantheism".

[5] There would not have been many Muslims prepared to identify with a pre-Islamic, pagan past. Sykes (1908), p. 454, found, for instance, that the Baban Kurds deeply revered their patron saint who, they said, had "converted them from Paganism and the worship of fire".

[6] "Eagle", p. 139.

was touched on only in the episodes of Pura Neschat and Atman's mother. Not to be outdone by Atatürk's progress in liberating women from the veil and other restrictions, he emphasizes that not only do modern Kurdish women walk free and unveiled, but throughout Kurdish history women have assumed important roles. He elaborates again on the ʿĀdila Khātun story and adds to it the story of Black Fatima who had allegedly led an army against the Ottomans in Erzurum.[7]

Kāmurān paints a picture of Kurdistan very much at odds with the reality of Kurdish cities, villages and the countryside devastated by revolts, deportations and neglect. For him, Kurdish cities represent a synthesis of traditional architecture and beauty, the sweet smell of ripening fruit, the sound of water rushing in fountains, with European style-houses, electrical appliance shops and a telephone booth on every corner.[8] Ever conscious of having to convince and charm the West—as Sekban had remarked only the living, blossoming tree will be admired and pitied if it falls ill—Kāmurān opts for imaginative enhancement.

In the pages of the "epilogue", Kāmurān expresses the Kurdish argument in the tone and rhetoric he and others would use for at least the following decade, stressing less the political aspects than the inherent virtues and abilities of the Kurdish people, their great cultural achievements and the rich resources of their land. He vigorously disputes the idea that the Kurds were "professional murderers, as people like to claim of the Kurds", or bound by the laws of vendetta, and provides examples to the contrary. Kurds were brave, honourable and freedom-loving, but also fair and forgiving towards their enemies.[9]

If he leaves the reader with a lasting impression of Kurdistan, it is less the figure of the dying Jado, surrounded by heroic freedom fighters, than the nation of arts and crafts, carpets, dance and song,

[7] "Eagle", pp. 140–141. Black Fatima was Kara Fatima Khanum, the female head of the Maraş tribe, who brought 300 fighters to İstanbul to fight alongside Ottoman troops in the Crimean War, as a proof of Maraş loyalty. In this way, Kara Fatima Khanum hoped to persuade the Sultan to free her husband from imprisonment, Bruinessen (2000, p. 15). Bruinessen's article is followed by a text from the *London Illustrated News*, entitled "Kara Fatima in Constantinople", April 22, 1854.

[8] "Eagle", p. 140.

[9] "Eagle", pp. 143–144.

a people which has survived the centuries with its authentic soul intact. In their alleged beliefs concerning the struggle between light and darkness, Kāmurān finds a metaphor for the Kurdish-Turkish struggle.

> Even today, the old Aryan light religion of Zoroaster is alive among the people. Everywhere, the primeval ethics are unforgotten; the Kurds still believe in the battle between Ormuzd, the bearer of light, and Ahriman, the bearer of darkness. And just as they do not deny the devil in their faith, but recognize him as a genuine opponent who must be fought, so they themselves live a life between light and darkness, but always in battle against darkness. Their feasts are bright in their native mountains; but foreign violence calls them darkly, again and again to battle. An old cultural nation with a thousand-year-old past, a proud people descended from a pure Aryan race, wild in their passions, hospitable and loyal, such are the Kurds. Glorious plateaus, fertile plains, the flowing Euphrates, artistic handiwork, nature-loving festivals—that is Kurdistan.[10]

In language evocative of tourist advertising, Kāmurān's closing remarks bring to mind Edward Said's comments on marketing the Orient for the Western consumer, presenting it as "one of the numerous wares beseeching his attention".[11] The limitations of the patriotic-militaristic novel could not be overcome merely by enriching it with folkloric details and other staples of Kurdish self-representation in the 1930's and the years to follow. Only with the romantic inventions of the "epilogue" is Kāmurān able to find a formula for marketing his version of the Kurds.

---

[10] "Eagle", p. 144.
[11] Said (1978), pp. 249–250.

CONCLUSION

"This is not about personal ambition. This is about the survival of a nation".[1] Thus responds the Kurdish rebel leader in *Der Adler von Kurdistan* to government attempts to buy his compliance by offering him an important political position. No doubt, most patriotic rebels would portray their motives similarly: as high-minded, noble, and independent of personal gain. However, it would be more accurate to view nationalist fervour and dedication as a result of the wedding of personal prospects and goals to those of the nation. In this study we saw that the Kurdish intellectual's anxiety about the allocation of positions and resources, both in the moribund Ottoman Empire or in whatever order would succeed it, was a prime mover in their nationalistic endeavours at the beginning of the 20th century. Delineating the we-group was also about defining the role of the educated in serving their compatriots, creating roles and positions for themselves. But lest we overemphasize the material aspect, the nationalist cause was also ennobling, conferring a sense of self-worth and dignity on those who espoused it. Certainly this latter aspect was what kept nationalist leaders such as Celādet and Kāmurān Bedir Khān active in the Kurdish cause long after political or financial gain could be hoped for.

In the latter part of the 19th century growing numbers of Ottomans saw modernization as the only effective cure for the ailing empire, and modern nationhood as the prerequisite for implementing the necessary reforms. Western powers were progressively making deeper inroads on Ottoman economic and political sovereignty. Pondering the reasons for European superiority, many Ottoman intellectuals concluded that the main sources of European strength were their citizen's patriotism and the sympathy and respect they were able to inspire in other nations. The Western powers represented an august circle of nations to which the Ottomans, including the Kurds as a distinct group, must gain membership or perish. For much of the period examined in this study, Kurdish intellectuals perceived the

[1] "Eagle", pp. 84–85.

situation of the Kurds as that of a test, with the European powers-that-be as a sort of examining board to determine if the Kurds were worthy of surviving as a distinct group.

This study focussed on how early Kurdish nationalists formulated answers to the crucial questions: Who are the Kurds, i.e. how are they distinct from others? Who and what are responsible for their backwardness? How can Kurds overcome the barriers to modernization?

Part One examined the efforts of aspiring Kurdish leaders to "awaken" their fellow Kurds to the necessity and benefits of the Kurdish cause. For over two decades, in the pages of their newspapers, intellectuals grappled with the many problems involved in defining the Kurds as a group distinct from their Muslim-Turkish brothers and articulating their specific needs. There were two main problem areas: the nature of the relationship to the Turks and the conditions in Kurdistan. Kurdish writers argued that recognizing and supporting a distinctively Kurdish identity in no way detracted from their loyalty to the Ottoman family; Kurdish administrators, officials and teachers would be required to manage the Kurdish leap into modernity. Kurdish writers had few illusions about the enormity of the task. Virtually every aspect of the dismal reality of Kurdistan posed an obstacle for modernizers. Perceiving pride and the respect of others to be necessary conditions for being considered a nation, Kurdish protagonists were overwhelmed at the apparent unviability of Kurdistan: tribal structures, nomadic way of life, illiteracy, ignorance and wildness. Moreover, most Kurds identified with their religious leader, ʿAbdülḥamīd, which made them incapable of comprehending that they were being manipulated by the Sultan. Until his deposition, ʿAbdülḥamīd was, for Kurdish nationalists, the inimical other, one of a long line of Ottoman despots who had crushed the Kurds and their culture, preventing their development.

In the Young Turk period the arguments for Kurdishness became more difficult to articulate. Kurdish leaders tried to navigate a course including both Kurdish and Ottoman concerns. Their main arguments for distinction and pride derived from the glorious days of the Kurdish emirates, the great epic poem *Mem ū Zīn*, and important historical figures who could be considered great Kurds, such as Saladin. In this period the educated class compiled a list of tasks that had to be accomplished, tasks which they saw themselves as singularly equipped to deal with: educating and enlightening the Kurdish masses, reforming the language, studying Kurdish history and writing books in Kurdish. As educated Kurds argued these needs, the lack of a positive image of contemporary Kurdishness was apparent. The masses of Kurds are represented sorrowfully, painted in the bleakest colors, as a group which can never, as it is, be invited to the banquet of progress and prosperity. Their civilization is a shambles. To be recognized, they must first become worthy; they must be remade. This constituted the project of Kurdish intellectuals and students.

Not until the Wilson Points were proclaimed, did Kurdish leaders gradually dispense with the notion of cultural development as a prerequisite for the right to be treated as a distinct entity. No longer were ethnic rights something to be earned. The Wilson Points contained a guarantee for the existence and autonomous development of ethnic minorities in the Ottoman Empire. However, now that Kurdishness had acquired an undeniably political character, there was more dissension than ever before about it. Nationalists saw the promise of autonomy as contingent on a separate identity and new allegiances. The vast majority of Kurds, however, did not want to part way with the Turks and other Muslims. There were many who joined forces with the Kemalists to drive out foreign occupiers and their sympathizers, hoping in this way to achieve Kurdish goals.

Part Two dealt with the rise of a new Kurdish movement in exile, mainly in Syria, where many of the Kurdish patriots, branded as traitors by the Kemalists, arrived. These Kurds tried to interpret what had happened and make sense of their changed circumstances, while creating new roles for themselves. They attempted to influence events in Turkey and play some part in the resistance to Mustafa Kemal. The exiled leaders felt that Kemal, in collusion with opportunistic Kurdish leaders, had violated Kurdish rights and betrayed their hopes. Nevertheless, in an open letter to Prime Minister İsmet İnönü written after the Sheykh Saʿīd-Revolt, the relationship of Turks and Kurds is cautiously characterized as brotherly.

Only with the establishment of *Khoybūn* in 1927 were a full-fledged nationalist identity and cause proclaimed. Arguing the legitimacy of the Kurdish revolts in the Turkish Republic, Ṯüreyyā Bedir Khān no longer portrayed the Kurds as a lamentable, duped and backward people who had to be awakened. They emerged, in Kurdish propaganda, as morally superior individuals forced to engage in resistance to the oppressors trying to destroy them. Turks were no longer depicted as brothers; the Kemalists were the latest in a long line of "evil Turks" who had, from time immemorial, striven to destroy the

Kurds. Kurdish writers, in particular Ṯüreyyā Bedir Khān, could now unrestrainedly project the cause of Kurdish suffering, recurring to stereotypes of the "evil Turk".

The failure of the *Khoybūn*-sponsored rebellion of Ararat and other frustrations brought about a change of heart in the prominent Kurdish leader, Dr. Şükrü Meḥmed Sekban, who published a refutation of all the arguments in the contemporary nationalist arsenal which could be deployed to advocate some form of rights for the Kurds. In its very negations, *La Question Kurde* illustrates, how Kurds in this period were putting forth their case for Kurdishness.

Other Kurdish leaders, most notably Celādet and Kāmurān Bedir Khān, remained in the service of their imagined nation, embarking, with French support, on the program of cultural nation-building, dealing with the problems of education, language and history which had been identified as crucial in the earlier Kurdish newspapers. They retained the *Khoybūn* image of the valiant, fighting Kurds, equipping them with the attributes which would allow them to join the club of modern nations. Cultural viability is perceived along the lines of the enthusiasm and interests of French Orientalists in traditional Kurdish culture: Kurdish music, folktales and songs, agricultural methods and way of life. Kurds could be proud of themselves and cherish their culture. They could be accepted unconditionally to the brotherhood of nations. While the Turkish enemy was still projected in derogatory stereotypes, the new emphasis was clearly on exploring and developing a positive image of Kurdishness. With few political options, the Kurdish patriot's new mission was to keep alive sympathy for the Kurds in the West and to carry on the cultural revival.

Part Three examined *Der Adler von Kurdistan*, Kāmurān Bedir Khān's venture into nationalist novel writing as part of the mission to promote the image of worthy Kurds, cruelly oppressed and struggling against extinction. The novel has certain superficial similarities with Franz Werfel's popular novel *The Forty Days of Musa Dagh*, and Kāmurān probably hoped that his novel would create interest and sympathy for the Kurds as Werfel's novel had done for the Armenians. However, Kāmurān's novel, published in German with the collaboration of a German writer, parallels in many respects the militaristic novels en vogue in Nazi Germany: the unquestioning submission of the patriotic masses to the will of the heroic leader and the corresponding necessity to destroy all traitors, i.e. those who oppose the leader in any way. The elements of the militaristic genre accommodated a good deal of *Khoybūn* ideology and practice; moreover, the fictional battle at Ararat presented a wishful version of what could have happened in the actual revolt. Although the novel is quite unremarkable in terms of literary quality, a close reading reveals a unique and fascinating attempt to fashion an image of Kurdishness incorporating the entire panoply of the imagined Kurdish nation and depicting their brave and just struggle for freedom. Kāmurān presented every aspect of Kurds and their culture which Kurds, from the end of the 1920's, included in their delineation of Kurdish identity: their heroism, patriotism, reverence for their land, identification with their mountains; their pride in their language and heritage; the beauty of their folk tales and songs, the rich variety of their material culture; their strong and patriotic women; the solidarity among Kurds from all backgrounds. Moreover, the entire cast of the nationalist drama was present: the heroes who lead the struggle, the patriots who support them, the traitors who opportunistically side with the enemy, and the enemies themselves, the perpetrators of unjust and brutal actions, who threaten the very existence of the nation.

Perhaps because of its similarities to German militaristic novels, *Der Adler von Kurdistan* was, in terms of impact, inconsequential. It does not seem to have either furthered the Kurdish cause or facilitated in any way Kāmurān Bedir Khān's later emergence as Kurdish spokesman. There is no evidence of any reaction to the book after it was published, first in German, then in French. Perhaps the author intended to later translate the book into Kurdish, thus giving the Kurds their first epic novel. At the very least *Der Adler von Kurdistan* was an eminent Kurdish nationalist's ambitious if misguided attempt to package and promote Kurdishness using the novel form. It seems that he should have received some recognition for trying.

BIBLIOGRAPHY

Periodicals

When I first embarked on the study of Kurdish newspapers, I was not aware of the excellent editions of *Jīn* and *Kürdistān* (1898–1902; or *Kurdistan* in Bozarslan's spelling) by Mehmet Emin Bozarslan. For *Kürdistān*, I used the edition of Kamal Fu'ād; for *Jīn*, I used the set at the Atatürk Kitaplığı (the former Belediye Kütüphanesi) 0/214 (which, e.g. in the case of the article "Zoḥāk Efsānesi" by Kurdī-yi Bitlīsī [no. 1, 7 Teşrīn-i ṯānī 1334/November 1918], has not the omissions of the Bozarslan edition because the latter's copy has misprints or has become unreadable). For *Hetavē Kurd* (0/360–9) and *Kürdistān* (1919; 0/354–8) I consulted the sets at the Atatürk Kitaplığı. *Kürd Teʿāvün ve Terakkī Gazetesi* (no. 1 only) is available at the University Library Tübingen; Bozarslan's edition of that newspaper appeared only in 1998.

Kürdistān. Appeared 1898–1902 in Cairo, Geneva, London, Folkstone, and again in Geneva. First no.: 30 Ḏūlkaʿde 1315/9 Nīsān 1314/April 22, 1898; last no.: 31: 6 Muḥarrem 1320/1 Nīsān 1318/April 14, 1902. With a few exceptions these numbers are available in the Staatsbibliothek Marburg (cf. Fuad [1970] XVIII, footnote 3). Reprint: Kamāl Fu'ād (Ed.): *Kūrdistān. Yēke mīn rūjnāma-i kūrdī 1898–1902.* Baghdād 1972 (missing numbers: 10, 12, 17, 18, 19). The edition of Bozarslan was published in 1991 (2 vols.).

Kürd Teʿāvün ve Terakkī Gazetesi. Dīnī, ʿilmī, siyāsī, edebī, ictimāʿī ġazetedir. İstanbul. Ṣāḥib-i imtiyāz ve müdir ve muḥarriri (editor and director): Süleymāniyelī Tevfīk, sermuḥarriri Diyārbekirlī Aḥmed Cemīl. No. 1: 11 Ḏūlkaʿde 1326/22 Teşrīn-i ṯānī 1324/December 5, 1908. At least eight nos. appeared. I had only access to no. 1. The edition of Bozarslan including the transcription of the Ottoman into Latin letters appeared in 1998.

Rojē Kurd. İstanbul. Only 3 nos. appeared: no. 1: 6 Hazīran 1329/14 Receb 1331/1913; no. 2: 6 Temmūz 1329/14 Şaʿbān 1331/1913; no. 3: 1 Ağustos 1329/11 Ramażān 1331/1913. Editor: ʿAbdülkerīm. The copies I have used are collected in the reprint: Jamāl Khaznadār (ed.): *Rojē Kurd 1913.* Baghdād: al-Mu'assasa al-ʿIrāqīya 1981. Uzun-Bedir-Han (1998), pp. 114–116, quote from no. 4 (September 11, 1913).

Hetavē Kurd. İstanbul. Continuation of *Rojē Kurd.* 10 nos appeared. Available to me: No. 1: 11 Teşrīn-i evvel 1329/23 Ḏīlkaʿde 1331/1913; no. 2: 21 Teşrīn-i ṯānī 1329/4 Muḥarrem 1332/December 3, 1913; no. 3: 29 Kānūn-u evvel 1329/13 Ṣafar 1332; nos. 4–5: 10 Mayıs 1330/27 Cemāḏiyilākhir 1332/1914; no. 10: 20 Ḥazīrān 1330/9 Şaʿbān 1332/1914. Ṣāḥib-i imtiyāz ve müdir-i mes'ūl: Bābān ʿAbdülʿazīz.

Jīn. Dīn, edebiyāt, ictimāʿiyāt ve iktṣādiyāt'tan baḥṯ eder. Türkçe Kürdce mecmūʿadır. Ṣāḥib-i imtiyāz ve müdür-i mes'ūl: Memdūḥ [Selīm]. İstanbul. No. 1: 7 Teşrīn-i ṯānī 1334/November 7, 1918; no. 25 (last issue): 2 Teşrīn-i evvel 1335/October 2, 1919. Bozarslan's edition was published 1985–1988 in 5 vols.

Kürdistān. Siyāsī, ictimāʿī, edebī, ʿilmī, usbūʿī ve müstakıll ül-fikr mecmūʿadır. Ṣāḥib-i imtiyāz ve müdür-i mes'ūl (Editor): Meḥmed Mihrī; sermuḥarriri: Arvāsīzāde Meḥmed Şefīk. İstanbul. At least 13 nos. published. Available to me: no. 8: 29 Mayıs 1335/28 Şaʿbān 1337/May 29, 1919; no. 9: 11 Ḥazīrān 1335/12 Ramażān 1337/June 11, 1919 [although in the subtitle a weekly appearance is mentioned the periodical, in fact, was only published twice a month, at least this can be concluded from the two issues avaible to me. If we take a semimonthly appearance for granted *Kürdistān* must have started in April 1919 and at least continued until August 1919].

Şarḳ ve Kürdistān. Şarḳın vażʿiyet-i siyāsiyesiyle ġarbın insāniyete ḳarşı şāʾibelerini muṣavvir ġazetedir ("Newspaper depicting the political situation of the Orient and the transgressions of the Occident against humanity"). No. 1: 25 Şawwāl 1326/November 20, 1908; no. 2: 29 Şawwāl 1326/November 24, 1908. Müʾessisleri: Hersekli Aḥmed Şerīf, Malaṭyalı Bedrī, Hersekli İsmāʿīl.

Articles and Books

Ahmad, Kamal Madhar (1994): *Kurdistan during the First World War.* Translated by Ali Maher Ibrahim. London: Saqi 1994 (first printed in Kurdish in Bagdad 1975; Turkish edition appeared under the title: Ahmed, Kemal Mazhar: *Birinci Dünya Savaşı Yıllarında Kürdistan.* 2.ed. Ankara 1992).

Alakom, Rohat (1995): *Bir Kürt Diplomatının Fırtınalı Yılları: General Şerif Paşa (1865–1944).* Stockholm: APEC 1995.

Anderson, Benedict (1993): *Die Erfindung der Nation. Zur Karriere eines folgenreichen Konzepts.* 2.ed. Frankfurt a.M., New York: Campus 1993 (English original: *Imagined Communities. Reflections on the Origin and Spread of Nationalism.* London 1983).

Andrews, Peter and R. Bennighaus (eds.) (1989): *Ethnic Groups in the Republic of Turkey.* Wiesbaden: Reichert 1989 (Beihefte zum Tübinger Atlas des Vorderen Orients/Reihe B Geisteswissenschaften. Nr. 60).

Anon. (1933–34): "Cümhuriyetin 10 cu yıl dönümü münasebetile neşrolunan af kanunu", No. 2330, *Sicilli Kavanini* 10 (1933–34), pp. 5–9.

Anon. (1938): "Af Kanunu", No. 3527, *Sicilli Kavanini* 19 (1938), pp. 748–749.

Anon.: "Oertel, Herbert", *Kürschners Literaturkalender* 49 (1939), p. 646.

Anon.: "Herbert Oertel", *Deutsches Literatur-Lexikon.* Vol. XI. Bern-Stuttgart 1988. Pp. 590–591.

Anter, Musa (1990): *Hatıralarım.* İstanbul: Doz 1990.

—— (1992): *Hatıralarım.* Vol. 2. İstanbul: Yön 1992.

Arfa, Hassan (1968): *The Kurds. An historical and political study.* London: Oxford University Press Repr. 1968.

Avineri, Shlomo (1978): "Politische und soziale Aspekte des israelischen und arabischen Nationalismus", in Winkler (1978), pp. 232–251.

Baṣrī, Mīr (1987): *Aʿlām al-siyāsa fī l-ʿIrāḳ al-ḥadīth.* London: Riad el-Rayyes Books 1987.

Bayrak, Mehmet (ed.) (1992): *Vet. Dr. Nuri Dersimi: Dersim'e ve Kürt Milli Mücadelesine dair Hatıratım.* Enlarged ed. İstanbul: Öz-Ge 1992.

—— (1993): *Kürtler ve Ulusal-Demokratik Mücadeleleri. Gizli Belgeler—Araştırmalar—Notlar.* Ankara: Öz-Ge 1993.

—— (ed.) (1994): *Açık-Gizli/Resmi-Gayrıresmi Kürdoloji Belgeleri.* Ankara: Öz-Ge 1994.

Bayrak, Orhan M. (1992): *Türkiye'yi Kimler Yönetti (1920–1992). Cumhuriyet'in 72 Yıllık Üstdüzey Yönetim Kadroları.* İstanbul: Yılmaz 1992.

[Bedir Khān, Celādet ʿĀlī].

Herekol Azīzan (1934): *De la question kurde. La loi de déportation et de dispersion des Kurdes.* Qelemşah 1934 (Hejmar 8).

Bedirxan, C. Ali (1978): *Türkiye Reisicumhuru Gazi M. Kemal Paşa Hazretlerine Açık Mektup (1933).* İstanbul: Komal 1978.

Bedir Khan, Emir Djeladet-Lescot, Roger (1986): *Kurdische Grammatik (Kurmanci-Dialekt).* Bonn: Verlag für Kultur und Wiss. 1986 (Untersuchungen zu den Sprachen und Kulturen der Welt: Sectio K, Untersuchungen zur kurdischen Sprache und Kultur, 1).

Bedirxan, Emir Celadet Ali (1992): *Bir Kürt Aydınından Mustafa Kemal'e Mektup*. İstanbul: Doz 1992.

Bedirhan, Celadet Âli (1995): *Günlük notlar 1922–1925*. Dilini sadeleştirerek yayına hazırlayan: Malmîsanij. Stockholm: APEC 1995.

[Bedir Khān, Kāmurān 'Alī].

Bedir Khān, Kāmurān and Bedir Khān, Celādet (1329/1913–14): *Edirne sükūṭunun iç yüzü*. İstanbul: Serbestī Maṭba'ası 1329/1913–14.

Bedr-Chan, Kamuran Ali (1924): *Das türkische Eherecht nach den Grundsätzen der hanafitischen Lehre unt. Berücks. d. türk. Familienrechtsgesetzes üb. Civilehe u. Scheidung v. 15.X.1917 u. des türk. Gesetzentwurfes üb. Eherecht v. 25.VIII. 1924, sowie d. Grundsätze d. deutschen Eherechts.* "[Maschinenschrift] 99, III S. 4E [Lag nicht vor.—Auszug nicht gedruckt.] Leipzig, Jur.Diss. v. 24. Febr. 1926" (from: *Jahresverzeichnis der an den deutschen Universitäten und Hochschulen erschienenen Schriften*, Bd. 42 (1926), Berlin: Preussische Staatsbibliothek 1928, Verzeichnisnr. U 26.4693) (not available at University Library Leipzig, either not delivered to the library by faculty, or burned in World War II).

Bedir-Khan, Prinz Kamuran Aali and Herbert Oertel (1937): *Der Adler von Kurdistan*. Potsdam: Ludwig Voggenreiter 1937.

Bedir-Khan, Emir Kamuran Aali (sic) et Adolphe de Falgairolle (1938?): *Le Roi du Kurdistan, roman épique kurde*. Gap: éditions Ophrys s.d. [1938?] (Collection Trésor du siècle)

Bedr Khan, Kamuran 'Ali (1949): "The Kurdish Problem", *JRCAS* 36 (1949), pp. 237–248.

Bedir Khan, K.: "Gerald Götting empfing kurdischen Gelehrten", *Neue Zeit* (Ost-Berlin), Nr. 208 (2.9.1960), 209 (6.9.1960).

Bedir Khan, Emir Kamuran Ali (1963): "Die Kurden. Überblick über die Geschichte, Soziologie, Kultur und Politik eines Volkes", *Bustan* 4 Jg./Heft 1 (1963), pp. 20–25.

Bedir Khan, Prinz Kamuran Aali (1968): *Der Schnee des Lichts. Kurdische Gedichte*. In deutschen Versen von Curt Wunderlich. Berlin 1935, Repr. Paris 1968.

[Bedir Khān, Ṯüreyyā].

Bedir Khan, Sureya (1928 a): *Les Massacres Kurdes en Turquie*. Cairo: Paul Barbey 1928 (Publication de la Ligue Nationale Kurde Hoyboun No. 2).

Bedir Khan, Sureya (by authority of Hoyboon, Supreme Council of the Kurdish Government) (1928 b): *The Case of Kurdistan against Turkey*. Philadelphia 1928.

Bedir Khan, Sureya (under pseudonym Dr. Bletch Chirguh): *La question kurde. Ses origines et ses causes*. Cairo 1930 (Publication de la Ligue Nationale Kurde Hoyboun no. 6).

Behrendt, Günter (1993): *Nationalismus in Kurdistan. Vorgeschichte, Entstehungsbedingungen und erste Manifestationen bis 1925*. Hamburg: Dt. Orient-Inst. 1993 (Politik, Wirtschaft und Gesellschaft des Vorderen Orients).

Berkes, Niyazi (1997): *Unutulan yıllar*. Yayına hazırlayan Ruşen Sezer. Second edition. İstanbul: İletişim 1997.

Beşikçi, İsmail (1970): *Doğu Anadolu'nun Düzeni. Sosyo-ekonomik ve etnik temeller*. Second ed. İstanbul: e yayınları 1970.

Beysanoğlu, Şevket (ed.) (1992): *Ziya Gökalp: Kürt Aşiretleri Hakkında Sosyolojik Tetkikler*. İstanbul: Sosyal 1992.

Blaschke, Jochen and Martin van Bruinessen (eds.) (1984): *Thema: Islam und Politik in der Türkei*. Berlin: EXpress Edition 1984 (Jahrbuch zur Geschichte und Gesellschaft des Vorderen und Mittleren Orients)

Blau, Joyce (1984): "Le Mouvement National Kurde", *Les Temps Modernes* 41. année, Nr. 456–457 (1984), pp. 447–461.

Boehm, Max Hildebert (1965): *Das eigenständige Volk. Grundlegung der Elemente einer europäischen Völkersoziologie*. Repr. Darmstadt: Wissenschaftliche Buchgesellschaft 1965 (first published Göttingen 1932).

Bois, Thomas (1985): *Kurdische Volksdichtung. Spiegel der kurdischen Seele.* Ed. by Yekta Geylanī. Bonn: Kurdisches Institut 1985.

Borck, Carsten, Eva Savelsberg and Siyamend Hajo (eds.) (1997): *Ethnizität, Nationalismus, Religion und Politik in Kurdistan.* Münster: Lit 1997 (Kurdologie, 1).

Bozarslan, Hamit (1994): "Au-delà de la abolition du Califat: Laicité, État-Nation et Contestation Kurde", *La Question du Califat. Les Annales de l'autre Islam* no. 2 (1994), pp. 225–235.

Bozarslan, Mehmet Emin (1968): *Mem u Zin.* İstanbul 1968.

Brentjes, Burchard (1964): "Zu einigen Problemen der Geschichte der kurdischen Nationalbewegung", in: *Wissenschaftliche Zeitschrift der Martin-Luther-Universität Halle-Wittenberg.* Gesellschafts- und Sprachwissenschaftliche Reihe. 13. Jg./9–10 (1964), pp. 679–694.

Brockelmann, Carl (1939): *Geschichte der islamischen Völker und Staaten.* München: Oldenbourg 1939.

Broder, Henryk M. (1994): "Verrat muß sein", *Kursbuch 116: Verräter* (Juni 1994), pp. 1–3.

Bruinessen, Maarten van (1978): *Agha, Shaikh and State. On the Social and Political Organization of Kurdistan.* Rijswijk n.d. (= Ph.D. diss. Utrecht 1978).

Bruinessen, Martin van (1981): *Origins and Development of Kurdish Nationalism in Turkey* (Arbeitsheft des Berliner Instituts für vergleichende Sozialforschung). Berlin 1981.

—— (1984): "Vom Osmanismus zum Separatismus: Religiöse und ethnische Hintergründe der Rebellion des Scheich Said", *Jahrbuch zur Geschichte und Gesellschaft des Vorderen und Mittleren Orients 1984. Thema: Islam und Politik in der Türkei.* Ed. by Jochen Blaschke and Martin van Bruinessen. Berlin: EXpress Edition 1984. Pp. 109–165.

—— (1989): *Agha, Scheich und Staat. Politik und Gesellschaft Kurdistans.* Berlin: Institut für Vergleichende Sozialforschung 1989 (Edition Parabolis).

—— (1989 a): "The Ethnic Identity of the Kurds", in: Andrews/Bennighaus (eds.) (1989), pp. 613–621.

—— (1992 a): *Agha, Shaikh and State. The Social and Political Structure of Kurdistan.* London and New Jersey 1992.

—— (1992 b): "Kurdish Society, Ethnicity, Nationalism and Refugee Problems", in: Kreyenbroek/Sperl (eds.) (1992), pp. 33–67.

—— (2000): "Von Adela Khanum zu Leyla Zana: Weibliche Führungspersonen in der kurdischen Geschichte", in: Savelsberg et al. (eds.) (2000), pp. 9–32.

Bucak, Mustafa Remzi (1991): *Bir Kürt Aydınından İsmet İnönü'ye Mektup.* İstanbul: Doz 1991.

Burton, H.M. (1944): "The Kurds", *JRCAS* 31/1 (1944), pp. 64–73.

CDTA = *Cumhuriyet Dönemi Türkiye Ansiklopedisi.* İstanbul 1983 sqq.

Chaliand, Gérard (ed.) (1988): *Kurdistan und die Kurden.* Vol. 1. Second ed. Göttingen and Wien 1988 (Reihe pogrom 105/106) (first published 1984).

Connor, Walker (1994): *Ethnonationalism. The Quest for Understanding.* Princeton: Princeton University Press 1994.

Çankaya, Ali Mücellidoğlu (n.d.): *Mülkiye Tarihi ve Mülkiyeliler. Hal tercemeleri kısmı 1860–1949.* II.–III.cilt. No year, no place (special edition).

Çoker, Fahri (n.d.): *Türk Parlamento Tarihi. Millî Mücadele ve T.B.M.M. I. Dönem 1919–1923. I. Dönem Milletvekillerinin Özgeçmişleri.* III. cilt. N.pl., n.d. (Türkiye Büyük Millet Meclisi Vakfı Yayınları No. 6).

Dağlı, Faysal (1996): *Ateşten Portreler.* İstanbul: Belge 1996.

Deny, Jean (1925): "Ziya Goek Alp", *Revue du Monde Musulman* 61 (1925), pp. 1–41.

Dersimi, Nuri (1992): *Dersim ve Kürt Milli Mücadelesine Dair Hatıratım.* Ed. Mehmet Bayrak. Ankara: Öz-Ge 1992.

Diner, Dan (1994): "Kontraphobisch. Über Engführungen des Politischen", *Kursbuch 116: Verräter* (Juni 1994), pp. 109–117.

Duguid, Stephen (1973): "The Politics of Unity: Hamidian Policy in Eastern Anatolia", *Middle Eastern Studies* 9 (1973), pp. 139–155.

Edmonds, Cecil John (1957): *Kurds, Turks and Arabs. Politics, Travel and Research in North-Eastern Iraq, 1919–1925.* London: Oxford University Press 1957.

Edmonds, C.J. (1958): "The Place of the Kurds in the Middle Eastern Scene", *JRCAS* 45 (1958), pp. 141–153.

—— (1971): "Kurdish Nationalism", *Journal of Contemporary History* 6 (1971), pp. 87–107.

EI (1) = *Enzyklopädie des Islam.* Leiden, Leipzig 1913 sqq.

EI (2) = *Encyclopaedia of Islam.* New edition. Leiden 1954 sqq.

Ekrem Cemil Paşa (1992): *Muhtasar Hayatım. Kemalizme karşı Kürt aydınının mücadelesinden bir yaprak.* 2.ed. Ankara: Beybun 1992.

Elphinston, W.G. (1952): "In Memoriam. The Emir Jeladet Aali Bedr Khan. The Passing of a Kurdish Prince", *JRCAS* 39/1 (1952), pp. 91–94.

Elwert, Georg (1989 a): "Nationalismus und Ethnizität. Über die Bildung von Wir-Gruppen", *Kölner Zeitschrift für Soziologie und Sozialpsychologie* 41 (1989), pp. 440–464.

—— (1989 b): *Nationalismus und Ethnizität. Über die Bildung von Wir-Gruppen.* Berlin: Das Arabische Buch 1989 (Ethnizität und Gesellschaft, Occasional Papers Nr. 22).

Empson, Ralph H.W. (1928): *The Cult of the Peacock Angel. A Short Account of the Yezīdī Tribes of Kurdistān.* London: Witherby 1928.

Ende, Werner (1984): "Wer ist ein Glaubensheld, wer ist ein Ketzer? Konkurrierende Geschichtsbilder in der modernen Literatur islamischer Länder", *Die Welt des Islams* 23–24 (1984), pp. 70–94.

Entessar, Nader (1992): *Kurdish ethnonationalism.* Boulder 1992.

Erdem, Hüseyin (1990): *Siyabend ile Xecê.* Yeniden anlatan ve Türkçe söyleyen Hüseyin Erdem. İstanbul: Belge 1990.

Fırat, M. Şerif (1961): *Doğu İlleri ve Varto Tarihi.* Second ed. Ankara: Milli Eğitim Basımevi 1961 (A fourth printing was published by Türk Kültürünü Araştırma Enstitüsü, Ankara 1981).

Fink, Gonthier Louis (1991): "Das Bild des Nachbarvolkes im Spiegel der deutschen und der französischen Hochaufklärung (1750–1789)", in: Giesen (ed.) (1991), pp. 453–492.

Fuad, Kamal (1970): *Kurdische Handschriften.* Wiesbaden: Franz Steiner 1970 (Verzeichnis der Orientalischen Handschriften in Deutschland XXX).

Fuccaro, Nelida (1997): "Die Kurden Syriens: Anfänge der nationalen Mobilisierung unter französischer Herrschaft", in: Borck et al. (1997), pp. 301–326.

—— (1997): "Ethnicity, state formation and conscription in postcolonial Iraq: the case of the Yezidi Kurds of Jabal Sinjar", *IJMES* 29 (1997), pp. 559–580.

Gellner, Ernest: *Nations and Nationalism.* Third printing. Ithaca-New York 1991 (Cornell Paperback).

Genelkurmay Belgelerinde Kürt İsyanları. 3 vols. İstanbul: Kaynak 1992.

Gerede, Hüsrev (1952): *Siyasī Hatıralarım 1. İran (1930–1934).* İstanbul 1952.

Ghassemlou, Abdul Rahman (1965): *Kurdistan and the Kurds.* Prague-London: Collet's 1965.

Giesen, Bernhard (ed.) (1991): *Nationale und kulturelle Identität. Studien zur Entwicklung des kollektiven Bewußtseins in der Neuzeit.* 2. ed. Frankfurt a.M: suhrkamp 1991 (suhrkamp taschenbuch wissenschaft 940).

Giesen, Bernhard and Kay Junge (1991): "Vom Patriotismus zum Nationalismus. Zur Evolution der 'Deutschen Kulturnation'", in: Giesen (ed.) (1991), pp. 255–303.

Göldaş, İsmail (1991): *Kürdistan Teāli Cemiyeti.* İstanbul: Doz 1991.

Gologlu, Mahmut (1971): *Türkiye Cumhuriyeti 1923.* Ankara: Başnur 1971.

Greenfeld, Liah (1992): *Nationalism. Five Roads to Modernity.* Second edition. Cambridge, Mass.: Harvard University Press 1992.

Haarmann, Ulrich (1988): "Ideology and History, Identity and Alterity: The Arab Image of the Turk from the 'Abbasids to Modern Egypt", *IJMES* 20 (1988), pp. 175–196.

Hanioğlu, Şükrü (1981): *Bir Siyasal Düşünür olarak Doktor Abdullah Cevdet ve Dönemi.* İstanbul 1981.
—— (1995): *The Young Turks in Opposition.* New York: Oxford University Press 1995.
Hansen, Gerda (1994): *Die Kurden und der Kurdenkonflikt. Literatur seit 1990. Eine Auswahlbibliographie.* Hamburg: Deutsches Übersee-Institut 1994 (Dokumentationsdienst Vorderer Orient: Reihe A, 22).
Hartmann, Martin (1898): "Zur kurdischen Literatur", *Wiener Zeitschrift für die Kunde des Morgenlandes* 12 (1898), pp. 102–112.
Hasanī, ʿAbd al-Razzāḳ al- (1988): *Tārīkh al-wizārāt al-ʿirāḳīya.* Baghdād: Wizārat al-Ṯaqāfa wa-l-Iʿlām 1988/1408 h.
Hassanpour, Amir (1989): *The Language Factor in National Development: The Standardization of the Kurdish Language, 1918–1985.* Ph.D. diss. University of Illinois 1989.
Hatemi, Hüsrev and Aykut Kazancıgil (eds.) (1991): *Ord. Prof. Dr. Tevfik Sağlam: Nasıl Okudum.* 3. ed. İstanbul: Nehir 1991.
Hilmi, Refik [Ḥilmī, Rafīq]: *Anılar. Şeyh Mahmud Berzenci Hareketi.* İstanbul 1995 (Arabic original: Baghdād 1956).
Hobsbawm, Eric J. (1990): *Nations and nationalism since 1780. Programm, myth, reality.* Cambridge, New York, Melbourne: Cambridge University Press 1990.
—— and Terence Ranger (eds.) (1983): *The Invention of Tradition.* Cambridge: Cambridge University Press 1983.
Hroch, Miroslav (1968): *Die Vorkämpfer der nationalen Bewegung bei den kleinen Völkern Europas. Eine vergleichende Analyse zur gesellschaftlichen Schichtung der patriotischen Gruppen.* Prag 1968 (Acta Universitatis Carolinae Philosophica et Historica, Monographia XXIV).
—— (1985): *Social Preconditions of National Revival in Europe. A Comparative Analysis of the Social Composition of Patriotic Groups among the Smaller European Nations.* Translated by Ben Fowkes. Cambridge: Cambridge University Press 1985.
Ibrahim, Ferhad (1983): *Die kurdische Nationalbewegung im Irak. Eine Fallstudie zur Problematik ethnischer Konflikte in der Dritten Welt.* Berlin: Klaus Schwarz 1983 (Islamkundliche Untersuchungen 88).
IJMES = International Journal of Middle East Studies
Iraq Directory, The 1936. n.p.
Istanbul Telefon Rehberi 1947. 27th ed.
Jaba, Auguste and Ferdinand Justi (1879): *Dictionnaire kurde-français.* St. Petersburg 1879.
Jeismann, Michael and Henning Ritter (eds.) (1993): *Grenzfälle. Über alten und neuen Nationalismus.* Leipzig: Reclam 1993.
JRCAS = Journal of the Royal Central Asian Society, London.
Judt, Tony (1994): "Der neue alte Nationalismus", *Merkur* 48. Jg./Heft 12 (1994), pp. 1047–1064.
Kadri Cemil Paşa (Zinar Silopī) (1991): *Doza Kurdistan (Kürdistan Davası). Kürt Milletinin 60 Yıllık Esaretten Kurtuluş Savaşı Hatıraları.* Ed. by Mehmet Bayrak. 2. ed. Ankara: Öz-Ge 1991 (1. ed. Beyrut 1969).
Karakaş, Şuayb (1988): *Süleyman Nazif.* Ankara 1988 (Kültür ve Turizm Bakanlığı Yayınları 968).
Kazancıgil, Aykut (ed.) (1991): *Binbaşı Elhaç Rıza Tahsin: Tıp Fakültesi Tarihçesi (Mirʾāt-ı Mekteb-i Tıbbiye).* 2 vols. İstanbul: Özel 1991.
Kendal (1988): "Türkisch Kurdistan", in: Chaliand (ed.) (1988), pp. 81–182.
Koçaş, M. Sadi (1990): *Kürtlerin Kökeni ve Güneydoğu Anadolu Gerçeği.* İstanbul: Kastaş 1990.
Kreyenbroek, Philip G. and Stefan Sperl (eds.) (1992): *The Kurds. A Contemporary Overview.* London and New York. Routledge 1992 (SOAS Politics and Culture in the Middle East Series).

Kreyenbroek, Philip G. (1992): "On the Kurdish language", in: Kreyenbroek/Sperl (eds.) (1992), pp. 68–83.
—— (1995): *Yezidism—Its Background, Observances and Textual Tradition.* Lewiston-Queenston-Lampeter: Edwin Mellen 1995 (Texts and Studies in Religion, 62).
—— and Christine Allison (eds.) (1996): *Kurdish Culture and Identity.* Atlantic Highlands, New Jersey 1996.
Kuran, Ercüment (1992): "Türkiye'de Kürt Meselesi", *Türk Dünyası Araştırmaları* 79 (1992), pp. 157–176.
"Kurden, Kurdistan", *EI* (1), vol. II, pp. 1212–1299.
"Kurds, Kurdistan", *EI* (2), vol. V, pp. 438–486.
Kushner, David (1977): *The Rise of Turkish Nationalism 1876–1908.* London: Frank Cass 1977.
Kutlay, Naci (1992): *İttihat Terakki ve Kürtler.* Enlarged 3. printing. Ankara: Beybun 1992.
Kutschera, Chris (1979): *Le Mouvement National Kurde.* Paris: Flammarion 1979.
Küchler, Hannelore (1978): *Öffentliche Meinung. Eine theoretisch-methodologische Betrachtung und eine exemplarische Untersuchung zum Selbstverständnis der Kurden.* Ph.D. diss. Freie Universität Berlin 1978.
Küçük, Yalçın (1990): *Kürtler üzerine tezler.* Ankara: Dönem 1990.
Lemberg, Eugen (1964): *Nationalismus.* 2 Bde. Reinbek: Rowohlt 1964 (rowohlts deutsche enzyklopädie).
Lescot, Roger and L.Ch. Wentzel (eds.) (1980): *Mam und Zin. Kurdisches Volksepos.* Zürich: Die Arche 1980.
Lewis, Bernard (1968): *The Emergence of Modern Turkey.* 2. ed. London-Oxford-New York 1968.
Lewis, G.L.: "D̲jewdet, ʿAbd Allāh", *EI* (2), p. 533.
Loewy, Ernst (ed.) (1969): *Literatur unterm Hakenkreuz. Das Dritte Reich und seine Dichtung. Eine Dokumentation.* Frankfurt/M.: Fischer 1969.
MacKenzie, David (1961): "The Origins of Kurdish", *Transactions of the Philological Society* (1961), pp. 68–86.
Makas, Hugo (1979): *Kurdische Texte und Kurdische Studien.* Repr. of the editions St.Petersburg/Leningrad 1897–1926 and Heidelberg 1900. 2 vols. in 1. Amsterdam: APA-PHILO Press 1979.
Malmîsanij (1991): *Said-i Nursi ve Kürt Sorunu.* 2.ed. İstanbul: Doz 1991.
—— (1993): *Bitlisli Kemal Fevzi ve Kürt örgütleri içindeki yeri.* 2.ed. İstanbul: Fırat 1993.
—— (2000): *Cızira Botanlı Bedirhaniler ve Bedirhani Ailesi Derneği'nin Tutanakları.* Second printing. İstanbul: avesta 2000 (first printing Stockholm 1994).
Mann, Oskar (1906): *Kurdisch-Persische Forschungen.* Abteilung IV, Band III, Teil I: Die Mundart der Mukri-Kurden. Berlin: Georg Reimer 1906.
Mardin, Şerif (1984): "'Bediüzzaman' Said Nursi und die Mechanik der Natur", in: Blaschke/Bruinessen (eds.) (1984), pp. 197–232.
—— (1989): *Religion and Social Change in Modern Turkey. The Case of Bediüzzaman Said Nursi.* Albany: State University of New York Press 1989.
—— (1991): "The Nakşibendi Order in Turkish History", in: Tapper (ed.) (1991), pp. 121–142.
McDowall, David (1996): *A Modern History of the Kurds.* London-New York: I.B. Tauris 1996.
Mevlânzâde Rıfat (1993): *Türkiye İnkılâbının İçyüzü.* Ed. by Metin Hasırcı. İstanbul: Pınar 1993.
Minorsky, Vladimir (1940): "Les origines des Kurdes", in: *Actes du XXe Congrès des Orientalistes 1938.* Louvain 1940. pp. 143–152.
MMZC = Meclis-i Mebʿūs̱ān Ẓabıṭ Cerīdesi

Moltke, von, Helmuth Karl (1892): "Das Land und Volk der Kurden", in: id.: *Gesammelte Schriften und Denkwürdigkeiten*. Vol. 2.: Vermischte Schriften. Berlin 1892. pp. 288–298.
Mommsen, Hans and A. Martiny (1971): "Nationalismus, Nationalitätenfrage", in: *Sowjetsystem und demokratische Gesellschaft. Eine vergleichende Enzyklopädie* 4 (1971), pp. 623–695.
Moradi, Golmorad (1992): *Ein Jahr autonome Regierung in Kurdistan. Die Mahabad-Republik 1946–1947. Geschichte der kurdischen Aufstandsbewegungen von der arabisch-islamischen Invasion bis zur Mahabad-Republik*. Bremen 1992 (= Ph.Diss. Heidelberg 1989).
[National Central Committee] (1930): "The Kurds of Iraq (Southern Kurdistan)", *The Near East and India*, September 25, 1930, p. 348.
Nazdar, Mustafa (1988): "Die Kurden in Syrien", in: Chaliand (ed.) (1988), pp. 395–411.
Nebez, Jemal (ed.) (1969): *Ahmad-i Chanie. Mam und Zin genannt Romeo und Julia der Kurden*. München: NUKSE 1969.
Nikitine, Basile (1925): "La féodalité kurde", *Revue du Monde Musulman* 60 (1925), pp. 1–26.
—— (1975): *Les Kurdes*. Paris 1956. Repr. 1975 (Editions d'aujourd'hui).
——: "Badrkhānī, T̲hurayyā (1883–1938) and D̲jalādat (1893–1951)", *EI* (2), vol. I, p. 871.
[Nūrī, İḥsān]
Nouri, Ihsan Pasha (1986): *La Revolte de l'Agri Dagh: Ararat (1927–1930)*. Préface de I.Ch.Vanly. Genève: Agrî Editions Kurdes 1986.
Olson, Robert (1989): *The Emergence of Kurdish Nationalism and the Sheikh Said Rebellion, 1880–1925*. Austin: University of Texas Press 1989.
Reso, Hemres (1978): "Materialien zur Entwicklung der kurdischen Literatur", in: Roth et al. (1978), pp. 81–99.
Rich, Claudius James (1836): *Narrative of a Residence in Koordistan*. 2 vols. London 1836.
Rondot, Pierre (1939): "Les Kurdes de Syrie", *La France Méditerranéenne et Africaine* vol. 2/1 (1939), pp. 81–126.
Roosevelt, Archie Jr. (1988): "Die kurdische Republik Mahabad", in: Chaliand (ed.) (1988), pp. 229–257 (German translation of: "The Kurdish Republic of Mahabad", *Middle East Journal* I/3 (July 1947), pp. 247–269).
Roth, Jürgen et al. (1978): *geographie der unterdrückten*. Hamburg: rororo 1978.
Rudenko, M.B. (ed.) (1962): *Aḥmad-i Ḫānī: Mam ū Zīn*. Moscow 1962.
Rusinek, Bernd-A./Volker Ackermann/Jörg Engelbrecht (eds.) (1992): *Einführung in die Interpretation historischer Quellen. Schwerpunkt: Neuzeit*. Paderborn-München-Wien-Zürich: Ferdinand Schöningh 1992 (UTB für Wissenschaft: Uni-Taschenbücher; 1674).
Ryan, Lawrence M. (1944): "Bibliography of the Kurdish Press", *JRCAS* 31 (1944), pp. 313–314.
Şadillili Vedat (1980): *Türkiye'de Kürtçülük Hareketleri ve İsyanlar*. Ankara: Kon 1980.
Safrastian, Arshak (1948): *Kurds and Kurdistan*. London 1948.
Şahiner, Necmeddin (1974): *Bilinmeyen Taraflariyle Bediüzzaman Said Nursī*. 3. ed. İstanbul: Yeni Asya 1974.
Şanlıer, Sinan (tr.) (1992): *Dr. Fritz: Kürtlerin Tarihi*. İstanbul: Hasat 1992.
Said, Edward (1978): *Orientalism*. London: Routledge and Kegan Paul 1978.
Sasuni, Garo (1986): *Kürt Ulusal Hareketleri ve Ermeni-Kürt İlişkileri (15. yy'dan Günümüze)*. Translated by Bedros Zartaryan and Memo Yetkin. Stockholm: Orfeus 1986.
Savelsberg, Eva/Siamend Hajo/Carsten Borck (eds.) (2000): *Kurdische Frauen und das Bild der kurdischen Frau*. Münster: LIT 2000 (Kurdologie; 3).
Savi, Saime İnal (1993): *Yusuf Ziyaeddin Paşa'nın El-Hediyyetü'l Hamīdiyye'sinde Osmanlıca-Türkçe Taraması*. Ankara: Elila 1993.
[Sekban, Şükrü Meḥmed].
Doktor Şükrü Meḥmed (1923): *Kürdler Türklerden ne istiyorlar? Nāfiʿa vekīli ve Diyarbakır mebʿūṯu Feyzî beye doktor Şükrü Meḥmed beyin bir mektūbu*. Ṭābʿ ve nāşiri: M. ʿ. No date, no place [Cairo 1923] (not mentioned in Özege).

Sekban, Dr. Chukru Mehmed (1933): *La Question Kurde. Des Problèmes des Minorités.* Paris: Presses Universitaires de France 1933.
Sekban, Şükrü Mehmet (1970): *Kürt Sorunu.* No place: Menteş 1970 (Belgelerle Türk Tarihi Dergisi-Yayın: 3).
Sekban, M. Şükrü (1979): *Kürt Meselesi.* Ankara: Kon 1979.
Semler, Christian (1994): "Der Weg ins Freie. Verrat und Identität der Linken", *Kursbuch 116: Verräter* (Juni 1994), pp. 25–36.
Serhat, Mustafa (1995): "Ehmedê Xanî (2)", *Özgür Ülke* January 27, 1995.
Sevgen, Nazmi: *Doğu ve Güneydoğu Anadolu'da Türk beylikleri. Osmanlı belgeleri ile Kürt Türkleri tarihi.* Ed. by Şükrü Kaya Seferoğlu and Halil Kemal Türközü. Ankara: Türk Kültürünü Araştırma Enstitüsü 1982.
Shakely, Ferhad (1992): *Kurdish Nationalism in Mam û Zin of Ahmad-i Khanî.* Brussels: Kurdish Institute of Brussels 1992 (originally Ph.Diss., University of Uppsala, see Hassanpour [1989], p. 462).
Shaw, Stanford J. and Ezel Kural Shaw (1977): *History of the Ottoman Empire and Modern Turkey.* Vol. II: *Reform, Revolution, and Republic: The Rise of Modern Turkey, 1808–1975.* Cambridge: Cambridge University Press 1977.
Sluglett, Peter and Marion Farouk-Sluglett (1991): *Der Irak seit 1958. Von der Revolution zur Diktatur.* Frankfurt/M.: edition suhrkamp 1991.
Soane, Ely Bannister (1913): *Grammar of the Kurmanji or Kurdish Language.* London 1913.
Soysal, İlhami (1985): *150'likler.* İstanbul: Gür 1985.
Strohmeier, Martin (1991): *Al-Kullīya aṣ-Ṣalāḥīya in Jerusalem. Arabismus, Osmanismus und Panislamismus im Ersten Weltkrieg.* Stuttgart: Franz Steiner 1991 (Abhandlungen für die Kunde des Morgenlandes, 49,4).
—— and Lale Yalçın-Heckmann (2000): *Die Kurden. Geschichte, Politik, Kultur.* München: Beck 2000 (Beck'sche Reihe 1329).
—— (forthcoming, 2002): "Das 'Erwachen' in kurdischen Zeitungen zu Beginn des 20. Jahrhunderts", in: *Querelles privées et contestations publiques. Le rôle de la presse dans la formation de l'opinion publique au Proche-Orient,* ed. by Michael Ursinus, Raoul Motika and Christoph Herzog (Aix-en-Provence 1996). İstanbul: İSİS 2002.
Sunguroğlu, İshak (1959): *Harput Yollarında.* Vol. 2. İstanbul 1959.
Süslü, Azmi (ed.) (1993): *Mesud Fāni (Bilgili)'ye göre Kürtler ve Sosyal Gelişimleri.* Ankara: Tanmak 1993 (French original: *La nation kurde et son évolution sociale.* Ph.D.diss. University of Paris 1933).
Sykes, Mark (1908): "The Kurdish Tribes of the Ottoman Empire", *Journal of the Royal Anthropological Institute of Great Britain and Ireland* 38 (1908), pp. 451–486.
Taneri, Aydın (1983): *Türkistanlı bir Türk boyu Kürtler. Kürtler'in kökeni-siyasî, sosyal ve kültürel hayatları. İbnü l'-Ezrak, Şeref Han ve Evliya Çelebi'nin eserlerinin değerlendirilmesi.* Second enlarged ed. Ankara: Türk Kültürünü Araştırma Enstitüsü 1983.
Tapper, Richard (ed.) (1991): *Islam in Modern Turkey. Religion, Politics and Literature in a Secular State.* London-New York: I.B. Tauris 1991.
TDEA = *Türk Dili ve Edebiyatı Ansiklopedisi,* İstanbul 1976 sqq.
Theweleit, Klaus (1977): *Männerphantasien.* Vol. 1: *Frauen, Fluten, Körper, Geschichte.* Frankfurt/M.: Roter Stern 1977.
Touraine, Alain (1974): *Soziologie als Handlungswissenschaft.* Darmstadt und Neuwied: Luchterhand 1974 (Soziologische Texte 59).
Tunaya, Tarık Zafer (1984, 1986): *Türkiye'de Siyasal Partiler.* Cilt I: *İkinci Meşrutiyet Dönemi, 1908–1918.* Second enlarged ed. İstanbul: Hilal 1984; Cilt II: *Mütareke Dönemi, 1918–1922.* Second enlarged ed. İstanbul: Kent 1986 (Hürriyet Vakfı Yayınları).
Tunçay, Mete (1981): *Türkiye Cumhuriyeti'nde Tek-Parti Yönetimi'nin Kurulması (1923–1931).* Ankara: Yurt Yayınları 1981.
Uzun, Mehmed (1989): *Siya Evīnē.* Stockholm: Orfeus 1989.
—— (1995): *Yitik Bir Aşkın Gölgesinde.* İstanbul: Belge 1995 [Turkish translation of Uzun (1989)].

—— (1998): *Im Schatten der verlorenen Liebe.* Zürich: Unionsverlag 1998 [German translation of Uzun (1989)].

Uzun, Mehmet and Rewşen Bedir-Han (eds.) (1998): *Mehmet Salih Bedir-Han. Defter-i A'malım. Mehmet Salih Bedir-Han'ın Anıları.* Istanbul: Belge 1998.

Vanly, Ismet Chérif (1986): *Kurdistan und die Kurden.* Vol. 2. Göttingen und Wien 1986 (pogrom Taschenbücher 1014).

Vanly, Ismet Chérif (1988): *Kurdistan und die Kurden.* Vol. 3. Göttingen und Wien 1988 (pogrom Taschenbücher 1017).

Vanly, Ismet Chériff (1992 a): "The Kurds in Syria and Lebanon", in: Kreyenbroek/Sperl (eds.) (1992), pp. 143–170.

—— (1992 b): "The Kurds in the Soviet Union", in: Kreyenbroek/Sperl (eds.) (1992), pp. 193–218.

Ward, Alan (ed.) (1961): *Mem u Zin—The Kurdish National Epic.* Amsterdam 1961.

Weiss, Stefan (1992): "Briefe", in: Rusinek/Ackermann/Engelbrecht (1992), pp. 45–60.

Wensinck, Arent Jan (1971): *A handbook of early Muhammedan tradition, alphabetically arranged.* Repr. Leiden 1971.

Wesendonk, O.G. von (1931): "Das kurdische Problem", *Preußische Jahrbücher* 223 (1931), pp. 117–130.

Winkler, Heinrich August (ed.) (1978): *Nationalismus.* Königstein 1978.

Yalçın-Heckmann, Lale (1991): *Tribe and Kinship among the Kurds.* Frankfurt am Main-Bern-New York-Paris: Lang 1991 (European university studies: Ser. 19: B; Bd. 27).

Yūsuf Ḍiyā' al-Dīn al-Ḫālidī (1892–93): *al-Hadīya al-ḥamidīya fī l-luġa al-kurdīya.* Derse'ādet: Şirket-i mürettebīye maṭba'ası 1310/1892–93 [The copy in the Bayerische Staatsbibliothek München carries the hand-written remark: "Geschenk von Abdurrezzaq Bey" ("present of Abdurrezzaq Bey"), this is most probably 'Abdürrezzāḳ Bedir Khān, d. 1918].

Zaza, Noureddine (1982): *Ma vie de Kurde ou le cri du peuple Kurde.* Lausanne: Favre 1982.

Zeki, M. Emin (1977): *Kürdistan Tarihi.* İstanbul: Komal 1977.

ANNEX

1. *The editor of Kürdistān petitions the Sultan to allow circulation of the newspaper*

Kürdistān no. 4 (12 Ḏūlḥicce 1316/21 Mayıs 1314/April 23, 1899), pp. 1–2.

My humble petition to his Majesty, Sultan ʿAbdülḥamīd II.
Number 1.

Owing to the importance attached by the Sultan to knowledge, I have succeeded in establishing and publishing the Kurdish newspaper *Kürdistān*. Because the Interior Ministry had communicated to the concerned officials by circular that the import of the newspaper into the Imperial Ottoman dominions was prohibited, I applied to the Grand Vizierate and to the head office of the Palace regarding the difficulties I had met in publishing and disseminating the abovementioned newspaper. In the application I submitted to you my request that you eliminate these difficulties. I informed you as well that I would bring the matter to your attention in case my requests, like similar ones previously, went unanswered.

Meanwhile, although enough time has passed to allow for an answer, no communication has been received. Therefore, I have been compelled to submit to the Imperial Threshold my humble request along with the first page of *Kürdistān* with the impression that the newspaper has been sacrificed to the interests of a few spiteful and influential persons whose names I can present later on if necessary.

My Sultan,
As is known to You, the Kurds are one of the most distinguished peoples of the eternal Ottoman Empire. Owing to its geographical position, Kurdistan has common borders with two states [Iran and Russia] and is especially equipped to prevent attacks by enemies in the direction of Anatolia and is able even to pose a threat to the enemy from that direction.

Although the Kurds occupy an important place in the world of politics and have long taken pride in their Ottoman nationality, not until You ascended the throne in the accustomed and auspicious way was their education and progress deemed worthy of attention.

As one of the distinguished Kurdish notables, bearing responsibility by virtue of the order of the Prophet "All of you are shepherds and all of you are responsible for the flock" and aiming to perform the duty which falls to me, I have produced and published this newspaper in the Kurdish language in order to encourage the Kurds in the study of arts and sciences and to keep them informed of the contemporary requirements.

Because I am one of the Kurdish leaders and because of my advice contained in the newspaper, it will have an extraordinary influence on the Kurds regarding their character and nationality. If ten years ago a newspaper like this had existed, the disturbances in Kurdistan which lead to foreign interventions and annoyances would not have happened. Some progress would have been achieved as well as modernizing projects.

My Sultan,
In the opinion of your humble servant this Kurdish newspaper is one of the most important tools for carrying out the necessary reforms in a speedy way and for preventing the oppression committed by some officials. This has been confirmed by many of those concerned. Because there is nothing harmful in the newspaper's contents, nothing stands in the way of the Exalted Government approving the request. In any case, putting my faith in your judgement, I request that the Sublime Porte issue an imperial decree permitting the newspaper to enter Kurdistan and other places where Kurds live. May the Sultan's decree be issued!

[no author is mentioned, but it is highly probable that the article was written by the editor Miḳdād Midḥat Bedir Khān]

2. *The Kurds are warned about the Sultan's manipulations and admonished to stop harrassing the Armenians*

Kürdistān no. 27 (22 D̲īlḳaʿde 1318/28 Şubāṭ-i evvel 1316/March 13, 1901)

To all Kurds

Kurds! Just as a human being has to prepare in the necessary ways to lead a private life as an individual, so the life of every individual, his interest and his happiness lie with the society to which he belongs, because it is impossible for man to live on his own and because it is a natural necessity to live bound to a society. Firstly, a man must work for the perpetuation of that society, protecting its honor and integrity, for it is more precious than his own life. The existence of the society is guaranteed if the soil—the fatherland—where he grows up and of which he is a part, is not trampled upon by the feet of enemies. Consequently, a person who is a genuine human being will first of all sacrifice his own life for the protection of the fatherland where he grew up, where he was nourished and whose air he breathes. Secondly, he can expect all kinds of benefits from the well-being of that society if he does his best for the continuation of the society of which he is a member. Thirdly, without going beyond the limits of that social framework he will secure the future of the members of his family.

For this reason every people acts after taking into consideration its national interests and finds its personal interests contained in the general national interests.

Despite the truth of this matter, you, the Kurds, have done nothing other than serve ʿAbdülḥamīd, his cruel officials and his accomplices. He has deprived you of all kinds of progress in civilization, of the happiness of knowledge and the blessing of freedom. Furthermore, he loathes you. To secure his personal interests and achieve his unjust aims, he brought about your infamy in this world and the next, by compelling you to massacre helpless Armenians, even children and women.

The supreme aspiration of the Padishah is to cover up, with these actions of yours, the many evils which he has perpetrated, taking advantage of the dark ignorance in which you exist. To that aim he has chosen some scoundrels from your midst and bestowed ranks and decorations which even dogs would not deign to accept and deceived all of you.

Kurds! Believe me, these things called rank and decoration presented to you as bringing honor and glory are but a smokescreen for hate and avarice. They obscure the realities and are good for nothing other than extinguishing your national guiding light and destroying your prosperity and future. Don't you know that with those pieces of metal [the aforesaid decorations] you are selling your personal honor and dignity which your grandfathers and fathers obtained for you by sacrificing their lives, their comfort and their tranquillity?

Kurds! You are the bravest, most intelligent and active of the Oriental peoples! What services have you performed to protect the holy soil on which you were nourished? Although you suffered greatly for the unlawful aims and interests of the Padishah whose biggest desire is to destroy you, how have you acted on behalf of the happiness of Kurdistan? You allow some thieving government agents to exploit your native land and you make all kinds of sacrifices for a wrongful despotic regime. Moreover, you help and serve these insects by pretending not to see, although every evil is right there in front of your eyes.

You have not yet understood that the Sultan whom you desire to follow saying "he is the Caliph", is a tyrant ruler whose dethronement is necessary. The cruelties he has perpetrated, sullying the holy name of the Caliph, are greater evils than those of Jengiz [Khān] and Timur. Although everybody else realizes this, you still have not understood it! Let us assume he is the Caliph. Does this force us to serve the oppressive agents he set on us and to submit stupidly to his oppression like sheep?

There are so many small nations who, as a result of continuous efforts, finally rescued themselves from the tyranny and oppression of the governments they were subjected to and became prosperous and happy. You, however, instead of protecting your well-being, comfort, honor and dignity by following the example of such nations, commit crimes equal to thrusting a dagger with your own hands into your heart and killing yourselves. In this way you have reduced your power and blindly provided the Sultan, your true foe, with the opportunity to oppress you. You have killed Armenians. Do these killings conform to your reputation for generosity and bravery? Even if they do, are you not ashamed vis-à-vis your ancestors who assured the comfort and prosperity of the Armenians for so many years, getting along with them in a brotherly manner? If they ask "Why did you torment our compatriots?" what are you going to answer? Are you not ashamed?

Does it befit humanity to be carried away to such a degree by the incitements of the Sultan who wants to present you to the civilized world as savages? Killing helpless Armenians, is this not tantamount to destroying your own country and your own home? Have the officials, provincial governors, under-governors and district officials who spurred you to pillage and plunder left anything in your possession? Did they not take your honor too, together with what was in your hands? Have you remained so ignorant as to become inspired by the passion to profit from killing and plundering which God and the Prophet have forbidden? Have you not, with your actions, ruined your chance to secure your place in heaven?

Some years ago a meeting was called on the order of the Sultan in Van. When it was decided to incite the Kurds to massacre the Armenians, Sheykh ʿUbaydullāh, who was present at the meeting, withdrew, declaring that such a decision could not be advantageous for the Sultan, because the killing of Armenians in such a way was against the orders of God, because a Sultan issuing such a decree would be a tyrant and a sinner and because a tyrant would deserve to be dethroned.

Kurds! Why has the sheykh's brave conduct not become a good example for you? Have you not already caused enough disgrace and calamity? How can your conscience allow blood stains to defile the dignity and honor which your ancestors acquired at great effort? Does it befit your patriotism to see the sacred soil of the fatherland, the means of your existence, trampled upon by the enemy? You must from now on endeavor to restore your old freedom and in so doing protect your honor and dignity so that you prove that you are descendants worthy of your ancestors! Instead of being an instrument of seizure by violence and plunder in the hands of officials acting as your leaders, and a vehicle for massacre and destruction, think about ways for salvation and shed your blood to this aim so that you may erase the shame resulting from the aforementioned painful events and behaviour and so that your fathers and ancestors will feel proud instead of being ashamed of you, their progeny.

In spite of this difficult situation, we must expect Kurdish notables and sheykhs to undertake the necessary steps. It is they who are responsible in this world and the next for the evils which were committed in Kurdistan. The little people, under any circumstances, can be excused because of their ignorance. But it is natural that those who did not try to stop these crimes and massacres, although they were able to understand the serious consequences, have done wrong. Those who, coveting ʿAbdülḥamīd's ranks and decorations, knowingly carried out his ruinous policies, are guilty of a truely inexcusable crime. It goes without saying that your Armenian compatriots have to be supported in order to put an end to the cruelties. You must try to cooperate with them and to live together in a brotherly fashion. Work for harmony and union! An initiative which is undertaken with good intentions is the prerequisite of God making us successful.

[Author's name not mentioned, most probably the editor ʿAbdurraḥmān Bedir Khān]

3. *The Kurds are lagging behind other members of the Ottoman family on the "highway to progress"*

Kürd Teʿāvün ve Teraḳḳī Ġazetesi, volume 1, no.1 (11 Ḏīlḳaʿde 1326/22 Teşrīn-i ṯānī 1324/December 5, 1908), p. 1.

When the Kurdish people assumed the highly esteemed name of Ottomans upon their own conscious request, it was a tumultuous time of invasion in which the culture of the milieu was read on the bejeweled engravings of swords, and scientific subjects were learned by heart to the accompaniment of side drums. Ability was equated with bravery, fame derived from strength and pride from attacks. The Kurds born in the matrix of this tumultuous Ottoman period, spent all their lives in this context; therefore, they acquired only religious strength and an ingrained heroism in their life struggle. Now the battles have subsided. The prosperity of civilization has opened another colorful page in the book of life for us. But we could say that misfortune has kept the eyes and even tongues of the Kurds closed and locked. As tent-dwellers, travelling through the wilderness they were subjected to oppressive and abhorrent acts of robbery and destruction. Today we see that all peoples are ahead of us on an open highway to progress, in an impressive state of advancement which dazzles proud Ottoman eyes.

We, struggling for so many years with the strength of a half-slaughtered being and incapacitated by our blindness, cannot find our way. Kurdistan, which has produced in the past great talents in arts and sciences, leaves as a heritage to its children only a copy of a religious book brought from India. We communicate with each other on important affairs by sending ignorant men of the sort "the meaning is in the stomach of the one who brings it". These men carry our messages on white paper stamped with the residue from our tobacco pipes; details are left to the narrative styles of the messengers. The *Kurdish Society for Elevation and Progress* has seen the nation of which it is a part in this terrible darkness and tragic dumbness and has made a vow of devotion to its Kurdish brothers who are a worthy member of the Ottoman family and who are the first bound to protect the honour of the Ottomans. Weeping for our history, but smiling vis-à-vis the future, the Kurds will move towards progress in every respect: knowledge, trade and industry. In short, they will acquire happiness commensurate with the exalted name of the Ottomans. A chant for determination and hope, a stirring call, this is our newspaper. May God grant us success!

Tevfīḳ [according to the title page this is Tevfīḳ M. Süleymānīyeli, from his "preface" to the first number of *Kürd Teʿāvün ve Teraḳḳī Ġazetesi*]

4. *The hierarchy of identities: Muslim, Ottoman, Kurdish; correcting the image of the Kurds*

Kürd Teʿāvün ve Teraḳḳī Ġazetesi vol. 1, no. 1 (11 D̲īlḳaʿde 1326/22 Teşrīn-i t̲ānī 1324/December 5, 1908, pp. 3–4.

The Kurds and Kurdistan

The Kurdish nation of whom I am a proud member has started to show signs of reform and animation. They, too, have decided to prosper and to safeguard their existence and to develop as a protector of an important branch of the pure Ottoman tree nourished by the blessed abundance of the bright sun of freedom. These pure people which constitute a very firm bastion and stronghold of the great Ottoman family and an eternal tributary of the full flowing and abundant stream of Islam, are first of all Muslims. Secondly, the Kurdish people are genuine and sincere Ottomans affirming the principles of the constitution which is the force behind the life of nations and the source of happiness in the world. Thirdly, they are Kurds; therefore, they strive to obtain their own national ideal and their own happiness all the while being a most important pillar, a most useful, fruitful and obedient element of that magnificent and holy family of Islam and of that revered family of Ottomans, never departing from that general principle in the slightest degree. Since they entered the salvation of Islam, that is since the first period of our religion, since the emergence of Islam, the Kurds have never rebelled against that holy faith, they do not now and they never will. Since the day they proudly and voluntarily entered the powerful Ottoman Empire on their own request and without being conquered, the Kurds have never shown a sign of treachery against the Ottomans, they do not now and they never will. The Kurds are still Kurds; they have not changed their nationality, the form of their external appearance and their material and moral identity in the slightest degree. Nevertheless, they have remained strongly attached to the Ottomans. No force in the world can be imagined which could succeed in destroying the old harmony between the Kurds and the Ottomans and their strong bonds. The Ottomans comprise the Kurds and the Kurds in return comprise the Ottomans; the meanings of these two words have merged beyond recognition. If the Ottomans—God forbid!—perish, not a trace of the Kurds will remain. If—God forbid!—the Kurds are annihilated, the Ottomans will become weak and ruined.

Nevertheless, in the previous period of despotism which must be banished to the terrible darkness of the past and the field of oblivion never to be recalled, this element of strength [the Kurds], which constitutes a pillar of the Ottoman state, had been oppressed and abused worse than other peoples of the Ottoman state. While the old government was absolutely an enemy of thought, regarding the Kurdish people it was an enemy of thought and an enemy of the language. Whereas it strove to cut only the head of other Ottoman peoples, it tried first to cut the tongue of the Kurds and along with the tongue its head. Indeed, permanent oppression makes the mind stupid; but cutting the tongue makes a nation not only dumb, but also dazed. The harshest oppression, the gravest irreparable destruction was this.

Having no tongue, the Kurds were not only about to lose their nationality, but also their religion. An excessive ignorance had enveloped many areas causing the loss of any human feelings. Under the influence of factors such as the lack of essential knowledge of religion, not only the lives of the miserable Kurds, but also their honor and national honour, which they hold more valuable than their existence, was in danger of being defiled. The previous government carried out various oppressive acts and injustices, ruined the country and its cultivated areas, encouraged plundering, and instigated massacres. Later, wishing to escape the consequences in a supposedly honest and pure way, it attributed all crimes to the savagery, fanaticism, blood-thirstiness and avarice of the Kurds. The world press, confusing the Kurdish people with the government, and the wretched oppressed who had been robbed of everything with bands of rebels, wrote Turks, when they meant the Ottoman government, wrote Kurds, when they meant the Kurdish region, rained lies and accusations on the innocent Kurdish individuals, drowning them in a flood of calumnies. The government remained silent, because it suited their interests to do so. The fate awaiting a herd whose silent shepherd is a wolf, is its demise.

One of the opprobrious misrepresentations of the Kurds is that they have long been mortal enemies of the Armenians. If we can disregard the recent past, it is impossible to find two neighbouring peoples with more friendly relations. Nothing was missing! And then came the charges by the Armenians against the Kurds. If the Kurds had really plotted against the lives of Armenians, would they not have carried out the alleged brutal acts before imagination gave birth to article 61 of the Treaty of Berlin? Would they not long ago have eliminated the Armenians who were almost made enemies by repeatedly being called enemies?

The Kurds, like other Ottomans, respect the life, property, honor and religion of their non-Muslim compatriots. Because the Kurds are Muslims, and also very devout Muslims, they have always understood, perhaps better than anyone else, the words of the Prophet: "Whatever is for us, is also for them, and whatever is incumbent on us, is also incumbent on them".[1]

However, let us now put aside these bitter memories! Let us rub the sponge over the shameful mistakes of the old government, and,

[1] I was not able to trace this quote; the *ḥadīṯ* consists only of prepositions, and Wensinck (1971) lists no prepositions.

saying "The future is ours", let us take up the hard work wholeheartedly. Yes, to work, to work day and night, to work continuously without resting. That is the first and last thing which we Orientals and, among the Orientals particularly the lagging Kurds, have to do.

In answer to the question of where we must start our work, it will have to be education. Then again education. And later? Later it is again education, education, education. May God give success to those who strive in this endeavour!

Bābānzāde
İsmāʿīl Ḥaḳḳī

5. *The task of "inventing" the Kurdish nation falls to the intellectuals*

Rojē Kurd no. 2 (14 Şaʿbān 1331/6 Temmūz 1329/July 19, 1913), pp. 2–5.

Your duty vis-à-vis your nation

To the enlightened Kurdish youth

In these lines I would like to address the Kurdish youth. My addressee is the educated part of the Kurdish youth. By that I mean the young men who have completed their higher education, or who are still busy with their studies on the benches of schools of higher education.

Today your people, like most of the Oriental peoples, must be brought back to life. In this era, to be able to protect the existence of a nation as a social organism, requires qualities and conditions of which your people are largely deprived. Your primary, your holiest duty is to work so that your nation acquires these qualities and conditions.

For the sake of simplicity let us classify these qualities and conditions into two groups: thought and economy. Today the life of nations is more than ever before dependent on competition, on the securing of supremacy in competition. But this struggle is carried out with the weapons of thought and economy in the area of livelihood. The nations and their individuals who are rather well-armed with these weapons make progress and become happy. The ones who are deprived of these weapons, however, will always be defeated in this contest, and will fall under the yoke of slavery of the victors in ideas and in economy, remaining a poor people and losing all kinds of moral and material qualities.

Therefore in this era the value of a nation and its capacity to learn can only be measured by assessing the condition of its members. That is to say, the importance of a national group is attached to the intellectual qualities and economic power each member possesses. Consequently, the wise men, intellectuals and patriots of every people know that their first duty is to strive to raise the intellectual and economic level of the group to which they belong and they work to carry out this duty with devotion.

Today you, the Kurdish intellectuals, understand better than anybody else that your people do not possess these intellectual and economic qualities to a notable degree. It is necessary to work very hard and in a very devoted manner in order to raise the level of the Kurdish people. This duty falls to you more than anyone else, and you are in a position to carry out this duty much better than anybody else.

Neither the laws of the country, nor the officials, nor even the great men whom your nation deems in accordance with its traditions to be a privileged class, in short, no other force but you can carry out this task successfully.

In order to be able to serve your nation, you must forego settling and remaining in cultural centres which are far away from the national milieu. On the contrary, you must return to the places where you grew up and reenter with an enlightened mind into the intimacy and cordiality of your native society.

If you stay far away from this milieu permanently and carry out your duty of enlightening and guidance from outside that milieu, then, believe me, your activities will be wasted; they will not bring about useful results on behalf of the nation. Your people will not consider you, the intellectual class, as in any way their own. It will always deal with you as a foreigner. Your attempt to provide guidance will be wasted.

You must always keep in mind that in this era the nations who have awakened or the nations who are about to awaken are those nations which keep the enlightened class at their breasts; furthermore, the enlightened class, embracing the nation, is always in contact with the various classes. The intellectuals suffer with the nation in times of catastrophe and there is mutual rejoicing in times of happiness. Now, if you understand the national duty in this way and start to carry it out accordingly, then you will have accomplished your task in its modern sense. You may be sure that in this way you will not only awaken the Kurdish nation, but you will also 'create' a Kurdish nation out of nothing.

Do not imitate in this respect the Ottoman-Turkish youth. They did not come down at all into their national milieu. They addressed the nation always from afar, from 'above'. They wanted to communicate to the nation ideas which it could not understand in a language which it could not understand. In times of national catastrophies they "beat their breasts" [in the way Shiites flagellate themselves during the Muḥarrem ceremony] far from the nation, from abroad. Therefore, they did not know the nation, and the nation did not know them. The nation always looked at them as foreigners. As result, the Turkish nation lived for centuries deprived of the illumination and guidance of the enlightened class. Intellectually and economically it decayed more and more. You must not make this mistake. You must learn a lesson from this disaster of the Turkish nation.

When you return to the national milieu the matter you will have to deal with is the establishment of elementary education on very strong and reasonable foundations. The number of elementary schools must be increased as much as possible. From the beginning you will be confronted with the problem of letters. The solution to that problem will not be easy. But you are the most competent element in the nation to solve the problem. You, the intellectuals, are the only force which can deal with the restrictions and conditions, and make brave judgements and decisions, taking into consideration the requirements of science and the exigencies of the century regarding the quick learning of reading and writing.

Give serious and careful attention to the establishment of primary education on sound principles. Regarding instruction, the most current principles of pedagogy should be your guide. Be aware, that in this century the object of primary education is not only for children to learn to read and write, but also to learn to reflect carefully and, especially, to reason correctly. Today the basis of intellectual education in the whole nation should consist of that. If you do not give attention to the training of primary school-teachers who will be able to provide this intellectual education, your elementary schools which you thought were most excellent will only educate to read and write.

The damage done to national efforts by the half-literate, deprived of intellectual education, is greater than that caused by utterly ignorant people.

Therefore, while you work to establish the basic principles of elementary education on the one hand, do not forget, on the other hand, to establish some excellent teacher training colleges, in which good teachers will be trained [one word unreadable].

On the day that you start to prepare your new generation in this way, you will have started to improve the intellectual qualities and abilities of the members of your nation. A nation which is composed of such members fully appreciates its rights and considers carefully how to protect and defend itself.

You state that your nation is dependent on the soil. The members of such a nation become farmers and cattle-breeders. They maintain their livelihood in one of the branches of these two basic areas. The economic improvement of persons who earn their livelihood in these ways is quicker than in other professional branches. If some practical, yet scientific methods are shown to them, they will become the first supporters of innovation and reforms in agriculture, because they will feel the profit immediately in their pockets and purses.

Now you are charged with the duty to enter the national milieu and to occupy yourself with these affairs. The means for real progress of a nation today is secured only with these methods; progress which is founded on such 'democratic' principles will never cease and will always increase.

If you do not act in such a way and want to stay like the Ottoman-Turkish youth outside the national milieu and to address the nation from 'above' and from abroad, then you leave yourself open to a heavy accusation. Everybody will surmise that you have fallen into the daydream of playing the part of the 'privileged intellectual class' of the nation and of founding an 'intellectual aristocracy' in the name of the nation. As if the two other classes of 'aristocrats' would not suffice for your nation [some words misprinted: "sizi de üçüncü bilā olm . . . üzere add etmekte herkes ḥakl olur"].

It is my heartfelt desire that the Kurdish enlightened youth should comprehend its duty vis-à-vis the nation according to the requirements of our time and that it hasten to do its duty in that manner.

Bulġāristānlı
Ṭoġan

6. *The focus of modernization efforts must be on rural Kurdistan; educated Kurds must leave the city for Kurdistan*

Hetavē Kurd no.1 (23 D̲īlḳaʿde 1331/11 Teşrīn-i evvel 1329/October 24, 1913), pp. 2–3.

To the writers of the newspaper *Hetavē Kurd*

Doubtlessly you are expending a lot of energy and ink in order to serve the Kurdish nation. But you are publishing this newspaper for literate nations. I am sure that, unfortunately, the literate among the Kurds are so few that one can count them on the fingers of one hand. Certainly, you would like the Kurds to be civilized, enlightened and capable of growth. There is no doubt that all of the Ottoman patriots longing for the strength and recovery of the Ottoman Empire also desire the strength and enlightenment of the ethnic groups they belong to.

But what follows from that wish? Wishes must be followed by action. For a youth who feels a strong compassion and a compassionate strength for his people in his heart, the first act of devotion must be to run to Anatolia. Here, in Istanbul, definitely nothing will come of mere talking and writing.

To the villages! To the villages! To eat cornbread, to drink goatmilk and to nourish the villagers with light, with the blessing of civilization. This must be your desire and it must be accompanied by the utmost courage and determination.

Let me ask you, I do not know, you'll tell me! How many Kurds are in the world? Where do they live? What are their crafts? What are their trades? In general, what is the nature of their economic life? Is the male population more numerous or the female? What is the literacy rate? What exists among the Kurdish people that deserves the name of industry? What is the proportion of them to other Ottoman peoples in terms of landownership? It is known that among the Kurds migration has started to America. How many migrants have there been? What is their situation in America in comparison to their Armenian fellow citizens? What are their enterprises with the neighboring peoples in possession of domestic animals? To what degree do they make use of animals and trade with them? To what degree have the Kurdish race and their customs been preserved? Where have Kurds established elementary schools by their own initiative and how many of these schools exist?

What is the proportion of the Kurds with and without landownership? Is the number of Kurds increasing or decreasing? What is the rate of births and deaths? What is the cause or what are the causes of deaths? How many marriages are there? How many divorces are there? What are the causes of divorce? How is it possible to facilitate marriage and to encourage a large number of children? And so on . . .

I would like to get answers to these questions from my patriotic Kurdish brothers.

I believe that these problems cannot be analyzed and solved at a desk. And I regret very much that our Exalted Government, too, has not paid the problems of life, conscience and emotional pain the attention they deserve. But perhaps the government has just not found the time.

Anatolia is full of bitterness and death: I would like to strike a painful blow to the breast of the leading government functionaries. And I would do the same to myself. This blow must be suffered without anger.

Only this year, in a recruitment medical examination, in a village in the province of Adana only 12 from among 744 persons were found to be free from syphilis.

Such is the dimension of the suffering: everyone and everything is affected [most probably one word misprinted; therefore translation doubtful]. In a decaying body there can be neither intelligence nor conscience.

Once flourishing places have become cemeteries. Hunger and poverty reign over our fertile land which once provided stores of grains to the houses with courtyards where people used to live. The responsibility for these calamities is ours, and we and the intellectuals must bear this burden.

Anatolia has been deprived of the most important of life's resources: knowledge. Knowledge means fresh air for civilized life. First of all, let us bring air.

If you would rather become founders and teachers of elementary schools in a Kurdish village than officials with the rank of head of a district or subdistrict in whatever places, only then, Kurdish youth, are you truly on the path which must be tread.

5 Teşrīn-i evvel 1913/October 5, 1913
Doḳtor ʿAbdullāh Cevdet

7. *Kurdish intellectuals should not be sent to Kurdistan without careful preparation*

Hetavē Kurd no. 2 (4 Muḥarrem 1332/21 Teşrīn-i ṯānī 1329/December 3, 1913), pp. 2–3.

[answer to Cevdet's article in *Hetavē Kurd* no. 1]

Social affairs:
To the respected founders of the newspaper *Hetavē Kurd*

The activities of *Hetavē Kurd* for the elevation and advancement of the Kurdish society deserve respect and appreciation. Naturally, this esteemed periodical through its editorial and organizational activities will "revive" the Kurdish nation, and if it accomplishes this then their efforts will have been worthwhile.

Looking at other nations we observe that all of them have created a national framework; they are occupied with advancing and elevating their societies. Peoples who do not know their nationality and who do not follow the national ideal, remain behind the others in the human family and remain spiritless. Imagine how deplorable a spiritless people is. How painful it is to be doomed to die and be swallowed by a civilized society.

Hetavē Kurd aims to perform a very sacred and exalted duty. It endeavours to save from oblivion the miserable Kurds, this consanguineous group of 6 or 7 million. Therefore I regard it as my duty to congratulate in the name of all Kurds those who have started this initiative. Meanwhile, regarding the improvement of the eastern provinces, initiatives and serious activities can be observed. The Armenians, who are of the same race as we, are seeking a better existence. We should know these people of the same race well and we must follow them in the full sense of the word.

[In the following two paragraphs the author mentions the common origins of Armenians and Kurds from the "Urdu-Urartu" people. After the Armenians adopted Christianity they went separate ways. In the recent past the Armenians had demonstrated progress and started to follow an "unknown" aim. The author hopes for cooperation and harmony between Kurds and Armenians and is confident that in the future both will be united]

The duty which now falls upon us Kurds, is to take care of our own affairs ourselves. Of course, no Kurd wants his race to die or be extinguished or be swallowed by persons of the same race. Consequently, every Kurd must agree with the sentence: "Let us take care of our own affairs ourselves".

What is needed to awaken the Kurds, to make them understand their existence, their right to live, and to put them on the road to progress? I do not share the opinion of the esteemed Doḳtor ʿAbdullāh Cevdet. Without a clear and definitive aim it is unnecessary and useless to scatter Kurdish youth across Anatolia. This suggestion is very premature. First of all, language is necessary to awaken the Kurds, to acquaint them with their existence, their right to live and to put them on the road to progress. The way to improve and propagate the language is by writing. In order to write the Kurdish language properly and to learn and teach it, it is necessary to revive and to improve our old letters, that is the Urdu letters [What Mevlānzāde calls "Urdu" should not be confused with the Indo-Aryan language which today is the official language of Pakistan; what he is obviously referring to is the above-mentioned Urdu/Urartu people and their language; Urartu was a language of non-Indo-European origin in Eastern Anatolia and Armenia in the 6–9 centuries B.C.].

We cannot master our language with the letters we use today. At present the pursuit of our aim is difficult and unfruitful. If we revive and improve our old letters, and if we can present a dictionary as well as books and grammars in the framework of a new method to our people whose situation is primitive, then the road to progress will be opened up. To secure these basic goals need not be so difficult. Today, thank God, we have among the Kurds some scholars, morally upright people with knowledge of language. They must come together and establish a scientific committee. Deeds in any case are stronger than words. I hope that the founders of *Hetavē Kurd* make this national duty their aim. The convening of this scientific committee in Istanbul will be more useful and reasonable than sending youth to Anatolia. In this respect I can use as an example the Armenians who are of the same race. When they felt the need for a national and social revolution they did not send their educated youth to the villages, to Anatolia. First of all, their scholars met in a city in Europe. They thought about the things they wanted to do, decided and afterwards they hurried to our region in order to communicate the objectives which had been agreed on. Let us do it in this way. Let us prepare in a reasonable way by first listing our objectives. Let us get ready first and then go to Kurdistan.

Mevlānzāde Rıfʿat

8. *The aims of Hēvī; urging Kurdish leaders to take action*

Hetavē Kurd no. 4–5 (27 Cemādiyilākhir 1332/10 Mayıs 1330/May 23, 1914), pp. 1–4.

Declaration of the "Kurdish Students Society *Hēvī*"

There was a time when the Kurds were an advanced and great nation. Today, all other nations have made great progress in science, crafts, trade and agriculture, but the Kurds have remained behind. Every nation has hundreds of schools and high schools in which thousands of children study arts and sciences. Each nation has books and journals which teach the methods and techniques of crafts, commerce and agriculture, in short, the way to live a good and comfortable life. We Kurds do not know anything about these things. For this reason everybody slanders and wrongly accuses us. In order to deliver ourselves from this situation we must inform ourselves as soon as possible about these things and seek remedies at once. As a matter of fact, our religion orders the Muslims to learn sciences and arts and to strive for progress and prosperity. God in the Holy Quran makes it a duty applicable to all Muslims to study, to engage in science and acquire knowledge. If we want to obey the will of God the Most High we must understand very well that there is no alternative to working for science, arts and progress. God has given the Kurds intelligence and all sorts of talents. We are capable of making great progress in a very short time. It is sufficient that we understand the state of the world and begin our work. The situation of the Kurds is so well known to all of us and the need to work is so evident that there is no need for long explanations.

Today each Kurd, big and little, rich and poor, understanding this duty to religion and the nation must live to fulfill this [some letters missing or unreadable]. To work separately is of no use. The best and most useful way is to work united. All nations which started to awaken began their task by first establishing "societies", [one word unreadable] and reached their goals by bringing about progress in their nations. We, the Kurdish youth, who have come together to obtain knowledge and study at the schools and colleges in Istanbul, in order to carry out our duty to our religion and our nation have founded with permission of the authorities a society with the name "Kurdish Students Society *Hēvī*". For the last two years this society has worked as hard as possible. In introducing itself today to all Kurds the Society wishes to explain thoroughly its aims.

The aims of our society are as follows:

1–To work jointly and united for the Kurds by making Kurdish students acquainted with each other
2–To present the Kurdish language and literature to the public
3–To open schools and colleges and to build mosques in Kurdistan
4–To teach poor children science and arts, to help the poor
5–In short, to work for the prosperity and happiness of the Kurds.

These aims, which we have worked day and night to achieve, are very important. Once a year many students come from Kurdistan to Istanbul and other places. At the new locations these students do not have the comforts and amenities of their home districts. Although there are many Kurdish students in one town they cannot assist each other because they do not know each other. They run into thousands of difficulties and suffer inconveniences. Consequently, they are not able to study. If they knew each other, they would without doubt suffer no trouble and study well. Thus, the Society intends to acquaint the students with each other.

Every nation has a language, with which it speaks, writes articles, and also prints books. Although in the past the Kurds had a perfect language for reading as well as for writing and speaking and although some books were written in this language, later it was gradually forgotten. Only outside the cities was it used again for speaking. In this way, Kurdish lost its former importance. However, a nation with half a language cannot exist. Such a nation can neither learn science nor acquire knowledge nor can it make progress. To make the Kurdish language suitable for reading and writing, to distribute it to every part of Kurdistan by writing books in that language, and in this manner to teach the Kurds science and knowledge is the first objective of the Society.

The reason for the present-day decay of the Kurds is ignorance.

In order to eliminate it, it is necessary immediately to get children started with reading at an early age. It is another principal aim of our Society to open schools for young children and to educate them in such a way that they are able to serve their religion, state and nation.

In summary, the aims of the Society are to serve the Kurds who are a strong pillar of Islam and thus to serve religion and the state. A nation which wants to exist and to advance, and, particularly, to escape from misery, tries first of all to accomplish these aims. If the Kurds work with determination and zeal they will surely advance within a short time. A nation which cannot do these things will attain nothing at all, and a nation which can do these things has the prospect of attaining happiness. That students form a society and openly address the Kurdish public is something which has not before been seen among us.

The purity and seriousness of our aim and intention is evident to a degree which does not leave any doubt and will help every Kurd. We ask for support from our people on behalf of the entire nation. O Kurdish scholars, sheykhs, leaders, great men!

You doubtlessly know and understand the things which we have put forward above much better than we do. You can understand and determine much better than we the state of the Kurds and the degree of their needs. Therefore we do not dare to guide you or to give you advice.

But, with your permission, we would like to mention that if there is one thing which the great Kurdish men have not been able to understand, it is the discord and quarreling between them, which harms the Kurdish cause even today. This malady has not served the well-being of the Kurds. There are no religious and national duties as important as the duties of the Kurdish scholars and leaders today. The fate of Islam is in your hands, to make this clear is a duty you are entrusted with. To open schools, to teach crafts and knowledge to some poor and intelligent children, to be instructed in book-printing; who other than you can do all these things which are the only means for the advancement of the nation?

The Creator says: "Are those who know and those who do not know equal?" [Arabic, Quran 39,9]

We may interpret this divine truth to mean: those who have knowledge and and those who do not have knowledge are not equal.

The punishment for a [unreadable] act is not the same for those who have knowledge and those who do not. Does not the Divine Wisdom "The master of the people is your servant" [Arabic][2] tell us that the real chiefs and leaders of a people are the ones who serve the people?

Moreover:
The sheep are not for the shepherd
but the shepherd serves the sheep
[Persian]

If we allow ourselves to be guided by the meaning of these words, then we will have paved most of the way to the source of happiness.

God will ask everybody about their sins. Everyone must do the religious and national duty he is entrusted with. Do not depend on others to carry out the service to your nation. This would clearly indicate your not wishing to serve the nation. For once you must realize that you owe your present prosperity and happiness to the nation you have refused to serve. What are the reasons which prevent you from carrying out this service?

It is one of the holy duties of those charged with responsibilities in high and favorable positions like you to work for the Kurdish cause, and to help and encourage those who work for the Kurds.

Now, esteemed elders, in view of the nobility of these aims, of the sincerity of these young people and of the needs of this nation, which of you can refuse to give support, which of you in view of the plight and needs of the nation will look on from a distance and remain insensitive and indifferent? Therefore we conclude:

If you want to carry out the duty and obligation to protect the life which is awakening among the Kurds, and the light which has started to glow, then there is a vast field for service. Here is the "Kurdish Students Society *Hēvī*"; the salvation and viability of Islam and the Kurds is a matter which is bound to your religious understanding, your patriotism and your love for the nation.

"Kurdish Students Society *Hēvī*"

Address: Istanbul, Şehzādebaşı [district of Istanbul]

---

[2] This is most probably a *ḥadīṯ*.

9. *The creation of the Kurdish nation is possible through education*

Kürdistān, birinci sene, ʿaded 8 (28 Şaʿbān 1337/29 Mayıs 1335/May 29, 1919), p. 98.

To keep the Kurdish nation and Kurdistan alive

The peoples able to demonstrate ability in this general examination which has been opened up to the unhappy peoples will attain privilege, a secure life and happiness according to their rights and abilities. There is no doubt that the Kurds, too, the most unjustly treated of peoples, who work tirelessly in the defense of their rights, will be able to demonstrate their abilities in this examination and thus gain rights which will allow them to achieve a great and holy life. But will the Kurds succeed in keeping that sacred Kurdistan alive once they have secured its existence? That is a point which deserves very serious thought!

Just as nobody can live without food, no country and no people can live without education. Unfortunately, the Kurds up to now have either not given adequate attention to education which is the nourishment for a country and people, or they have not succeeded in creating anything useful. Therefore the lack of this vital necessity makes it difficult to continue and to develop the life of the Kurds and Kurdistan. What will happen then? Will Kurdistan, ready for birth but not yet born, die shortly after birth? In the case of such a catastrophe—God forbid—will not all Kurds become murderers? Will not all Kurds commit suicide? The patriotism of the Kurds, their attachment to their nation are very strong. But I would like to say with great sorrow that there has been no continuity in Kurdish efforts to achieve common goals. It is due to this lack of consistent efforts that the Kurds for many years have experienced suffering and catastrophes. The Kurds who have suffered greatly under slavery and gone through catastrophes, are now struggling with all their strength for their salvation. But there are some shortcomings in these efforts. If the shortcomings are not eliminated at once, all present efforts will, in the end, be wasted. Therefore, as long as there is still time, Kurdish intellectuals and youth must unite to produce a sustained effort and, by relying on teaching, must establish Kurdish education. Because education is the prime mover of everything, there will be no resistance to correcting the situation. Then the sustenance to prolong and develop the life of the Kurds and Kurdistan will have been provided.

Bedir Khān
Meḥmed ʿOṯmān

10. *The revival of Hēvī in 1919: criticism of the Kurdish leadership, styling of the Kurdish youth as the avantgarde of the nation*

Jīn birinci sene, ʿaded 20, 4 Ḥazīrān 1335/June 5, 1919, pp. 4–10, here: 8–10.

Two laudable initiatives: The "Society for the Elevation of Kurdish Women" and the "Kurdish Students Society *Hēvī*" [Hope]

The other laudable initiative which strengthens our hopes is the "Kurdish Students Society *Hēvī*". We observe with gratitude and pride that it has started again its activities. After an interval of four and a half to five years due to the Great War it has taken up its work again. *Hēvī* aroused great hope and confidence with its three-year efforts [1912–1915] in the Kurdish world. It lost extremely valuable members in a war brought about by a government which accumulated and spread disasters. Four and a half years ago the country's entire educated youth was gathered at the ground of the War College to be dragged into the fire of war. Hundreds of these young men who had brought *Hēvī* to life submitted to the heavy chains of a careless and ambitious militarism. The legacy of *Hēvī* was entrusted to God and two young men. *Hēvī* lived in their hearts as a bright hope for tomorrow.

Yes, *Hēvī* was a "hope" for the Kurds. Seven years ago,[3] when all serious-minded people and great men dozed in their corners, when everybody was timid and hesitating, when everybody said yes to everything, the *Hēvī* youth dared only in low voices to discuss the prospects which can be talked about loudly today. They poured out

[3] *Hēvī* was founded in 1912.

their grievances to one another about what they thought could be achieved with only a small effort.

Hēvī was a beginning. A regime which accumulated and spread catastrophes could not hope to turn *Hēvī* into an instrument serving the governments' interests or even to make *Hēvī* indebted to the government by giving hush money. Therefore, *Hēvī* members were dragged under a pretext to police stations and their voices were silenced in prison.

While in Syria Arabs were being hung,[4] *Hēvī*-members in Istanbul were being sought by the authorities. Who knows what their fate would have been, if the war had not eliminated the necessity of erecting gallows in Istanbul or preparing places of exile in Anatolia or prison cellars.

Today, among those who raise again the *Hēvī*-flag, there are almost none of the older brothers from those days. However, the spirit of determination and continuation which *Hēvī* spread before the war has not disappeared, but has gained strength and magnitude. As one of our esteemed thinkers expressed at the revival ceremony of *Hēvī*: 'Our youth have shown that they are totally free from and superior to the spirit and mentality of the Orient. They have not, like Orientals, destroyed existing structures. They have demonstrated the qualities of steadfastness, perseverance and determination by enlarging the structure on the foundation they had already established.'

Every time I see how fervently and affectionately the *Hēvī*-members are devoted and committed to each other and their duty, at every moment of every day, the bright and strong future of Kurdistan rises before my eyes.

After this interval of four and a half, five years, *Hēvī*'s mission is now entrusted to today's *Hēvī*-members. Given the magnitude of the task all that is needed is that they are neither pessimistic, nor optimistic nor hopeless: They must regard only the facts and understand the consequences. They must strive to avoid illusion and greed, while working towards what is real and possible. Illusion and greed have never won. Hopes derived from reality and practicability will sooner or later provide minds with an enthusiasm for moving forward, tenacity of spirit and divine inspiration which should be theirs by nature.

[4] Arab nationalists sentenced to death by Jemāl Pasha and hung in Beirut and Damascus in 1915/16.

Hēvī should not forget the bitter poison of illusion and greed which result in frustration and disappointment. To these saviours I convey my honour and respect . . .

Memdūḥ Selīm Begi May 26, 1919

11. *A Kurdish intellectual remembers the early Kurdish nationalist Şükrü Mehmet Sekban*

Anter (1990), pp. 74–76:

Doctor Mehmet Şükrü Sekban

He was originally from Maden, which is now a district in the province of Elazığ. He was a dermatologist and held a position which today we call associate professor at the Cerrahpaşa Hospital. He participated in all Kurdish activities in Istanbul. He made a lot of money. He supported all Kurdish societies and periodicals. He was at the top of the list which Atatürk called the group of 150. Sekban, like others from that group, fled the country . . . I got to know Doctor Sekban after the amnesty. Our relationship continued until his death. He explained his reason for writing the book "The Kurds are Turks" [*La Question Kurde*] which made him feel ashamed and which in his opinion had not been understood, in the following way:

"In 1925 Kurdistan lacked a protector. It was exposed to all kinds of oppression and genocide. There came not the least support or protest either from Europe or from the Islamic world. The initiative was compeletely left to the fascist regime in Ankara. Abroad we could not do anything. The truth of the matter is that the movements which the Turks call rebellions were a reaction against the agreements with Atatürk which had not been carried out. For the Kurds had been saved from the cruel treatment of the Party of Union and Progress and the sultans and expected to be treated in a humane fashion when the Turkish Republic was established. But then they realized that the Republican administration oppressed them even more heavily. Because I knew Nuri Said Pasha from the time in Istanbul, I became health minister in the cabinet which he headed in Iraq at the time of King Faysal I. It was surely due to distress that I became weak and came down with tuberculosis. I went to

Germany for treatment. Amidst all my sorrow I thought: The ignorant people in Ankara call the whole world 'Turkish'. If I say, 'The Kurds are Turks', maybe the oppression against the Kurds will diminish. In the hospital I wrote my thoughts on paper napkins. After my release from hospital I had the manuscript printed at the press of the Sorbonne University in Paris. But my friends were very upset. After my return Celadet Bedirxan and I had dinner together in Damascus. When an Arab dish came which I was not familiar with I asked Celadet Bey, 'What is that?' He replied, 'Doctor, that is eggplant, but you can call it zucchini'. I realized that Celadet Bey was alluding to my book. Later, more ordinary criticisms were put forward. That I had allegedly been under the influence of my Circassian wife who was from Istanbul. That I had written the book because my wife missed Istanbul very much, and my intention was to be pardoned by Atatürk . . . But I swear that's not the way it was."

It may sound like self-praise, but the Doctor liked me very much. Nuri Sait Pasha was both Sekban's and Menderes' friend. When Menderes welcomed Nuri Sait at Yeşilköy airport, Sait allegedly said to him, 'My dear brother Menderes, there is a friend of mine, Doctor Mehmed Sekban, whom I like as much as I like you. I would like to see Sekban at your side when I get off the plane [in Istanbul]. Then my heart would feel even more joyful.' Nuri Sait was suffering from a heart ailment, and had a lot of faith in Şükrü Sekban. After that event Menderes summoned the Doctor; he made him a doctor at the Istanbul Electric Power, Funicular and Streetcar Board with a high salary. Everytime Nuri Sait came to Istanbul Menderes took Sekban with him to the airport.

It was the last journey of Nuri Sait to London via Istanbul in 1958. At the airport, he had given a present to the Doctor. The Doctor phoned me and asked me to come to his office. I went there. He said: 'Look, my son, Musa; these are presents from Sait Pasha: dates, tea and coffee. Neither I nor my wife will make use of the dates or the tea. I will just take some coffee, you take the rest home!' I took the present and said to him: 'Uncle, since you are so close to Nuri Said Pasha, why don't you tell him to help the Kurds in Iraq?' He laughed and with his famous oath he said, 'I'll be damned, if I don't tell him on his return'.

Nuri Sait went to London and returned. One Sunday, a police jeep stopped in front of my house in Suadiye. I laughed and asked the commissar, 'I hope nothing's wrong! Do we have to go the police station again?' He answered, 'No, no, we are just leaving; you just make sure that you are at this address no later than 12 o'clock.' I looked at the address; it was the doctor's house. Thinking that he was ill I went there immediately. When I arrived at the entrance to the street where his house was located, I saw that strict security measures were being enforced. I told the police that I was going to visit Doctor Sekban. They let me pass. When I entered the house the Doctor met me at the door and took me in saying, 'My dear nephew, come and see who I will introduce you to.' I knew Nuri Said from photographs. He brought me directly to the face I recognized and said, 'Look, my Pasha, this is the Kurdish youth, who has been complaining about you'. The Pasha spoke Turkish because he had graduated from Galatasaray High School. He got up, I shook his hand and he kissed me. He seated me beside him and said, 'Look, my nephew, I swear it is true; you are right but only because you are not familiar with the events. Be assured that I repeatedly helped Kurds, not only in ordinary arrest situations, but also when they were sentenced to death. The truth of the matter is that I am not an Arab. My ancestors are Kurds from the region of Siirt. I will never lose sight of your wish. In the presence of your uncle, the Doctor, I give my word . . .'.

But shall I say it was a pity; or shall I say thank God? I really must say thank God; after the return of the *beyefendi* to Baghdad the revolution broke out and he was executed. Our tea and dates had not yet been consumed!

12. *Anter (1992), pp. 24–25, in the second volume of his memoirs* quotes Sekban on why he wrote his *La Question Kurde*

In the 1930's, Kemal Pasha and the Government in Ankara tried to assimilate the Kurds. All government authorities and the press in unison expressed the ridiculous opinion that, 'The Kurds are Turks'. On the other hand, like a pack of hungry wolves falling upon a herd of sheep at the height of winter, they subjected the Kurds, who had been left without a sheperd or protector, to a brutal genocide. I was one of the 150 persons whom Atatürk deemed to be traitors to the fatherland. I fled and took refuge with the Prime Minister of Iraq, Nuri Sait Pasha, who had studied at Galatasaray High School. But because of the Ankara Government's mistaken perception not only of me but also of all Kurds, and because of the oppression, genocide and expulsions I developed tuberculosis in six months. I was treated in one of the most excellent sanatoriums in Germany. The German newspapers wrote everyday about the brutal events in Turkey. I thought, the ruling Turkish politicians are ignorant; if, therefore, I say, 'The Kurds are Turks', Kemal Pasha, who appears to be particularly interested in this issue, might stop killing Kurds. With this thought I wrote the fallacious and fabricated book.

ILLUSTRATIONS
1–XII

ژوپر ١ | سالا عوّلي | عدد ١

حجي كاغذك ڤي ريكه
دڤي ريكت مصري سر
ناف خويي ڤي جريده يي
لاو بدرخان پاشا
مقداد مدحت بكي
هر جار دوهزار جريده يا
بي پره آزي ريكم
كردستاني ده بدن خلكي
پازده روژا جاركي تيت
نقيساندن

كردستان

١٣١٥

عنوان
مصرده «كردستان» غزته سي
صاحب ومحرري بدرخان
پاشا زاده
❊ مقداد مدحت ❊
هر طبعنده ٢٠٠٠ نسخه كردستان
ولات مظانه ارسال ووسائط ايله
قرا وقصبانه نشر وتعميم اولنه جقدر

كردستان خارجنده هر بر
ابونه سنه لك ابونه بدلي
٨٠ غروشدر
كردستان داخلنده خصوصي
اشخاصه مجاناً كوندريلور

❊ كردلري ايقاظ وتحصيل صنايعه تشويق ايچون شمدلك ❊

❊ اون بش گونده بر نشر اولنور كردجه غزته در ❊

❊ روژا پنجشنبيده ٣٠ ذوالقعده سنه ١٣١٥ پنجشنبه في ٩ نيسان سنه ١٣١٤ ❊

بسم الله الرحمن الرحيم

صد هزار شكر وحمد ژ خدى تعالى ره آم مسلمان خلق بكرن . وظائفنا علم ومعرفتيره هش وزكا دامه . در حقا علماندنا علم ومعرفتيره گلك آيتين جليله واحاديث شريفه هنن دنيايده چقاس مسلمان هبن گوند وبازيرين تمياده مكتب ومدرسه وجريده هنن دنيايده چه دبه چه نابه جريده دنفيسن . حيفامن تيت ژ كردا ره كرد ژ گلك قوما زيده تر خويي هش وزكانه جامبرن دبنين خوده راست وقوينه خورتن ودِيسا وكه قومين دي نه خوندانه نه دولاندن دنيايده چه دبه جيران وان موسقوف چاوه يه وى چه بكه نظانن لوما ريا خديده من آف جريده ياها نفيسي باذنا خدى تعالى پاش نهو هر پازده روژاده جاركي آزي جريده كي بنفيسم . ناف في من كريه (كردستان) ڤي جريده يده آزي بحثا قنجيا علم ومعرفتا بكم

لكودري مروف دعلمه لكودرى مدرسه ومكتبن قنج هنه آزي نيشا كردا بكم لكودري چه شر دبه دولتين معظم چه دكن چاوه شر دكن تجارت چاوه دبه ازي حميا حكات بكم حتى نهو كسي جريده كي هولي نفيسي يه آف جريده يا مناها يا عوّلي يه لوما وي گلك كيمايي هبتن . ازهيڤي دكم كيمايا جريده يي ژمنره بنفيسن حمي رتشت وكي نو چه دبن ركين پاشي رهنكي دچه دكوه ريده آفه ايدي آزي دست مقصدى بكم . (ومن الله التوفيق)

حضرت پيغمبر عليه الصلوة والسلام گوتي يه «العلماء ورثة الانبياء» آنكو علما وارثين انبيانه ژ طرف خديده مامورن وعظ ونصيحتي بدن خلكى ريا قنج نيشا وان بكن لوما گلي علمايين كردا چاره اون وعظ ونصيحتا نميژى ددن ولى دڤي اون مير وآغا وكرمانجين دناسن وان تشويقا ظانينا علم ومعرفتي بكن ريا قنج نيشا وان بكن هكي اون وي نكن گنهى حميا سطوى وه يه

Ill. I. *Kürdistān* ʿaded 1, 30 Ḏūlḳaʿde 1315/9 Nīsān 1314/April 22, 1898.

کرد

تعاون وترقی غزته‌سی

١٣٢٤

جمعیتك واسطهٔ نشر افكاریدر

تاریخ تأسیسی ١٣٢٦ — ١٣٢٤

نومرو ١ ❧ شمدیلك هفته‌ده بردفعه نشر اولنه‌جق دینی، علمی، سیاسی، ادبی، اجتماعی غزته‌در ❧ جلد ١

مندرجات

درسعادت

سلانیك مطبعه‌سی

١٣٢٤

Ill. II. *Kürd Teʿāvün ve Teraḳḳī Ġazetesi* cild 1, numero 1, 11 Ẕīlḳaʿde 1326/22 Teşrīn-i s̱ānī 1324/December 5, 1908.

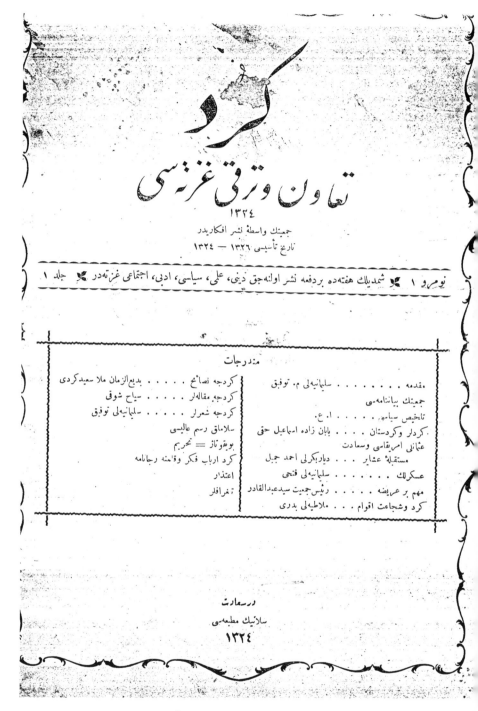

صاحب امتياز :
و مدير مسئول
عبدالكريم

عدد : ١

روژ کرد

تاريخ تأسيسى :
١٣٣١

جلد : ١

١٤ رجب سنه ١٣٣١ — شيمديلك آيده بر نشر اولنور — ٦ حزيران سنه ١٣٢٩

صاعقه طوغوره ، خارقهٔ خلقت عالم !
بير سن كيبي فرزند ديكر ، مادر اعصار .

دهاة اكراددن : سلطان صلاح الدين ايوبى

Ill. III. *Rojē Kurd* cild 1, ʿaded 1, 14 Receb 1331/6 Ḥazīrān 1329/June 19, 1913; showing Sultan Saladin.

صاحب امتياز
ومدير مسئول :
بابانزاده عبد العزيز
آثار نه نوسري نادرستو
عدد : ۱

هتاوی کرد

تاريخ تأسيسي :
غرهٔ ذی القعده
۱۳۳۱
درج اولنميان آثار اعاده اولنمز
ژماره : ۱

۲۳ ذی القعده سنه ۱۳۳۱ شیمدیلك آیده بر نشر ایدیلور ۱۱ تشرین اول سنه ۱۳۲۹

Ill. IV. *Hetavē Kurd* ʿaded 1, 23 Ḏīlḳaʿde 1331/11 Teşrīn-i evvel 1329/October 24, 1913; showing Bābānzāde ʿAbdürraḥmān.

صاحب امتیاز
ومدیر مسئول :
بابان عبدالعزیز

آثار نەنوسری نادریتوه
عدد : ۲

هتاوکرد

تاریخ تأسیسی :
غرهٔ ذی القعده
۱۳۳۱

درج اولنمیان آثار اعاده اولنمز
زمار : ۲

٤ محرم الحرام سنه ۱۳۳۲ شیمدیلك آیده بر نشر اولونور ۲۱ تشرین ثانی سنه ۱۳۲۹

شامده ملیتنی محافظه ایدن کردلردن بر عائله

استانبول
رسملی کتاب مطبعه‌سی
۱۳۲۹

Ill. V. *Hetavē Kurd* ʿaded 2, 4 Muḥarrem 1332/21 Teşrīn-i ṯānī 1329/December 3, 1913; showing "Une famille Kurde"; subtitle: "Şāmda milliyetini muḥāfaẓa eden Kürdlerden bir ʿāʾile" ("a Kurdish family in Damascus which has retained its nationality").

برنجی سنه ۲۹ مايس ۱۳۳۵ عدد ۸

كردستان

سنه‌لكی ۲۰۰ آلتی آيلغی ۱۲۰ اوچ آيلغی ۷۰ غروشدر.

ماليه ۲۰۰ شش ماهه ۱۲۰ ۳ ماهه ۷۰ غروشانه.

سياسی ، اجتماعی ، ادبی ، علمی اسبوعی و مستقل الفكر مجموعه‌در

مندرجات

مقالات	لسان	محررلری
مستر آرنورپوت وود حضرتلرينه	تورکجه	
فضولی جواب		محمد مهر
وضعيت عموميهٔ اكراده بر نظر	»	ابن الرشيد
عائلهٔ اقوام	»	لاوی دلال
كوردلك وكوردستانی يشاته بيلمك	»	محمد عثمان
كورد (هی‌وی) طلبه جمعيتك احياسی	»	توفيق. ح
كوكل ايستركه ا . .	»	عبدالواحد
بر حقيقتی تنوير	»	م. سليم بگی
باسمه سبحانه	عربجه	محمد شفيق
ای كلی كردان	كوردجه	ياملكی‌زاده: م.
شينا ملا حمزه خدی بهلی	»	كاكه حه
شئونات: شريف پاشا حضرتلرينك تلغرافی تورکجه		كوردستان

نسخه‌سی ۵ غروشدر نسخاوی پنج قروشانه

نجم استقبال مطبعه‌سی

Ill. VI. *Kürdistān* birinci sene, ʿaded 8, 28 Şaʿbān 1337/29 Mayıs 1335/May 29, 1919.

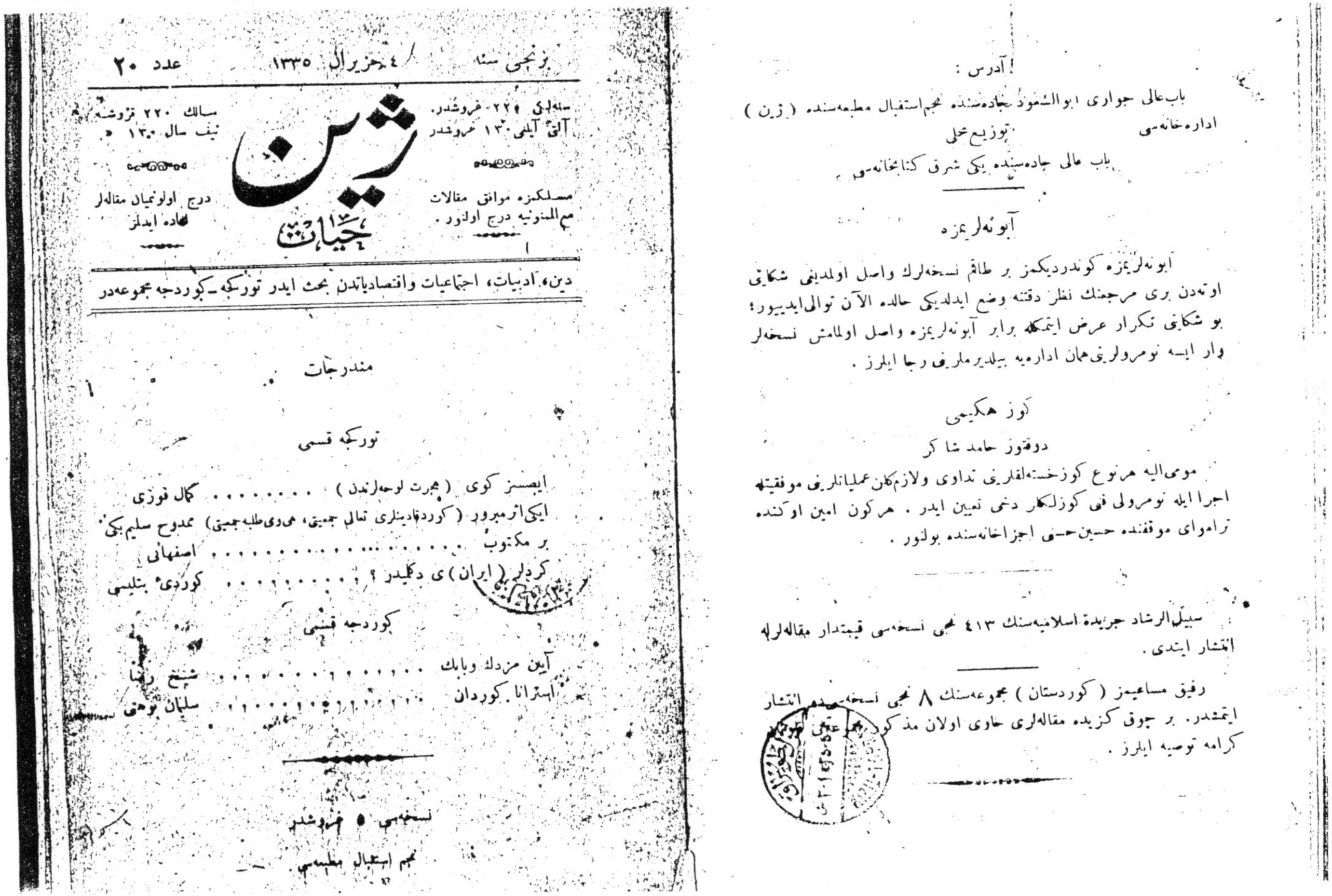
برنجی سنه ٤ حزیران ١٣٣٥ عدد ٢٠

ژین
حیات

سنه‌لکی ٢٢٠ غروشدر. آلتی آیلغی ١٣٠ غروشدر
مسالك ٢٢٠ [illegible] نیف سال ١٣٠

مسلکمزه موافق مقالات مع الممنونیه درج اولنور.
درج اولونمیان مقاله‌لر اعاده ایدلمز

دینی، ادبیات، اجتماعیات واقتصادیاتدن بحث ایدر تورکجه ـ کوردجه مجموعه‌در

مندرجات

تورکجه قسمی

ایبسز کوی (هجرت لوحه‌لرندن) .... کمال فوزی
ایکی اثر مبرور (کوردتعالی جمعیتی، کورد طلبه جمعیتی) ممدوح سلیم بک
بر مکتوب .... اصفهانی
کردلر (ایران)ی دکلیدر؟ .... کوردی بتلیسی

کوردجه قسمی

آیین مزدك وبابك .... شیخ رضا
ایستانا کوردان .... سلیمان نوحی

نسخه‌سی ٥ غروشدر
نجم استقبال مطبعه‌سی

آدرس :
باب عالی جواری ابوالسعود جاده‌سنده نجم استقبال مطبعه‌سنده (ژین) اداره‌خانه‌سی
توزیع محلی
باب عالی جاده‌سنده ینی شرق کتابخانه‌سی

آبونه‌لریمزه

آبونه‌لریمزه کوندردیکمز بر طاقم نسخه‌لرك واصل اولمدیغی شکایتی اوته‌دن بری مرجعنك نظر دقتنه وضع ایدلدیکی حالده الآن توالی ایدییور؛ بو شکایتی تکرار عرض ایتمکله برابر آبونه‌لریمزه واصل اولمامش نسخه‌لر وار ایسه نومرولرینی همان اداره‌یه بیلدیرملرینی رجا ایلرز.

کوز حکیمی
دوقتور حامد شاکر

مومی الیه هرنوع کوزخسته‌لقلرینی تداوی ولازم‌کلن عملیاتلرینی موفقیتله اجرا ایله نومرولی فنی کوزلکلر دخی تعیین ایدر. هرکون امین اوکنده ترامونای موقفنده حسین حسنی اجزاخانه‌سنده بولنور.

سبیل الرشاد جریده اسلامیه‌سنك ٤١٣ نجی نسخه‌سی قیمتدار مقاله‌لرله انتشار ایتدی.

رفیق مساعیمز (کوردستان) مجموعه‌سنك ٨ نجی نسخه‌سی ده انتشار ایتمشدر. برچوق کزیده مقاله‌لری حاوی اولان مذکور [illegible] کرامه توصیه ایلرز.

Ill. VII. *Jīn* birinci sene, ʿaded 20, 4 Ḥazīrān 1335/June 5, 1919.

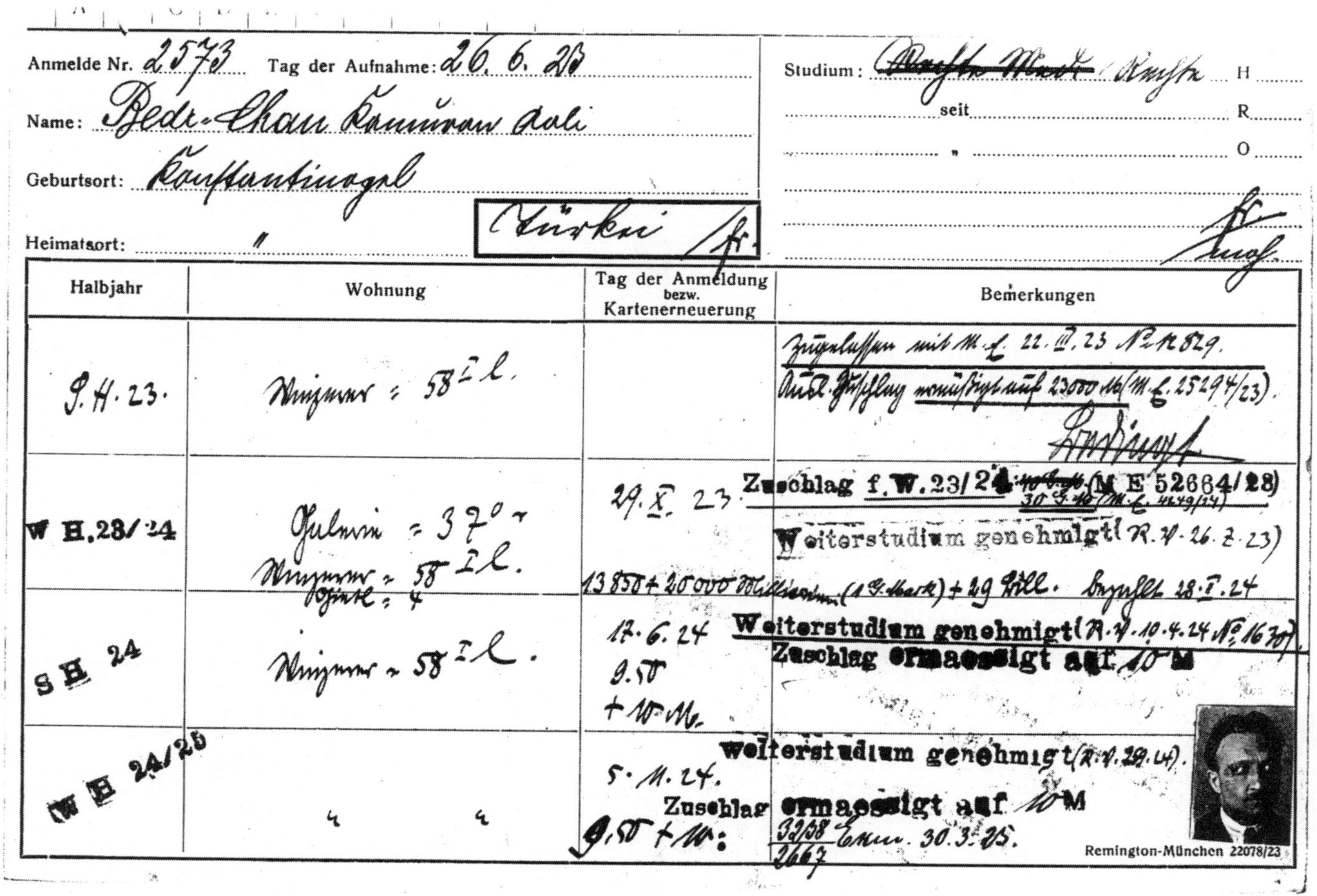

Anmelde Nr. 2573 Tag der Aufnahme: 26. 6. 23

Name: Bedr-Chan Kamuran Aali

Geburtsort: Konstantinopel

Heimatsort: " Türkei

Studium: ~~Rechts Wiss~~ Rechte H

seit R

" O

Halbjahr	Wohnung	Tag der Anmeldung bezw. Kartenerneuerung	Bemerkungen
S.H. 23.	Kaiserstr. 58 I l.		Zugelassen mit M. E. 22. III. 23 Nr. 12829. Ausl. Zuschlag ermäßigt auf 23000 M (M. E. 25294/23).
W H. 23/24	Ohlmüllerstr. 37 o r Kaiserstr. 58 I l.	29. X. 23.	Zuschlag f. W. 23/24 (M E 52664/28) Weiterstudium genehmigt (R. V. 26. X. 23) 13850 + 20000 Millionen (1 G. Mark) + 29 Mill. bezahlt 28. I. 24
S H 24	Kaiserstr. 58 I l.	17. 6. 24 9.50 + 10 M.	Weiterstudium genehmigt (R. V. 10. 4. 24 Nr. 1630) Zuschlag ermaessigt auf 10 M
W H 24/25	" "	5. 11. 24. 9.50 + 10 M.	Weiterstudium genehmigt (R. V. 29. 10.) Zuschlag ermaessigt auf 10 M 32/38 2667 Exm. 30. 3. 25.

Remington-München 22078/23

Ill. VIII. Registration card of ''Bedr-Chan Kamuran Aali'' from Constantinople; he studied law at the University of Munich from spring 1923 to spring 1925.

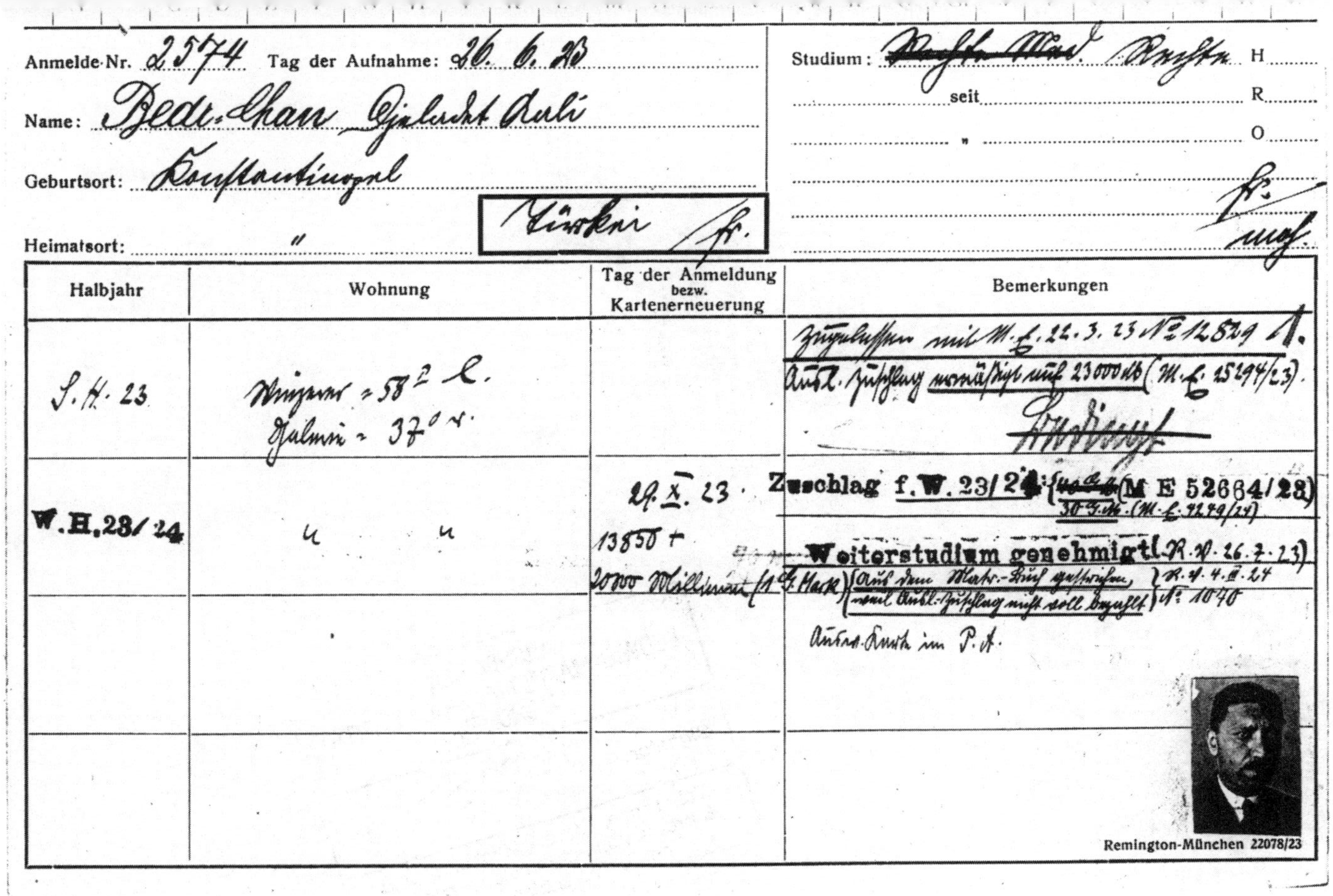

Anmelde-Nr. 2574 Tag der Aufnahme: 26. 6. 23

Name: Bedr-Chan Djeladet Aali

Geburtsort: Konstantinopel

Heimatsort: "

Studium: Rechte

seit

Halbjahr	Wohnung	Tag der Anmeldung bezw. Kartenerneuerung	Bemerkungen
S. H. 23			
W. H. 23/24	" "	29. X. 23. 13850 +	Zuschlag f. W. 23/24: (M E 52684/28) Weiterstudium genehmigt

Remington-München 22078/23

Ill. IX. Registration card of "Bedr-Chan Djeladet Aali" from Constantinople; he studied law at the University of Munich from spring 1923 to spring 1924.

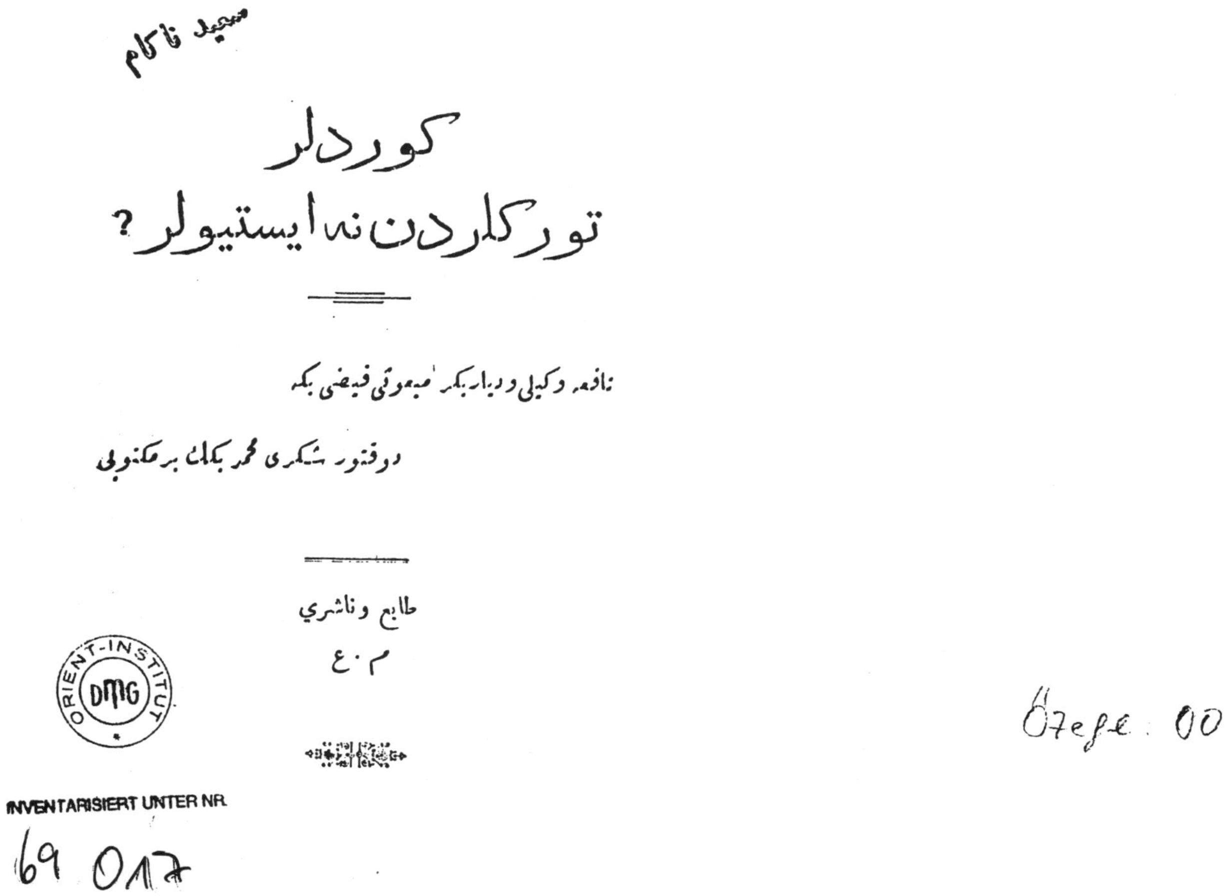

سعيد ناكام

كوردلر
توركلردن نه ايستيولر ؟

نافعه وكيلي ودياربكر مبعوثي فيضي بكه

دوقتور شكري محمد بكك بر مكتوبي

طابع وناشري
م٠ع

Ill. X. Front page of *Kürdler Türklerden ne istiyo(r)lar? Nāfiʿa vekīli ve Diyārbekir mebʿūṯu Feyżī Beye Doḳtor Şükrü Meḥmed Beyin bir mektūbu.* Tābiʿ ve nāşiri M.ʿ. [Cairo 1923].

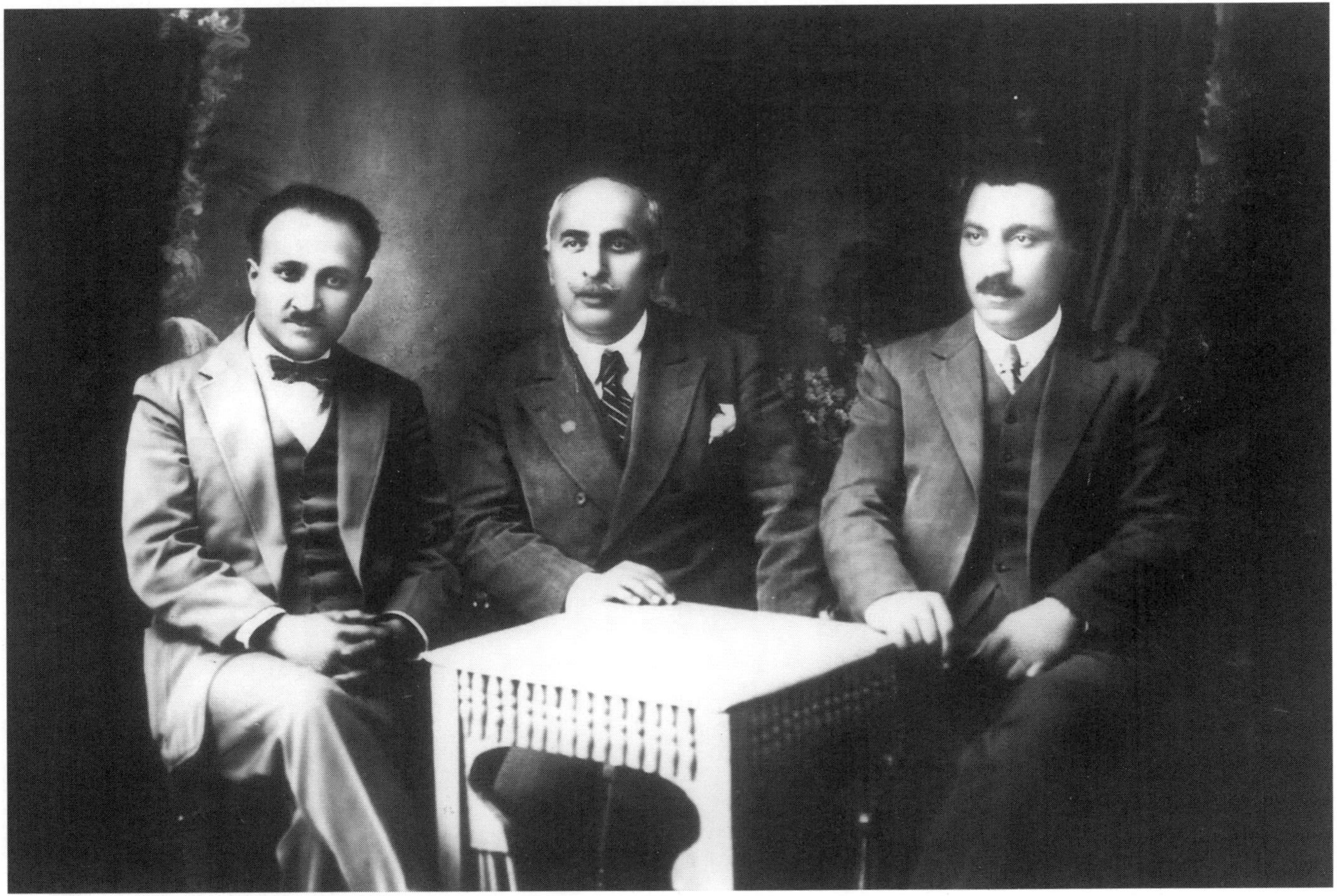

Ill. XI. Kāmurān, T̲üreyyā and Celādet Bedir Khān (courtesy of Institut Kurde, Paris).

Dr. Şükrü Mehmet Sekban

Ill. XII. Photograph of Dr. Şükrü Mehmet Sekban, taken from: Dr. Chukru Mehmed Sekban: *La Question Kurde. Des Problèmes des Minorités.* Paris 1933.

INDEX

SOCIAL, ECONOMIC AND POLITICAL STUDIES OF THE MIDDLE EAST AND ASIA

1. Nieuwenhuijze, C.A.O. van. *Sociology of the Middle East.* A Stocktaking and Interpretation. 1971. ISBN 90 04 02564 2
6. Khalaf, S. and P. Kongstad. *Hamra of Beirut.* A Case of Rapid Urbanization. 1973. ISBN 90 04 03548 6
7. Karpat, K.H. (ed.). *Social Change and Politics in Turkey.* A Structural-Historical Analysis. 1973. ISBN 90 04 03817 5
9. Benedict, P., E. Tümertekin and F. Mansur (eds.). *Turkey.* Geographic and Social Perspectives. 1974. ISBN 90 04 03889 2
10. Entelis, J.P. *Pluralism and Party Transformation in Lebanon:* Al-Kata'ib, 1936-1970. 1974. ISBN 90 04 03911 2
14. Landau, J.M. *Radical Politics in Modern Turkey.* 1974. ISBN 90 04 04016 1
15. Fry, M.J. *The Afghan Economy.* Money, Finance, and the Critical Constraints to Economic Development. 1974. ISBN 90 04 03986 4
19. Abadan-Unat, N. (ed.). *Turkish Workers in Europe, 1960-1975.* A Socio-Economic Reappraisal. 1976. ISBN 90 04 04478 7
20. Staffa, S.J. *Conquest and Fusion.* The Social Evolution of Cairo A.D. 642-1850. 1977. ISBN 90 04 04774 3
21. Nieuwenhuijze, C.A.O. van (ed.). *Commoners, Climbers and Notables.* A Sampler of Studies on Social Ranking in the Middle East. 1977. ISBN 90 04 05065 5
23. Starr, J. *Dispute and Settlement in Rural Turkey.* An Ethnography of Law. 1978. ISBN 90 04 05661 0
24. el-Messiri, S. *Ibn al-Balad.* A Concept of Egyptian Identity. 1978. ISBN 90 04 05664 5
25. Israeli, R. *The Public Diary of President Sadat.* 3 parts
    1. The Road to War. 1978. ISBN 90 04 05702 1
    2. The Road of Diplomacy: The Continuation of War by Other Means. 1978. ISBN 90 04 05865 6
    3. The Road of Pragmatism. 1979. ISBN 90 04 05866 4
29. Grandin, N. *Le Soudan nilotique et l'administration britannique.* Éléments d'interprétation socio-historique d'une expérience coloniale. 1982. ISBN 90 04 06404 4
30. Abadan-Unat, N., D. Kandiyoti and M.B. Kiray (ed.). *Women in Turkish Society.* 1981. ISBN 90 04 06346 2
31. Layish, A. *Marriage, Divorce and Succession in the Druze Family.* A Study Based on Decisions of Druze Arbitrators and Religious Courts in Israel and the Golan Heights. 1982. ISBN 90 04 06412 5
34. Atiş, S.M. *Semantic Structuring in the Modern Turkish Short Story.* An Analysis of *The Dreams of Abdullah Efendi* and Other Short Stories by Ahmet Hamdi Tanpinar. 1983. ISBN 90 04 07117 2
36. Kamali, M.H. *Law in Afghanistan.* A Study of the Constitutions, Matrimonial Law and the Judiciary. 1985. ISBN 90 04 07128 8
37. Nieuwenhuijze, C.A.O. van. *The Lifestyles of Islam.* Recourse to Classicism—Need of Realism. 1985. ISBN 90 04 07420 1
38. Fathi, A. (ed.). *Women and the Family in Iran.* 1985. ISBN 90 04 07426 0

40. Nieuwenhuijze, C.A.O. van, M.F. al-Khatib, A. Azer. *The Poor Man's Model of Development.* Development Potential at Low Levels of Living in Egypt. 1985. ISBN 90 04 07696 4
41. Schulze, R. *Islamischer Internationalismus im 20. Jahrhundert.* Untersuchungen zur Geschichte der islamischen Weltliga. 1990. ISBN 90 04 08286 7
42. Childs, T.W. *Italo-Turkish Diplomacy and the War over Libya, 1911-1912.* 1990. ISBN 90 04 09025 8
45. Lipovsky, I.P. *The Socialist Movement in Turkey 1960-1980.* 1992. ISBN 90 04 09582 9
46. Rispler-Chaim, V. *Islamic Medical Ethics in the Twentieth Century.* 1993. ISBN 90 04 09608 6
47. Khalaf, S. and P. S. Khoury (eds.). *Recovering Beirut.* Urban Design and Post-War Reconstruction. With an Introduction by R. Sennett. 1994. ISBN 90 04 09911 5
48. Mardin, Ş (ed.). *Cultural Transitions in the Middle East.* 1994. ISBN 90 04 09873 9
49. Waart, P.J.I.M. de. *Dynamics of Self-Determination in Palestine.* Protection of Peoples as a Human Right. 1994. ISBN 90 04 09825 9
50. Norton, A.R. (ed.). *Civil Society in the Middle East.* 2 volumes.
    Volume I. 1995. ISBN 90 04 10037 7
    Volume II. 1996. ISBN 90 04 10039 3
51. Amin, G.A. *Egypt's Economic Predicament.* A Study in the Interaction of External Pressure, Political Folly and Social Tension in Egypt, 1960-1990. 1995. ISBN 90 04 10188 8
52. Podeh, E. *The Quest for Hegemony in the Arab World.* The Struggle over the Baghdad Pact. 1995. ISBN 90 04 10214 0
53. Balım, Ç. *et al.* (eds.). *Turkey: Political, Social and Economic Challenges in the 1990s.* 1995. ISBN 90 04 10283 3
54. Shepard, W.E. *Sayyid Qutb and Islamic Activism.* A Translation and Critical Analysis of *Social Justice in Islam.* 1996. ISBN 90 04 10152 7
55. Amin, S.N. *The World of Muslim Women in Colonial Bengal, 1876-1939.* 1996. ISBN 90 04 10642 1
56. Nieuwenhuijze, C.A.O. van. *Paradise Lost.* Reflections on the Struggle for Authenticity in the Middle East. 1997. ISBN 90 04 10672 3
57. Freitag, U. and W. Clarence-Smith. *Hadhrami Traders, Scholars and Statesmen in the Indian Ocean, 1750s to 1960s.* 1997. ISBN 90 04 10771 1
58. Kansu, A. *The Revolution of 1908 in Turkey.* 1997. ISBN 90 04 10791 6
59. Skovgaard-Petersen, J. *Defining Islam for the Egyptian State.* Muftis and Fatwas of the Dār al-Iftā. 1997. ISBN 90 04 10947 1
60. Arnon, A. *et al. The Palestinian Economy.* Between Imposed Integration and Voluntary Separation.1997. ISBN 90 04 10538 7
61. Frank, A.J. *Islamic Historiography and 'Bulghar' Identity among the Tatars and Bashkirs of Russia.* 1998. ISBN 90 04 11021 6
62. Heper, M. *İsmet İnönü. The Making of a Turkish Statesman.* 1998. ISBN 90 04 09919 0
63. Stiansen, E & M. Kevane (eds.) *Kordofan invaded.* Peripheral Incorporation and Social Transformation in Islamic Africa. 1998. ISBN 90 04 11049 6
64. Firro, K.M. *The Druzes in the Jewish State.* A Brief History. 1999. ISBN 90 04 11251 0

65. Azarya, V, A. Breedveld and H. van Dijk (eds.). *Pastoralists under Pressure?* Fulbe Societies Confronting Change in West Africa. 1999. ISBN 90 04 11364 9
66. Qureshi, M. Naeem. *Pan-Islam in British Indian Politics.* A Study of the Khilafat Movement, 1918-1924. 1999. ISBN 90 04 11371 1
67. Ensel, R. *Saints and Servants in Southern Morocco.* 1999. ISBN 90 04 11429 7
68. Acar, F. and Günes-Ayata, A. *Gender and Identity Construction.* Women of Central Asia, the Caucasus and Turkey 2000. ISBN 90 04 11561 7
69. Masud, M. Kh. (ed.) *Travellers in Faith.* Studies of the Tablīghī Jamāʿat as a Transnational Islamic Movement for Faith Renewal. 2000. ISBN 90 04 11622 2
70. Kansu, A. *Politics in Post-Revolutionary Turkey, 1908-1913.* 2000. ISBN 90 04 11587 0
71. Hafez, K. (ed.) *The Islamic World and the West.* An Introduction to Political Cultures and International Relations. 2000. ISBN 90 04 11651 6
72. Brunner, R. & Ende, W. (eds.) *The Twelver Shia in Modern Times.* Religious Culture and Political History. 2001. ISBN 90 04 11803 9
73. Malik, J. (ed.) *Perspectives of Mutual Encounters in South Asian History, 1760-1860.* 2000. ISBN 90 04 11802 0
74. Ahmed, H. *Islam in Nineteenth Century Wallo, Ethiopia.* Revival, Reform and Reaction. 2001. ISBN 90 04 11909 4
75. Fischbach, M.R. *State, Society and Land in Jordan.* 2000. ISBN 90 04 11912 4
76. Karpat, K.H. (ed.) *Ottoman Past and Today's Turkey.* 2000. ISBN 90 04 11562 5
77. Jahanbakhsh, F. *Islam, Democracy and Religious Modernism in Iran (1953-2000).* From Bāzargān to Soroush. 2001. ISBN 90 04 11982 5
78. Federspiel, H. M. *Islam and ideology in the emerging Indonesian state :* The Persatuan Islam (PERSIS), 1923 to 1957. 2001. ISBN 90 04 12047 5
79. Saleh, F. *Modern Trends in Islamic Theological Discourse in 20th Century Indonesia.* A Critical Survey. 2001. ISBN 90 04 12305 9
80. Küçük, H. *The Role of the Bektāshīs in Turkey's National Struggle.* 2002. ISBN 90 04 12443 8
81. Karpat, K.H. *Studies on Ottoman Social and Political History.* Selected Articles and Essays. 2002. ISBN 90 04 12101 3
82. Ali El-Dean, B. *Privatisation and the Creation of a Market-Based Legal System.* The Case of Egypt. 2002. ISBN 90 04 12580 9
83. Bos, M. van den. *Mystic Regimes.* Sufim and the State in Iran, from the late Qajar Era to the Islamic Republic. 2002. ISBN 90 04 12815 8
85. Carré, O. *Mysticism and Politics.* A Critical Reading of *Fī Ẓilāl al-Qur'ān* by Sayyid Quṭb (1906-1966). 2003. ISBN 90 04 12590 6
86. Strohmeier, M. *Crucial Images in the Presentation of a Kurdish National Identity.* Heroes and Patriots, Traitors and Foes. 2003. ISBN 90 04 12584 1
88. White, P.J. and Jongerden, J. *Turkey's Alevi Enigma.* A Comprehensive Overview. 2003. ISBN 90 04 12538 8